DOWN BY THE WATER

A Collection Of Recipes From The Junior League Of Columbia, Inc.

DOWN BY THE WATER

A Collection Of Recipes From The Junior League Of Columbia, Inc.

Down By The Water: A Collection Of Recipes From The Junior League Of Columbia, Inc.

Copyright© 1997 by The Junior League of Columbia, Inc.
2926 Devine Street
Columbia, South Carolina 29205
(803) 252-4552

Betsy Thompson Bakhaus, Photographer
Susan Fuller Slack, CCP, Food Stylist and Prop Coordinator

Library of Congress Catalog Number: 97-073965
ISBN: 0-9613561-1-1-1

Edited, Designed and Manufactured by Favorite Recipes® Press
an imprint of

PO Box 305142, Nashville, Tennessee 37230, (800) 358-0560

Book Design: David Malone
Art Director: Steve Newman
Project Manager: Debbie Van Mol
Project Production: Sara Anglin

Manufactured in the United States of America
First Printing: 1997   25,000 copies

DEDICATION

The Junior League dedicates this book to "Smart Matters" children, those aged

six and younger who represent the finest our future can offer.

MISSION

The Association of Junior Leagues International, Inc., is an organization of women committed

to promoting voluntarism, developing the potential of women, and improving communities through the effective action and

leadership of trained volunteers. Its purpose is exclusively educational and charitable.

VISION

The Junior League of Columbia, Inc., seeks to strengthen the well-being and future of Columbia's children

through the dedicated action of trained volunteers.

Smart Matters, a Junior League program, helps the community prepare

children for school and encourages parents to help their children in this mission.

Smart Matters logo denotes recipes of interest to children.

ABOUT THE ARTIST

The cover painting, Congaree Dusk, *is by the artist Blue Sky, and is in the permanent collection of Price Waterhouse LLP. Copyright 1997 by Blue Sky. Blue Sky painted* Tunnelvision, *a mural measuring fifty-by-seventy-five feet. This internationally acclaimed mural, the work for which he is best known, is housed in the Farm Credit Bank in Columbia, South Carolina. A resident of Columbia, he attended the University of South Carolina where he received his bachelor's and master's degrees. He also studied at the Art Students League in New York and the University of Mexico in Mexico City. Sky's paintings have been exhibited in New York, Chicago, New Orleans, Washington, D.C., Boston, and countless other museums and galleries in the eastern United States. His work is in the collections of the White House, the Smithsonian, the Federal Reserve Bank, IBM, Wachovia Bank, Carolina First, R.J. Reynolds, the South Carolina State Museum, the Columbia Museum, and numerous other museums and public and private collections. He has received numerous awards and endowments and his work has been widely published. Over a dozen books document his work.*

CONTENTS

You hold more than a cookbook in your hands. You hold a heritage. Between the covers of *Down By The Water* await the culinary treasures and discoveries of South Carolina's finest cooks. The Junior League members worked hard on this book, and they searched for favored recipes that, like rivers, lakes, and streams, endure and shape our lives.

Great cooking has long come from the Low Country and its rice, indigo, and Sea Island cotton cultures. "The Salt" possesses its own cuisine, thanks to the blue crabs, shrimp, fish, and oysters. And wonderful cooking has long simmered off the home fires of the Mountain Province with its silvery, cold streams.

And simple but exquisite meals distinguish the Piedmont and the Sandhills where cattails fringe the ponds and lakes where hopes of a fish fry actually materialize at the end of a cane pole.

Food and water. Does not a meal taste better by the water?

The relationship between food, cooking, and water is inseparable. It's as stimulating as the smell of morning coffee, and it has many facets. It begins when rain moistens the earth and nurtures the tender shoots of vegetables. It continues where clear brook water shelters and sustains trout. It surges where the ebb and flood tides enrich the sea's nursery—the estuary.

We steam, boil, poach, simmer, and stew with it. And chill and cool with it. And drink it—in many forms. Do not the wine's grapes contain the rain?

Between Appalachia and the Atlantic, throughout the Palmetto heartland, a great feast is forever being prepared. This volume celebrates that feast. Food and water—the great inseparables, bound for you between the covers of this book. Let's dine now, *Down By The Water*.

ACKNOWLEDGMENTS

Ace Glass
Adventure Carolina
Emily Bakhaus
John Bakhaus
John John Bakhaus
Barron's Fishing and Hunting Center
Sharon Besley
Nancy Bunch
China Berry
Creative Kids
Eric Crissey
Elizabeth Davis
Clarke and Trish DuBose
The Gourmet Shop

Mrs. Hugh Graham
Gudmundson and Buyck Jewelers
Andrew Hackney
David Hartfield
M. Boyle Interiors, Inc.
Mais Oui, Ltd.
Diane Mylander
Ozzie Nagler
Non(e) Such
Peggy Peier
Pier One Imports
Bruce Sacino
Richard Seabrook
Senn Brothers Produce

Blue Sky
Colonel Richard C. Slack
South Carolina Governor's Mansion
Sparling Specialties
Fonda Powell Stroud
Sylvan Jewelers
Rajeev and Bhavna Vasudeva and family
Virginia Lee Interiors
Mary Frances Wendt
Jane Whiteside
The Windemere Club
Woodly and Associates

SPECIAL THANKS TO

Jimmy Stevenson, owner of Southern Way Catering, for "Main Events" food preparation and for being a special friend. ♦ Tom Poland, author of *South Carolina—A Natural Heritage* and *South Carolina—A Timeless Journey*, for so eloquently introducing our book and describing our photography. ♦ Carol J. G. Ward, Food Editor, *The State Newspaper*, for informing the public about the production of our book. ♦ Jamie Walker for posing as the sportsman he is. ♦ Linda Hewlette, owner of City Cafe, for preparing the desserts in the photograph "Desserts On The Patio." ♦ Jean Pierre Chambas, Director of Fine Wines and Spirits, Southern Wines & Spirits of South Carolina, for his overview of wines and beverages. ♦ Peter Fawcett and the staff of Capital Wine and Beverage Distribution for selecting wines to grace our menus. ♦ Susan Fuller Slack, CCP, for food styling and prop coordination.

APPETIZERS & BEVERAGES

APPETIZERS & BEVERAGES

APPETIZERS AT DUSK

As the sun sets over Finlay Park, the city's lights come alive.

Opposite:

Smoked Salmon Gâteau

Fillet-Topped Baguettes with Walnut Parsley Pesto

Bubba's Shrimp on a Stick

Tomato Galette with Fresh Rosemary

CUCUMBER ROUNDS

1 large loaf thinly sliced
   white or wheat bread

1 cup mayonnaise

2 teaspoons dried minced
   onion

1 1/2 teaspoons seasoned
   salt

Thinly sliced cucumbers

Paprika to taste

- Cut the bread into rounds with a biscuit cutter.
- Combine the mayonnaise, onion and seasoned salt in a bowl and mix well.
- Spread the mayonnaise mixture over the bread rounds. Top with a cucumber slice and sprinkle with paprika.
- For 150 sandwiches, spread a mixture of 1 1/2 quarts mayonnaise, 2 1/2 ounces seasoned salt and 2 ounces dried minced onion on 6 large loaves thinly sliced bread.

Twenty-Five Servings

GREEN OLIVE TAPENADE

1 (10-ounce) jar pitted
   green olives, drained

1 (2-ounce) can anchovy
   fillets, drained

2 large cloves of garlic

1 teaspoon drained
   capers

1/4 cup olive oil

1 1/2 teaspoons fresh
   lemon juice

1/8 teaspoon cayenne

- Combine the olives, anchovies, garlic and capers in a food processor container.
- Process until smooth. Add the olive oil gradually, processing constantly until of the consistency of a paste; scrape the side of the work bowl occasionally. Add the lemon juice and cayenne.
- Process until blended. Spoon into a serving bowl. Serve with toasted bread slices.
- May be prepared up to 1 week in advance and stored, covered, in the refrigerator.

**Makes Twelve (Two-Tablespoon)
Servings**

FILLET-TOPPED BAGUETTES WITH WALNUT PARSLEY PESTO

Walnut Parsley Pesto

*2/3 cup chopped fresh
    Italian parsley*

*1/2 cup chopped walnuts,
    toasted*

*1/2 cup grated imported
    Parmesan cheese*

1/3 cup packed fresh basil

1 large clove of garlic

*1/2 cup (about) extra-virgin
    olive oil*

Salt to taste

Beef

*1 pound rare fillet of beef,
    chilled*

*1 French baguette, cut
    diagonally into 1/2-inch
    slices*

- For the pesto, combine the parsley, walnuts, cheese, basil and garlic in the container of a food processor fitted with a steel blade.

- Add the olive oil gradually, processing constantly until a soft paste forms. Add salt. Process until blended.

- Chill, covered, for 8 to 10 hours to allow the flavors to marry. Store in the freezer after 2 weeks.

- For the beef, cut the fillet into thin slices.

- Place a mound of the beef on each bread slice; top with some of the pesto. Arrange on a serving platter.

- Serve immediately.

Eight to Ten Servings

To intensify the flavor of basil used in pesto and other sauces, bruise the leaves by placing them in a sealable plastic bag and pounding with a meat mallet. This mimics the classic method of preparing basil with a mortar and pestle.

FRESH DILL DIP FOR CRUDITES

For an easy and delicious appetizer, mix 1 cup mayonnaise, 1 cup sour cream, 1/4 cup fresh minced dillweed, 2 tablespoons minced onion, 1 tablespoon lemon juice and 1/8 teaspoon salt, or salt to taste, in a bowl. Chill, covered, for 8 to 10 hours to allow the flavors to marry. Serve with fresh vegetables of your choice.

SALMON CANAPES WITH FRESH DILL

6 ounces cream cheese, softened

3/4 cup finely chopped spring onions (white part only)

3 tablespoons drained capers

2 tablespoons packed chopped fresh dillweed

4 teaspoons Dijon mustard

1 tablespoon fresh lemon juice

Salt and freshly ground pepper to taste

24 thin slices French baguette

6 ounces thinly sliced smoked salmon, cut into 24 portions

Sprigs of fresh dillweed

- Combine the cream cheese, spring onions, capers, 2 tablespoons dillweed, Dijon mustard and lemon juice in a bowl and mix until of spreading consistency. Season with salt and pepper.
- Spread the cream cheese mixture over the bread. Top each canapé with 1 portion of the salmon and a sprig of fresh dillweed. Arrange on a serving platter.

Twenty-Four Servings

APRICOT BRIE SPREAD

1/2 cup water

1/4 cup chopped dried apricots

2 teaspoons brandy

1 (15-ounce) round Brie cheese

2 tablespoons chopped pecans

- Combine the water, apricots and brandy in a saucepan. Bring to a boil over medium heat.
- Cook for 5 minutes or until the apricots are tender, stirring constantly.
- Remove the top rind of the Brie to within 1/4 inch of the edge. Arrange the Brie on a baking sheet. Spread with the apricot mixture and sprinkle with the pecans.
- Broil 8 inches from the heat source for 2 to 4 minutes or until the cheese is soft.
- Transfer the Brie to a serving platter. Serve with gingersnaps or lightly sweetened crackers.

Eight to Ten Servings

CHEESE TORTA

16 ounces cream cheese, softened

1/4 cup unsalted butter, softened

4 ounces basil-tomato feta cheese, crumbled (optional)

3/4 cup pesto

3/4 cup finely chopped oil-pack sun-dried tomatoes

- Oil a deep 3-cup mold. Line with moistened cheesecloth, leaving a slight overhang.
- Process the cream cheese, butter and feta cheese in a food processor until smooth. Divide the mixture into 6 portions.
- Spoon 1 portion of the cheese mixture into the prepared mold, spreading evenly to cover the bottom. Spread with 1/4 cup of the pesto, another portion of the cheese mixture and 1/2 of the sun-dried tomatoes. Repeat the layers. Layer 1 portion of the cheese mixture, the remaining pesto and the remaining cheese mixture over the prepared layers. Cover with the cheesecloth.
- Chill for several hours or until set. Invert onto a serving platter and discard the cheesecloth.
- Garnish with additional pesto, sun-dried tomatoes or Belgian endive. Serve with assorted party crackers and/or Belgian endive.
- May layer the pesto and sun-dried tomatoes in any order.

Twelve (or More) Servings

INSTANT HERBED CHEVRE

Goat cheese goes gourmet with the addition of these flavorful seasonings! Serve as an appetizer with toasted sliced French bread or slice and serve as an accompaniment to a special salad. Garnish each slice with an edible flower petal if desired.

1 log fresh chèvre

Finely chopped fresh basil, thyme, dillweed and/or marjoram

Coarsely ground pepper or lemon pepper

Chopped toasted hazelnuts, walnuts or pine nuts

- Roll the chèvre in 1 of the herbs or a combination of the herbs.
- Roll in the pepper; coat with the hazelnuts.
- Slice and serve immediately.
- May store the log, loosely covered, in the refrigerator until serving time.

Four Servings

JALAPENO CHEESE SPREAD

Tastes like a complicated recipe, but so easy!

2 cups shredded Cheddar cheese

2 cups chopped pecans

8 to 10 spring onions, chopped

1 tablespoon (about) mayonnaise

1 (10-ounce) jar jalapeño jelly

- Combine the cheese, pecans, spring onions and mayonnaise in a bowl and mix well. Spread in an 8x12-inch dish.
- Chill, covered, for several hours. Spread with the jalapeño jelly just before serving.
- Serve the spread with assorted party crackers.

Sixteen Servings

MUSHROOM PATE

8 ounces mushrooms,
   chopped

1/2 small onion, chopped

8 ounces cream cheese,
   softened

1 tablespoon (or more)
   chopped fresh rosemary

Salt and pepper to taste

- Sauté the mushrooms and onion in a nonstick skillet until tender.
- Combine the mushroom mixture, cream cheese, rosemary, salt and pepper in a food processor container.
- Process until blended, scraping the work bowl occasionally. Spoon into a serving bowl.
- Chill, covered, until serving time. Garnish with additional fresh rosemary.
- Serve with toast points and/or assorted party crackers.

Twelve to Sixteen Servings

PEPPER CHEESE

2 cups shredded
  Monterey Jack cheese,
  at room temperature

8 ounces cream cheese,
  softened

1 clove of garlic, minced

1 teaspoon fines herbes

1 teaspoon
  Worcestershire sauce

1 teaspoon minced
  chives

Seasoned pepper to taste

- Combine the Monterey Jack cheese, cream cheese, garlic, fines herbes, Worcestershire sauce and chives in a bowl and mix well.

- Shape into a 1/4-inch-thick square or any desired shape on waxed paper. Coat all sides with seasoned pepper.

- Chill, covered, until serving time. Serve with Champagne crackers and wheat crackers.

- Fines herbes is a blend of chervil, parsley, chives and tarragon. This blend can be purchased in most supermarkets.

Sixteen Servings

PIMENTO CHEESE WITH A TWIST

The Grand Marnier gives this pimento cheese a unique taste.

1 (4-ounce) jar chopped
  pimentos, drained

1/2 cup mayonnaise

1/4 cup Durkee sauce

3 tablespoons Grand
  Marnier

2 cloves of garlic, minced

1 1/2 teaspoons Dijon
  mustard

1/4 teaspoon cayenne

1 pound sharp Cheddar
  cheese, shredded

- Combine the pimentos, mayonnaise, Durkee sauce, liqueur, garlic, Dijon mustard and cayenne in a bowl and mix well. Add the cheese, stirring until mixed.

- Chill, covered, for 8 to 10 hours.

- Serve with assorted crackers or slices of French bread, or as a stuffing for celery.

Makes Three Cups

SMOKED SALMON GATEAU

2 tablespoons freshly grated
  Parmesan cheese

3 tablespoons butter

1 cup each chopped onion
  and red bell pepper

16 ounces cream cheese,
  softened

1/3 cup whipping cream

4 eggs

8 ounces smoked salmon,
  chopped

2 ounces Swiss cheese,
  shredded

3 tablespoons freshly grated
  Parmesan cheese

1 tablespoon fresh lemon
  juice

1 teaspoon minced fresh
  dillweed, basil, marjoram
  and/or chives

1/8 teaspoon hot pepper sauce

Salt and freshly ground
  pepper to taste

1 bunch parsley, minced

- Coat the bottom and side of an 8-inch springform pan with butter; sprinkle with 2 tablespoons Parmesan cheese. Wrap foil around the outside bottom and 2 inches up the side of the pan.

- Heat 3 tablespoons butter in a skillet over medium heat until melted. Add the onion and red pepper. Sauté for 5 minutes or until tender. Let stand until cool.

- Beat the cream cheese, whipping cream and eggs in a mixer bowl until smooth.

- Stir the salmon, Swiss cheese and 3 tablespoons Parmesan cheese into the onion mixture. Add the lemon juice, 1 of the herbs or a combination of the herbs, hot pepper sauce, salt and pepper and mix well. Fold into the cream cheese mixture.

- Spoon into the prepared springform pan. Place the pan in a larger baking pan. Add boiling water to the larger pan to a depth of 2 inches.

- Bake at 300 degrees for 1 hour or until set. Turn off the oven. Remove the springform pan from the water. Return the springform pan to the oven.

- Let stand in the oven with the door closed for 1 hour.

- Cool on a wire rack for 2 hours. Remove the side of the pan. Place the gâteau on a serving platter. Press the parsley lightly into the side of the gâteau.

- Serve with assorted party crackers or sliced baguette.

Thirty Servings

Decorate the Smoked Salmon Gâteau with vegetable flowers using eggplant peel for the petals, leeks for the stems and leaves and chive blossoms for the blossom center. Press minced fresh parsley around the side of the gâteau.

BLACK BEAN AND CORN SALSA

Very versatile dish. Serve as an appetizer or cold salad, or as a topping for burritos, chicken or fish. Increase the quantity of spices and vinegar according to taste.

3 (15-ounce) cans black beans, rinsed, drained

1 (16-ounce) package frozen white Shoe Peg corn, thawed

1 onion, finely chopped

1 yellow bell pepper, chopped

1 red bell pepper, chopped

1 cup red wine vinegar

1 tablespoon olive oil

1 tablespoon dried cilantro

$1/2$ teaspoon chili powder

$1/2$ teaspoon cumin

2 cloves of garlic, chopped

Tortilla chips or flour tortillas

- Combine the black beans, corn, onion, yellow pepper and red pepper in a bowl and mix well.

- Combine the wine vinegar, olive oil, cilantro, chili powder, cumin and garlic in a bowl and mix well. Add to the bean mixture, tossing to coat.

- Chill, covered, until serving time. Serve with tortilla chips or heated flour tortilla wedges.

- May omit the olive oil to decrease the number of fat grams in the recipe.

Fifty Servings

BLACK-EYED PEA SALSA

Serve as a dip with corn chips or as a side dish with grilled pork or chicken.

2 (15-ounce) cans black-eyed peas, rinsed, drained

6 to 8 Roma tomatoes, chopped

2 large cucumbers, peeled, seeded, chopped

2 teaspoons minced jalapeño

$1/2$ cup white wine vinegar

$1/2$ cup olive oil

1 teaspoon basil

1 teaspoon sugar

1 clove of garlic, minced

Salt and pepper to taste

- Combine the peas, tomatoes, cucumbers and jalapeño in a bowl and mix gently.

- Combine the wine vinegar, olive oil, basil, sugar, garlic, salt and pepper in a bowl and mix well. Add to the pea mixture, tossing to coat.

- Serve with assorted chips.

- The flavor is enhanced if the salsa is prepared 1 day in advance.

Thirty Servings

Sun-Dried Tomato Dip
With Roasted Red Peppers

Commercially packed roasted red bell peppers are a great convenience, but peppers are also easily roasted at home. There are many methods of doing this, such as skewering the red pepper on the tines of a long-handled fork and holding over the flame of a gas stove until charred on all sides, or charring the red pepper under the broiler unit of your stove, turning until blackened on all sides. Regardless of the method you use, the end result is worth the effort.

8 sun-dried tomato halves

2 (7-ounce) jars roasted red
   bell peppers, drained

1 clove of garlic, minced

1 tablespoon fresh lemon
   juice

2 tablespoons chopped fresh
   flat-leaf parsley

4 ounces cream cheese,
   softened

1/2 cup sour cream

1/8 teaspoon salt

Pepper to taste

Pita chips

- Combine the sun-dried tomatoes with enough hot water to cover in a bowl.

- Let stand for 5 minutes. Drain and pat dry.

- Pat the red peppers dry with a paper towel.

- Combine the sun-dried tomatoes, red peppers, garlic, lemon juice and parsley in a food processor container.

- Process until smooth. Add the cream cheese, sour cream, salt and pepper.

- Process until blended. Spoon into a serving bowl.

- Chill, covered, until serving time. Garnish with additional chopped fresh parsley. Serve with pita chips.

Makes Two Cups (About)

Roasted Red Peppers

Choose fresh firm red bell peppers with smooth skins. Slice the peppers lengthwise into halves. Discard the stems, seeds and ribs. Slice each half into thirds. Arrange the peppers flesh side down on a broiler rack. Broil for 7 to 8 minutes or until charred on all sides, turning frequently. Place immediately in a nonrecycled brown paper bag or a covered bowl. Seal the bag or cover the bowl. Let stand for 10 to 15 minutes to allow the peppers to steam. Discard the skins. Store, covered, in the refrigerator for up to 5 days.

HOT SPINACH DIP

Mix 8 ounces softened cream cheese, 8 ounces shredded Monterey Jack cheese at room temperature, 10 ounces drained thawed frozen chopped spinach, 1/3 cup half-and-half, 3/4 chopped onion, 2 chopped tomatoes, 1 tablespoon chopped jalapeño and 1/8 teaspoon Tabasco sauce in a bowl. Spoon into a baking dish. Bake at 400 degrees for 20 to 25 minutes. Serve with tortilla chips or corn chips.

ARTICHOKE PARMESAN PHYLLO BITES

3 (6-ounce) jars marinated
   artichoke hearts
1/2 cup freshly grated
   Parmesan cheese
1 clove of garlic, minced
10 sheets frozen phyllo
   pastry, thawed
10 teaspoons freshly grated
   Parmesan cheese

- Drain the artichokes, reserving the marinade.

- Combine the artichokes, 1/2 cup cheese and garlic in a food processor container fitted with a steel blade.

- Pulse 4 times or until the artichokes are finely chopped.

- Place 1 sheet of the phyllo on a sheet of waxed paper, leaving the remaining pastry covered with a damp cloth to prevent drying out.

- Brush the phyllo lightly with some of the reserved marinade. Sprinkle with 2 teaspoons of the 10 teaspoons cheese. Top with another sheet of phyllo and brush lightly with the reserved marinade.

- Cut the phyllo sheets lengthwise into halves. Cut each half crosswise into thirds, resulting in six 5x6-inch sections.

- Spoon 1 heaping teaspoon of the artichoke mixture in the center of each phyllo section. Gather the corners over the filling and gently twist to enclose the filling. Place on a lightly greased baking sheet. Repeat the procedure with the remaining ingredients.

- Bake at 350 degrees for 14 minutes or until golden brown.

- Serve immediately.

Thirty Servings

SPICY CORN FRITTERS WITH CREME FRAICHE

1 (10-ounce) package frozen
    corn, thawed, drained

1/2 cup chopped onion

3 scallions, coarsely chopped

2 cloves of garlic

1 teaspoon Tabasco sauce

Salt and pepper to taste

1/2 cup flour

1/2 cup chopped fresh parsley
    or cilantro

2 eggs

Vegetable oil for frying

Crème fraîche

Sprigs of fresh parsley or
    cilantro

- Combine the corn, onion, scallions, garlic, Tabasco sauce, salt and pepper in a food processor container.

- Process until mixed. Add the flour, 1/2 cup parsley and eggs. Process just until mixed.

- Heat 1/4 inch oil in a skillet until hot but not smoking. Drop the corn mixture by tablespoonfuls into the hot oil.

- Fry for 5 minutes or until golden brown on both sides, turning once. Drain on paper towels.

- Top each fritter with crème fraîche and a sprig of parsley or cilantro.

- May substitute chick-peas for the corn, sour cream or yogurt for the crème fraîche and sprinkle with caviar for a special occasion.

- Reheat at 200 degrees if prepared in advance.

Thirty-Five Servings

BUTTERED PECANS

Prepare Buttered Pecans by drizzling 1/2 cup melted butter over the bottom of a baking pan. Spread 4 cups pecan halves in a single layer in the prepared pan, turning to coat. Bake at 350 degrees until the pecans are crisp, turning every 10 minutes. Spread on paper towels to drain. Sprinkle with salt.

MARINATED CHICKEN WINGS

2 to 3 dozen chicken
  wings or drumettes

Garlic salt to taste

1 cup soy sauce

1/4 cup white wine

1/4 cup vegetable oil

1 tablespoon sugar

1 teaspoon ground ginger

- Sprinkle the chicken generously on all sides with garlic salt. Arrange in a deep baking pan.
- Combine the soy sauce, white wine, oil, sugar and ginger in a bowl and mix well. Pour over the chicken, turning to coat.
- Marinate, covered, in the refrigerator for 12 to 16 hours, turning occasionally.
- Bake at 325 degrees for 1 1/2 to 2 hours or until cooked through.

Eight to Twelve Servings

JALAPENO PIE

1 (7-ounce) can
  jalapeños, drained

8 ounces coarsely
  shredded sharp
  Cheddar cheese

4 eggs

Salt and ground red
  pepper to taste

- Seed the jalapeños. Cut lengthwise into thin slivers.
- Line the bottom and side of a 9-inch pie plate with the jalapeño slivers. Press the cheese over the peppers.
- Beat the eggs, salt and red pepper in a mixer bowl until blended. Pour over the prepared layers.
- Bake at 350 degrees for 25 to 30 minutes or until set.
- Cut into wedges and serve from the pie plate.

Sixteen Servings

GOAT CHEESE QUESADILLAS WITH ROASTED RED PEPPER SAUCE

Roasted Red Pepper Sauce

2 red bell peppers

1 small onion, coarsely chopped

3 cloves of garlic, chopped

3 tablespoons olive oil

2 tablespoons chopped fresh basil

Salt and pepper to taste

Quesadillas

6 (9- or 10-inch) flour or whole wheat tortillas

4$^{1}/_{2}$ ounces soft mild goat cheese, cut into 4 portions

$^{1}/_{4}$ cup basil pesto

1 small onion, thinly sliced

2 tablespoons unsalted butter, softened

- For the sauce, arrange the red peppers on a broiler rack. Broil 2 inches from the heat source for 15 to 20 minutes or until the skins are charred and blistered on all sides, turning every 5 minutes.

- Let stand, covered, in a bowl until cool. Peel the peppers. Remove tops and discard seeds and ribs.

- Cook the onion and garlic in 1 tablespoon of the olive oil in a skillet over medium heat until tender, stirring constantly.

- Combine the red peppers, onion mixture, remaining 2 tablespoons olive oil, basil, salt and pepper in a food processor container.

- Process until smooth. Spoon into a bowl.

- Store, covered, in the refrigerator for up to 3 days.

- For the quesadillas, spread 1 tortilla with 1 portion of the goat cheese. Top with 1 tablespoon pesto and $^{1}/_{4}$ of the onion. Repeat the layering process. Top with a tortilla. Spread the top and bottom of the quesadilla with 1 tablespoon of the butter. Repeat the process with the remaining ingredients for 1 more quesadilla.

- Heat a griddle or 10-inch skillet over medium-high heat until hot. Cook the quesadillas 1 at a time on the griddle for 4 minutes per side or until golden brown, pressing gently with a metal spatula.

- Cut each quesadilla into 8 wedges. Serve warm with the sauce.

Four to Eight Servings

MUSHROOM PIROSHKI

Mushroom Filling

1 large onion, chopped

3 tablespoons butter

8 ounces mushrooms, chopped

1/2 teaspoon salt

1/2 teaspoon pepper

1/4 teaspoon thyme

2 tablespoons flour

1/4 cup sour cream

Piroshki

9 ounces cream cheese, softened

1/2 cup margarine, softened

1 1/2 cups sifted flour

- For the filling, sauté the onion in the butter in a skillet until light brown. Stir in the mushrooms.

- Cook for 3 minutes, stirring constantly. Add the salt, pepper and thyme and mix well. Sprinkle in the flour and mix well. Stir in the sour cream.

- Cook over medium heat until thickened, stirring constantly.

- For the piroshki, mix the cream cheese and margarine in a bowl until blended. Add the flour and mix well.

- Chill, covered, in the refrigerator.

- Roll 1/8 inch thick on a lightly floured surface. Cut into 3-inch rounds with a cutter.

- Spoon 1 teaspoon of the filling onto the center of each round. Fold over to enclose the filling; press the edges with a fork to seal. Arrange on a baking sheet.

- Bake at 450 degrees for 15 to 20 minutes or until brown.

Ten to Twelve Servings

HOT ONION SOUFFLE

16 ounces cream cheese, softened

1/2 cup mayonnaise

2 cups finely chopped onions

2 cups grated Parmesan cheese

- Combine the cream cheese and mayonnaise in a bowl and mix well. Stir in the onions and Parmesan cheese. Spoon into a baking dish.

- Bake at 425 degrees for 15 to 20 minutes or until brown and bubbly.

- Serve the soufflé with assorted party crackers.

Sixteen to Twenty Servings

PAINTED DESERT PINWHEELS

These colorful appetizer pinwheels taste every bit as good as they look. Reprinted from Mexican Medley with permission from Susan Fuller Slack and The American Cooking Guild.

2 New Mexico chiles, roasted, peeled, seeded

1 jalapeño, chopped

1 clove of garlic

1 to 2 tablespoons chopped fresh cilantro

8 ounces cream cheese, softened

1/4 teaspoon salt

5 (10-inch) flour tortillas

15 rectangular paper-thin slices ham

20 (3 1/2-inch-square) paper-thin slices Monterey Jack cheese

5 green onions, trimmed

10 oil-pack sun-dried tomato halves, drained, cut into strips

1/2 cup finely chopped black olives

- Combine the chiles, jalapeño, garlic and cilantro in a food processor container fitted with a steel blade. Process until chopped.
- Add the cream cheese and salt. Process until blended.
- Spread 3 tablespoons of the cream cheese mixture over each tortilla. Arrange 3 slices of the ham and 4 slices of the cheese over the cream cheese mixture, leaving 1/2 inch uncovered at the top edge. Place 1 green onion, sun-dried tomato strips and olives in a strip near the bottom edge of each tortilla. Roll starting from the bottom to enclose the filling. Spread the edge with additional cream cheese mixture to seal. Wrap each tortilla roll individually in plastic wrap.
- Chill for 1 to 10 hours. Trim ends from tortillas. Cut each roll into 6 to 8 slices.
- May substitute thin slices of turkey or beef for the ham. May substitute one 4-ounce can green chiles for the New Mexico chiles and 1 small red bell pepper for the sun-dried tomatoes.

Thirty to Forty Servings

CINNAMON SUGAR PECANS

Spread 1/2 cup melted butter in a baking pan. Beat 2 egg whites and 1/4 teaspoon salt in a mixer bowl until foamy. Add 1 cup sugar and 1 1/2 teaspoons cinnamon gradually, beating constantly until soft peaks form. Add 1 pound pecan halves, stirring until coated. Spread in prepared pan. Bake at 325 degrees for 30 minutes or until crisp, turning every 10 to 12 minutes. Slide a metal spatula under pecans to loosen. Cool in pan.

ICED ALMONDS

Heat 1 cup blanched whole almonds, 1/2 cup sugar and 2 tablespoons butter in a skillet over medium heat for 15 minutes or until the almonds are toasted and golden brown, stirring constantly. Stir in 1/2 teaspoon vanilla extract. Spread the almonds in a single layer on a baking sheet lined with foil. Sprinkle with 3/4 teaspoon salt. Let stand until cool. Break into small clusters.

GREEK SPINACH SQUARES

1 (10-ounce) package frozen chopped spinach, thawed, drained

1 medium onion, chopped

6 green onions with tops, chopped

3 tablespoons olive oil

1 1/2 cups small curd cottage cheese

3/4 cup crumbled feta cheese

4 eggs, beaten

1/3 cup yellow or white cornmeal

1/3 cup self-rising flour

2 teaspoons sugar

1 teaspoon baking powder

6 tablespoons melted butter

2 eggs

- Squeeze the moisture from the spinach.

- Sauté the onion and green onions in the olive oil in a skillet until tender. Stir in the spinach.

- Cook over medium heat until all of the liquid is absorbed, stirring frequently. Spoon into a bowl. Add the cottage cheese, feta cheese and 4 eggs and mix well.

- Combine the cornmeal, flour, sugar and baking powder in a bowl and mix well. Stir into the spinach mixture. Spoon into a greased 9x13-inch baking pan.

- Whisk the butter and 2 eggs in a bowl until blended. Spread evenly over the prepared layer.

- Bake at 350 degrees for 45 minutes. Let stand for 10 minutes before cutting into squares.

Twenty-Four Servings

Aunt Sallee's Vegetable Pizza

2 (8-count) cans crescent
  rolls

8 ounces cream cheese,
  softened

3/4 cup mayonnaise

1 envelope ranch salad
  dressing mix

3 cups finely chopped
  broccoli, purple onion, red
  bell pepper, green bell
  pepper, fresh mushrooms,
  tomatoes, black olives,
  green olives and/or lettuce

8 ounces mozzarella cheese,
  finely shredded

- Unroll the crescent roll dough into a large rectangle on a lightly greased baking sheet, pressing edges and perforations to seal.
- Bake at 375 degrees for 10 minutes. Cool on the baking sheet on a wire rack for 20 minutes or until completely cool.
- Combine the cream cheese, mayonnaise and salad dressing mix in a food processor container.
- Process until blended. Spread the cream cheese mixture over the baked layer.
- Sprinkle with the chopped vegetables. Top with the mozzarella cheese.
- Chill, covered, for 4 to 10 hours. Cut pizza into bite-size pieces.

Forty-Eight (Two-Inch) Squares

If you spread the cream cheese mixture over the baked crust of this vegetable pizza before the crust has been allowed to cool, the crust will become soggy and inedible. Be sure to cool the crust at least twenty minutes before proceeding with the recipe. Cool the baking sheet on a wire rack so that cool air can circulate underneath the hot pan.

CAJUN SHRIMP

3 quarts water

1 large lemon, sliced

4 pounds unpeeled large
   fresh shrimp

2 cups vegetable oil

1/4 cup hot pepper sauce

1 tablespoon minced
   garlic

1 tablespoon olive oil

1 1/2 teaspoons salt

1 1/2 teaspoons seafood
   seasoning

1 1/2 teaspoons basil

1 1/2 teaspoons oregano

1 1/2 teaspoons thyme

1 1/2 teaspoons minced
   fresh parsley

- Bring the water and lemon slices to a boil in a stockpot. Add the shrimp.

- Cook for 3 to 5 minutes or until the shrimp turn pink; drain. Rinse with cold water and drain. Place in a bowl.

- Chill, covered, in the refrigerator.

- Peel and devein the shrimp. Place the shrimp in a large heavy-duty sealable plastic bag.

- Combine the vegetable oil, hot sauce, garlic, olive oil, salt, seafood seasoning, basil, oregano, thyme and parsley in a bowl and mix well. Pour over the shrimp and seal the bag.

- Marinate the shrimp in the refrigerator for 8 hours, turning the bag occasionally.

- Drain and spoon the shrimp into a serving bowl.

Twenty-Five Servings

SHRIMP AND FETA CUPS

8 ounces white
   mushroom caps,
   finely chopped

4 ounces feta cheese,
   crumbled

5 to 8 ounces shrimp,
   cooked, peeled,
   deveined

1 egg, lightly beaten

24 uncooked tart shells

- Sauté the mushrooms in a nonstick skillet until tender; drain. Spoon into a bowl.

- Add the feta cheese, shrimp and egg and mix well.

- Arrange the tart shells on a baking sheet. Fill the shells with the shrimp mixture.

- Bake at 350 degrees for 12 to 15 minutes or until brown. Serve immediately.

Twenty-Four Servings

Bubba's Shrimp On A Stick

8 bamboo skewers

16 (1x6-inch) paper-thin slices Canadian bacon or country ham

16 uncooked large shrimp, peeled, deveined

1/2 cup Dijon mustard

1/4 cup Jack Daniel's or other bourbon

1/4 cup packed light brown sugar

Vegetable oil

- Soak the bamboo skewers in enough water to cover in a bowl for 30 minutes; drain.

- Wrap 1 slice of the Canadian bacon around each shrimp. Thread 2 shrimp onto each skewer. Arrange on a baking sheet.

- Combine the Dijon mustard and bourbon in a bowl and mix well. Brush both sides of the shrimp with the mustard mixture.

- Marinate in the refrigerator for 30 minutes to 2 hours.

- Press 2 tablespoons of the brown sugar through a sieve over the shrimp. Turn the shrimp. Repeat the process with the remaining brown sugar.

- Let stand at room temperature for 15 minutes.

- Brush the grill rack with oil. Arrange the shrimp on the rack.

- Grill over medium-high heat for 3 minutes per side or until cooked through. Remove to a serving platter.

- Serve immediately.

Eight Servings

Cocktail Sauce for Shrimp or Crudites

Combine 1/4 cup chili sauce, 1 cup mayonnaise, 1/2 teaspoon minced onion, 1 teaspoon lemon juice, 1 teaspoon curry powder, 1/2 teaspoon Worcestershire sauce, 1/2 teaspoon red pepper sauce, salt and pepper to taste and mix well. Store in the refrigerator until serving time. Serve with steamed shrimp or with your favorite shrimp salad.

TOMATO GALETTE WITH FRESH ROSEMARY

For a tasty variation, sprinkle three or four tablespoons coarsely chopped niçoise olives over the galette before baking.

1 sheet frozen puff pastry

1 egg, lightly beaten

1 tablespoon milk

3 tablespoons anchovy paste, or to taste

1½ cups shredded mozzarella cheese

6 medium red or yellow tomatoes, cut into ½-inch slices

1 medium red onion, thinly sliced

1 teaspoon finely minced garlic

¾ cup grated imported Parmesan cheese

Fresh rosemary leaves

Sprigs of fresh basil

• Thaw the puff pastry in the refrigerator.

• Roll the pastry into a 12x16-inch rectangle on a lightly floured surface. Cut four 1x16-inch strips from the pastry rectangle.

• Place the rectangle on a nonstick baking sheet. Brush the edges of the pastry lightly with water. Press the pastry strips onto the edges of the pastry all around the rectangle, trimming the ends of the pastry strips as needed. Prick lightly with a fork.

• Whisk the egg and milk in a bowl until blended. Brush the decorative top strips with the egg mixture.

• Spread the anchovy paste over the pastry bottom; sprinkle with ¾ cup of the mozzarella cheese. Arrange the tomatoes and onion over the cheese. Sprinkle with the garlic, remaining mozzarella cheese, Parmesan cheese and a few rosemary leaves.

• Bake at 350 degrees for 18 to 20 minutes or until the pastry puffs and turns golden brown.

• Cool on the baking sheet for 5 minutes. Remove to a serving platter. Decorate with sprigs of rosemary or basil.

Eight Servings

LAZY MAN'S SPANAKOPITA

1 (10-ounce) package frozen
  chopped spinach, thawed,
  drained

3/4 cup thinly sliced green
  onions

1 tablespoon olive oil

1 1/4 cups crumbled feta
  cheese

1 tablespoon fresh lemon
  juice

1/4 teaspoon nutmeg

Salt and pepper to taste

1 egg yolk, lightly beaten

1 sheet frozen puff pastry,
  thawed

Milk

- Squeeze the moisture from the spinach.

- Sauté the green onions in the olive oil in a skillet over medium heat for 1 minute. Transfer to a bowl. Let stand until cool.

- Add the spinach, feta cheese, lemon juice and nutmeg to the green onions and mix well. Season with salt and pepper. Stir in the egg yolk.

- Roll the pastry into a 13-inch square on a lightly floured surface. Cut the pastry lengthwise into halves, creating two 6 1/2x13-inch strips.

- Divide the spinach mixture into 2 equal portions. Spread each spinach portion evenly over each pastry half, leaving 1-inch border on all sides. Brush the edges with milk.

- Roll as for a jelly roll to enclose the filling, pressing the edges firmly to seal.

- Place the pastries seam side down on a buttered baking sheet. Cut 1-inch-long crosswise score lines every 3/4 inch. Brush with milk.

- Bake the pastries at 400 degrees for 25 minutes or until golden brown.

- Cool slightly on the baking sheet. Transfer the pastries to a cutting board. Cut into slices at the score lines. Serve warm.

Thirty-Six Servings

To express the liquid from spinach, use a potato ricer. Squeeze hard enough to press out most of the liquid, but not so hard that you "rice" the spinach.

GRANOLA

This recipe originated in an inn in New England.

2 cups honey

1³/4 cups vegetable oil

1 (42-ounce) package
   quick-cooking oats

2 cups nonfat dry milk
   powder

2 cups sliced almonds

1 cup sunflower kernels

1 cup untoasted wheat germ

1 cup shredded coconut

1 cup raisins

- Combine the honey and oil in a microwave-safe dish.
- Microwave for 7 minutes.
- Mix the oats, milk powder, almonds, sunflower kernels, wheat germ, coconut and raisins in a large disposable roasting pan. Add the honey mixture and mix well.
- Bake at 300 degrees for 45 minutes, stirring every 15 minutes.
- Let stand until cool.
- Store in airtight containers or sealable plastic bags in the refrigerator.
- May store in the freezer for future use.

Twenty-Six (One-Cup) Servings

BLOODY MARY

1 (46-ounce) can tomato
  juice

18 to 20 ounces vodka

1 (14-ounce) can beef
  bouillon

1/4 cup fresh lemon juice

2 tablespoons
  Worcestershire sauce

1 tablespoon sugar

1 teaspoon celery salt

1/2 teaspoon Jane's Crazy
  Salt

1/4 teaspoon seasoned
  pepper

8 to 10 drops of Tabasco
  sauce

Lime wedges

- Combine the tomato juice,
  vodka, bouillon, lemon juice,
  Worcestershire sauce, sugar,
  celery salt, Jane's Crazy Salt,
  pepper and Tabasco sauce in a
  large container and mix well.

- Pour over ice in glasses. Top each
  glass with a lime wedge.

Ten to Twelve Servings

HENRY'S BEST EGGNOG

12 egg yolks

1 cup sugar

2 cups bourbon

1 cup brandy

1 pint vanilla ice cream

4 cups milk

2 cups whipping cream

12 egg whites

Freshly grated nutmeg
  to taste

- Beat the egg yolks and sugar in
  a mixer bowl until thickened and
  pale yellow. Stir in the bourbon,
  brandy, ice cream, milk and
  whipping cream.

- Beat the egg whites in a mixer
  bowl until stiff peaks form. Stir
  in the nog.

- Ladle into cups. Sprinkle with
  nutmeg to taste.

Twelve to Fifteen Servings

BRAY'S LEMONADE

Simple Syrup

4 cups cold water

2 cups sugar

Lemonade

3 cups lemon juice

3 cups cold water

3 cups club soda

Sprigs of fresh mint

- For the syrup, bring the cold water and sugar to a boil in a saucepan over high heat, stirring with a wooden spoon until the sugar dissolves.

- Boil for 5 minutes longer. Remove from heat.

- Let stand until cool. Store, covered, in a container in the refrigerator for 3 to 4 weeks.

- For the lemonade, combine 1½ cups of the lemon juice, cold water and 1 cup of the Simple Syrup in a pitcher and mix well.

- Pour into ice cube trays. Freeze until firm.

- Combine the remaining 1½ cups lemon juice, remaining Simple Syrup and club soda in a pitcher and mix well. Pour over the lemonade ice cubes in a glass. Top each serving with a sprig of mint.

Six Servings

PIEDMONT PUNCH

This is a drink made famous throughout the South on the now defunct Piedmont Airlines.

2¼ cups white grape juice

2¼ cups apple juice

2 cups pineapple juice

½ cup water

2 tablespoons fresh lemon juice

2 teaspoons fresh lime juice

½ teaspoon almond extract

- Combine the grape juice, apple juice, pineapple juice, water, lemon juice, lime juice and flavoring in a pitcher and mix well.

- Pour over ice cubes in a glass.

Ten Servings

ROSLYN DRIVE MINT TEA

2 cups boiling water

5 family-size
   decaffeinated tea bags

24 sprigs of mint

2 cups sugar

2 cups boiling water

1 cup lemon juice

12 cups cold water

- Pour 2 cups boiling water over the tea bags and mint in a heatproof pitcher. Steep for 20 minutes.

- Combine the sugar, 2 cups boiling water and lemon juice in a 1-gallon heatproof container, stirring until the sugar dissolves.

- Strain the tea and add to the sugar mixture. Add the cold water and mix well.

- Chill, covered, until serving time.

- Pour over ice in glasses.

- May substitute 4 family-size caffeinated tea bags for 5 decaffeinated tea bags.

Sixteen (Eight-Ounce) Servings

RUM SLUSH PUNCH

1 cup sugar

1 (46-ounce) can
   pineapple juice

1 (2-liter) bottle
   lemon-lime soda

2 (12-ounce) cans frozen
   orange juice
   concentrate

1 (16-ounce) jar
   maraschino cherries

$1/2$ cup rum

- Dissolve the sugar in a small amount of hot water in a bowl.

- Combine the sugar water, pineapple juice, lemon-lime soda, orange juice concentrate, undrained cherries and rum in a large bowl and mix well.

- Pour into 4 sealable freezer bags and seal tightly. Arrange the bags flat on a freezer rack.

- Freeze for 48 hours.

- Thaw slightly or just until of a slush consistency. Pour into a punch bowl.

- Ladle into punch cups.

- The punch will not freeze solid because of the alcohol content.

Twenty to Twenty-Five Servings

BEYOND THE IRON

Water plumes rise above the grounds of the Governor's Mansion. In time, these waters will make their way seaward, and the cycle of Carolina waters will begin anew.

SALADS

SALADS

THE LACE HOUSE AND LEMONS IN WATER

Just out of view, double piazzas and fences of elaborate, embellished ironwork distinguish the Lace House, the official guest house of the Governor's Mansion.

Opposite:

*Macadamia Cream Tarts
with Papaya Apricot Glaze*

*Lime Cilantro Shrimp with
Sliced Kiwifruit*

Instant Herbed Chevre

Marinated Sesame Asparagus

ROYAL ANNE CHERRY SALAD

1 envelope unflavored gelatin

$^1/_4$ cup cold water

2 (6-ounce) packages lemon gelatin

$^1/_3$ cup sugar

$^1/_2$ cup boiling water

1 (16-ounce) can Royal Anne cherries

1 (16-ounce) can crushed pineapple

1 (8-ounce) can crushed pineapple

Juice and grated peel of 1 orange

Juice and grated peel of $^1/_2$ lemon

- Soften the unflavored gelatin in the cold water and mix well.
- Dissolve the lemon gelatin and sugar in the boiling water and mix well.
- Drain the cherries, reserving 1 cup of the juice. Cut the cherries into halves.
- Drain the pineapple, reserving 1 cup of the juice.
- Combine the unflavored gelatin, lemon gelatin mixture, cherries, reserved cherry juice, pineapple, reserved pineapple juice, orange juice, orange peel, lemon juice and lemon peel in a bowl and mix well. Pour the gelatin mixture into a shallow dish.
- Chill until set.

Ten to Twelve Servings

CRANBERRY GINGERSNAP SALAD

Great salad for a special holiday meal.

2 cups crushed gingersnaps

$^1/_4$ cup melted butter or margarine

8 ounces cream cheese, softened

1 (16-ounce) can whole cranberry sauce

1 (8-ounce) can crushed pineapple, drained

1 cup sour cream

1 tablespoon brown sugar

$^1/_2$ cup sour cream

- Combine the gingersnaps and butter in a bowl and mix well. Pat $^2/_3$ of the crumb mixture over the bottom of a greased 8x8-inch dish.
- Beat the cream cheese at medium speed in a mixer bowl until smooth and creamy. Stir in the cranberry sauce, pineapple, 1 cup sour cream and brown sugar. Spread over the prepared layer.
- Freeze, covered, until firm. Let stand at room temperature for 20 to 25 minutes before serving.
- Cut into squares. Top with $^1/_2$ cup sour cream and the remaining crumb mixture.

Eight Servings

MELON, CUCUMBER AND TOMATO SALAD

Dressing

5 tablespoons salad oil

3 tablespoons wine vinegar

2 teaspoons sugar

Salt and pepper to taste

Salad

1 large cucumber

Salt to taste

1 cantaloupe

1 pound fresh tomatoes

1¹/₂ tablespoons chopped
fresh mint

1 tablespoon chopped fresh
parsley

1 tablespoon chopped fresh
chives

- For the dressing, combine the salad oil, wine vinegar, sugar, salt and pepper in a jar with a tightfitting lid. Shake until blended.

- For the salad, peel and chop the cucumber into bite-size pieces. Spread on a plate and sprinkle with salt. Cover with another plate.

- Let stand for 30 minutes; drain. Rinse with cold water and drain.

- Cut the cantaloupe and tomatoes into bite-size pieces.

- Combine the cucumber, cantaloupe and tomatoes in a bowl and mix gently. Add the dressing, tossing to coat.

- Chill, covered, for 2 to 3 hours, stirring occasionally.

- Stir in the mint, parsley and chives just before serving. Transfer to a serving bowl using a slotted spoon.

- May substitute any type of melon for the cantaloupe.

Six Servings

ROAST BEEF AND HERB CHEESE WITH MIXED BABY GREENS

12 to 16 thin slices rare
   roast beef

6 ounces cream cheese,
   softened

6 ounces soft goat cheese

3 spring onions, chopped

1/2 cup finely chopped red
   bell pepper

2 teaspoons coarsely ground
   pepper

1 teaspoon minced garlic
   chives

1/2 cup plus 1 tablespoon
   olive oil

1/4 cup red wine vinegar

3 tablespoons chopped
   shallots

1 tablespoon chopped
   fresh basil, tarragon,
   parsley, thyme and/or a
   combination of herbs

Salt and pepper to taste

10 to 12 cups mesclun

- Line 6 teacups with plastic wrap, leaving an overhang. Line each with 2 slices of beef, crossing in the middle and extending over the rim of the cups. May add extra beef if needed to fill in holes.

- Combine the cream cheese, goat cheese, spring onions, red pepper, pepper and chives in a bowl and mix well. Spoon into the teacups, dividing equally; press gently. Fold the beef over to make a small meat package. Fold over the plastic wrap.

- Chill for 8 to 10 hours. Invert onto a plate. Discard the plastic wrap wrap.

- Heat 1 tablespoon of the olive oil in a skillet over medium heat until hot. Add the meat packages flat side down.

- Cook, covered, for 5 minutes or until the cheese is soft when you press top of the meat bundle. Remove to a plate.

- Let stand for 1 hour.

- Combine the wine vinegar and shallots in a bowl. Add the remaining 1/2 cup olive oil in a fine stream, whisking constantly until mixed. Stir in the fresh herbs. Season with salt and pepper.

- Line 6 salad plates with the mixed greens. Place the meat packages on the greens. Drizzle with the dressing.

Six Servings

CHARLESTON CHICKEN SALAD

Kristian Niemi of Mr. Friendly's New Southern Cafe was most generous to share this recipe.

Honey Dijon Dressing

1 cup mayonnaise

1/3 cup Dijon mustard

1/3 cup honey

1 tablespoon cider vinegar

Chicken

2 tablespoons top-quality
  curry powder

2 tablespoons vegetable oil

4 boneless skinless chicken
  breasts

Salad

Mixed baby greens

Peach Chutney (at right)

Thinly sliced red onion

Tomato wedges

Toasted almonds

- For the dressing, whisk the mayonnaise, Dijon mustard, honey and cider vinegar in a bowl until blended. Store, covered, in the refrigerator.

- For the chicken, combine the curry powder and oil in a bowl and mix well. Spread over both sides of the chicken. Chill, covered, in the refrigerator until just before grilling.

- Grill over hot coals until firm but not dry. Press with your finger on the thickest part of the chicken breast while it is cooking. If it feels spongy, it is not quite done. If it feels firm and springy, it is done. Chicken breasts can be juicy and flavorful, but people have a tendency to overcook. If in doubt, take the chicken off the grill and make an incision in the thickest part—if it is pink, then the chicken is not cooked through.

- For the salad, arrange the mixed greens on salad plates. Slice the chicken and lay across the greens. Top with the Peach Chutney; drizzle with the dressing. Arrange the sliced red onion and tomato wedges decoratively around the edges of the plates. Sprinkle with the almonds.

Four to Six Servings

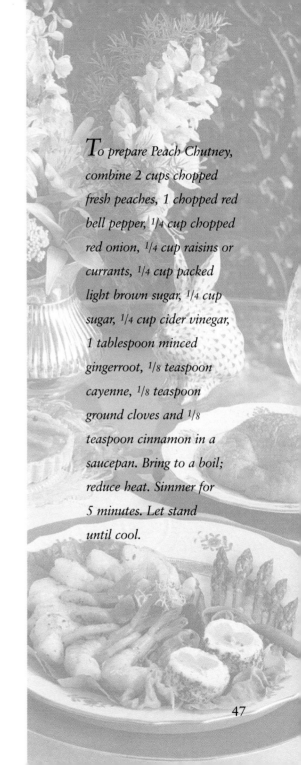

To prepare Peach Chutney, combine 2 cups chopped fresh peaches, 1 chopped red bell pepper, 1/4 cup chopped red onion, 1/4 cup raisins or currants, 1/4 cup packed light brown sugar, 1/4 cup sugar, 1/4 cup cider vinegar, 1 tablespoon minced gingerroot, 1/8 teaspoon cayenne, 1/8 teaspoon ground cloves and 1/8 teaspoon cinnamon in a saucepan. Bring to a boil; reduce heat. Simmer for 5 minutes. Let stand until cool.

CHICKEN SALAD WITH A TWIST

6 ounces rotini

3 cups chopped cooked chicken

$^1/_2$ cup Italian salad dressing

$^1/_2$ cup mayonnaise

3 tablespoons lemon juice

1 to 2 tablespoons prepared mustard

Salt and pepper to taste

- Cook the corkscrew pasta using package directions; drain.

- Combine the pasta and chicken in a bowl and mix gently.

- Combine the salad dressing, mayonnaise, lemon juice and mustard in a bowl and mix well. Add to the pasta mixture, stirring to mix. Season with salt and pepper. Chill until serving time.

- Vary the salad by adding 1 or more of the following ingredients: chopped onion, sliced black olives, canned mushrooms, chopped cucumber, pepperoni, chopped red or green bell pepper, cooked shrimp, artichoke hearts and/or hearts of palm.

Eight to Ten Servings

CHICKEN SALAD WITH BLACK BEANS AND CORN

1 (15-ounce) can black beans, rinsed, drained

1 (11-ounce) can Mexicorn, drained

1/2 (10-ounce) package mixed greens, torn into bite-size pieces

6 ounces sliced smoked chicken breast, cut into strips

1/2 cup thinly sliced red onion

1/3 to 1/2 cup creamy garlic salad dressing

Tortilla chips (optional)

- Combine the black beans, Mexicorn and mixed greens in a bowl and mix gently. Stir in the chicken and onion.

- Add the salad dressing, tossing to coat. Top with tortilla chips.

- May substitute Italian salad dressing for the creamy garlic salad dressing.

Four Servings

THREE RIVERS CHICKEN SALAD

Serve as a salad or spread on croissants.

Chicken Salad Dressing

1 to 1 1/2 cups mayonnaise

3 tablespoons honey

3 tablespoons prepared mustard

1 teaspoon cayenne

Salad

5 boneless skinless chicken breasts, cooked, chopped

1 (15-ounce) package golden raisins

1 cup chopped pecans

1/2 cup sweet pickle cubes

1 small onion, finely chopped

3 or 4 ribs celery, chopped

- For the dressing, combine the mayonnaise, honey, mustard and cayenne in a bowl and mix well.

- For the salad, combine the chicken, raisins, pecans, pickle cubes, onion and celery in a bowl and mix well.

- Add the dressing, tossing to coat.

- Store, covered, in the refrigerator until serving time.

Ten Servings

Use warm oil when preparing spice-infused oils with peppercorns, chiles or ginger. Combine one cup oil with four teaspoons freshly ground peppercorns or dried hot chiles, or with about 1/3 cup very finely chopped peeled gingerroot in a heavy saucepan. Starting on the lowest possible heat, bring the mixture to a temperature of 140 degrees and maintain that temperature for ten minutes, using a deep-fry or candy thermometer to ensure the mixture stays at that temperature. Pour the oil carefully into a bowl and let stand at room temperature for a day or longer. Strain into a jar and refrigerate for up to one month.

PAELLA SALAD

1 1/2 cups water

Salt to taste

Onion wedges

1 or 2 bay leaves

8 ounces medium shrimp

1 (5-ounce) package yellow rice mix

1/4 cup tarragon vinegar

2 tablespoons olive oil

1/4 to 1/2 teaspoon curry powder

1/8 teaspoon each dry mustard and white pepper

2 cups chopped cooked chicken breasts

1/2 cup frozen peas, thawed

1/3 cup sliced celery

1/4 cup minced onion

1 (2-ounce) jar chopped pimento, drained

Chopped tomato

Black pepper to taste

Lemon slices

1 (15-ounce) can asparagus spears, drained

- Bring the water, salt, onion wedges and bay leaves to a boil in a saucepan. May add other seasonings as desired to the water. Add the shrimp.

- Cook for 3 to 5 minutes or until the shrimp turn pink. Drain, discarding the onion and bay leaves.

- Chill, covered, in the refrigerator. Peel and devein the shrimp.

- Prepare the rice using package directions and omitting the butter. Spoon into a bowl. Let stand until cool.

- Combine the vinegar, olive oil, curry powder, dry mustard and white pepper in a bowl and mix well. Stir into the rice. Add the shrimp, chicken, peas, celery, 1/4 cup onion, pimento and tomato and mix gently. Season with salt and black pepper.

- Chill, covered, until serving time. Top with lemon slices and asparagus spears.

- Serve with cheese straws and a layered fresh fruit salad.

- May be prepared early in the day and stored, covered, in the refrigerator. Add the peas just before serving.

- For variety, add artichoke hearts and/or black or green olives.

Six Servings

SHRIMP AND ORZO SALAD

Dill Dressing

1/4 cup packed fresh
dillweed

3 tablespoons lemon
juice

3 tablespoons olive oil

1 1/2 tablespoons red wine
vinegar

1 1/2 cloves of garlic

1/2 teaspoon salt

1/8 teaspoon freshly
ground pepper

Salad

1 pound shrimp

3/4 cup orzo

1 cup pitted black olives,
sliced

3 1/2 ounces feta cheese,
crumbled

3 spring onions, chopped

- For the dressing, process the
  dillweed, lemon juice, olive oil,
  wine vinegar, garlic, salt and
  pepper in a blender until smooth.

- For the salad, cook the shrimp in
  boiling water in a saucepan until
  pink. Pour the shrimp into a
  colander. Top with ice to stop the
  cooking process.

- Cook the pasta using package
  directions; drain. Let stand
  until cool.

- Combine the pasta, shrimp,
  olives, feta cheese and spring
  onions in a bowl and mix gently.
  Add the dressing, tossing to coat.

- Chill, covered, for 3 hours.

Four Servings

CHUTNEY TUNA SALAD

2 (6-ounce) cans white
tuna, drained

1 tablespoon chopped
scallions

1 tablespoon chopped
fresh parsley

1 rib celery, minced

2 tablespoons mango
chutney

2 tablespoons raisins

2 tablespoons sliced
almonds

1/2 cup low-fat
mayonnaise

1 teaspoon curry powder

- Combine the tuna, scallions,
  parsley, celery, chutney, raisins
  and almonds in a bowl and
  mix well.

- Combine the mayonnaise and
  curry powder in a bowl and mix
  well. Add to the tuna mixture,
  stirring just until mixed.

- Spoon the salad onto 4 lettuce-
  lined salad plates.

Four Servings

ASPARAGUS CONGEALED SALAD

2 envelopes unflavored
   gelatin

1/2 cup cold water

1 cup water

3/4 cup sugar

1/2 cup wine vinegar

1 (15-ounce) can cut
   green asparagus

1 cup chopped celery

1/2 cup chopped pecans

2 tablespoons grated
   onion

2 pimentos, chopped

1 teaspoon salt

Juice of 1 lemon

- Soften the gelatin in 1/2 cup
  cold water.

- Bring 1 cup water, sugar and
  wine vinegar to a boil in a
  saucepan. Boil until the sugar
  dissolves, stirring occasionally.
  Stir in the gelatin mixture. Let
  stand until cool.

- Add the undrained asparagus,
  celery, pecans, onion, pimentos,
  salt and lemon juice to the
  gelatin mixture and mix well.
  Pour into a shallow dish.

- Chill until set.

  Ten Servings

BLACK BEAN SALAD

Perfect to serve with fajitas or as a dip with tortilla chips.

Juice of 1 large lemon

1/2 large avocado,
   chopped

1 (16- to 19-ounce) can
   black beans, rinsed,
   drained

1 (11-ounce) can
   Mexicorn, drained

1 tablespoon chopped
   fresh cilantro

1/4 teaspoon salt

1 head Boston lettuce,
   separated

- Pour the lemon juice into a bowl.
  Stir in the avocado, black beans,
  Mexicorn, cilantro and salt.

- Line 4 salad plates with the
  Boston lettuce. Top with the
  bean mixture.

  Four Servings

CABBAGE SALAD

2 (3-ounce) packages any
flavor ramen noodles
with flavor packets

2 (10-ounce) packages
finely shredded
cabbage

1 cup slivered almonds

1 cup sunflower kernels

1 bunch green onions,
chopped (optional)

1/2 cup light olive oil or
canola oil

1/2 cup sugar

1/3 cup white vinegar

- Break the noodles into small
pieces by striking the unopened
packages with a meat mallet.
Reserve the flavor packets.

- Combine the ramen noodles,
cabbage, almonds, sunflower
kernels and green onions in a
bowl and mix well.

- Combine the olive oil, sugar,
white vinegar and reserved flavor
packets in a bowl and mix well.
Pour over the cabbage mixture,
tossing to coat.

- If the salad is made in advance,
add the ramen noodles 30
minutes before serving if a
crunchier texture is desired.

- May substitute 3 1/2 teaspoons
sugar substitute for the sugar.

Twelve to Fifteen Servings

SLAW FOR BARBECUE

1 large head cabbage,
shredded

1 large white onion,
shredded

1 large green bell pepper,
shredded

1 cup sugar

1 cup vinegar

3/4 cup salad oil

1 tablespoon salt

1 teaspoon dry mustard

1 teaspoon celery seeds

- Layer the cabbage, onion and
green pepper in the order listed
in a bowl. Sprinkle the sugar
over the top; do not stir.

- Combine the vinegar, salad oil,
salt, dry mustard and celery seeds
in a saucepan and mix well. Bring
to a boil, stirring occasionally.

- Pour the hot vinegar mixture
over the cabbage mixture; do
not stir.

- Chill, covered, for 4 to 10 hours;
do not stir.

- For variety, add shredded carrots,
yellow bell pepper and purple
onion or substitute these ingredients for the cabbage, white
onion and green bell pepper.

- This salad will stay crisp for
several days if stored, covered,
in the refrigerator.

Ten to Twelve Servings

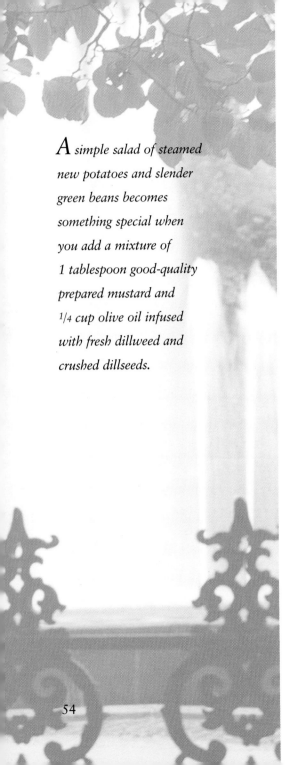

A simple salad of steamed new potatoes and slender green beans becomes something special when you add a mixture of 1 tablespoon good-quality prepared mustard and 1/4 cup olive oil infused with fresh dillweed and crushed dillseeds.

Mrs. Chandler's Potato Salad

8 medium unpeeled potatoes, boiled

1 1/2 cups mayonnaise

1 cup sour cream

1 1/2 teaspoons prepared horseradish

1 teaspoon celery seeds

1/2 teaspoon salt

2 medium onions, finely minced

1 cup chopped fresh parsley

Salt to taste

Chopped fresh parsley to taste

- Peel the potatoes and cut into 1/8-inch slices.
- Combine the mayonnaise, sour cream, horseradish, celery seeds and 1/2 teaspoon salt in a bowl and mix well.
- Combine the onions and 1 cup parsley in a bowl and mix well.
- Layer the potatoes, salt to taste, mayonnaise mixture and onion mixture in the order listed 1/2 at a time in a glass serving bowl. Sprinkle with parsley to taste.
- Chill, covered, for 8 hours or longer. May be prepared 1 day in advance and stored, covered, in the refrigerator.

Eight to Ten Servings

Mixed Greens With
Goat Cheese And Pine Nuts

10 tablespoons basil-flavor
olive oil

5 tablespoons balsamic
vinegar

Salt and pepper to taste

8 cups packed mixed baby
greens

2 heads Belgian endive, sliced

1 small head radicchio, torn
into bite-size pieces

1 cup packed fresh basil

5 ounces soft goat cheese,
crumbled

2 tablespoons pine nuts

- Whisk the olive oil into the balsamic vinegar in a bowl
  until blended. Season with salt and pepper.
- Mix the baby greens, endive, radicchio and basil in a
  bowl. Add the vinaigrette, tossing to coat. Sprinkle with
  the goat cheese and pine nuts.
- Montrachet or feta cheese may be used.
- May substitute olive oil for the basil-flavor olive oil.

Eight Servings

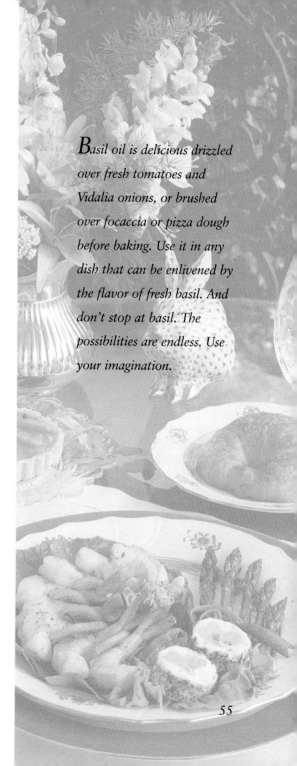

*Basil oil is delicious drizzled
over fresh tomatoes and
Vidalia onions, or brushed
over focaccia or pizza dough
before baking. Use it in any
dish that can be enlivened by
the flavor of fresh basil. And
don't stop at basil. The
possibilities are endless. Use
your imagination.*

Prepare Mom's Potato Salad for your next picnic or patio party. Peel and chop 5 or 6 medium potatoes. Combine with enough water to cover in a saucepan. Cook over low heat for 15 minutes or just until tender; drain. Mix the potatoes, 5 chopped hard-cooked eggs, 7 ounces chopped Spanish olives, 1 to 1½ cups mayonnaise and ⅛ teaspoon paprika. Store in the refrigerator until serving time.

PONT NEUF SALAD

Vinaigrette

⅓ *cup red wine vinegar*

2 tablespoons Dijon mustard

⅔ *cup olive oil*

Sea salt to taste

Freshly ground pepper to taste

Salad

¾ *cup chopped pecans*

2 to 3 tablespoons melted butter

4 heads Belgian endive, sliced

½ *head romaine, torn into bite-size pieces*

5 ounces (or less) bleu cheese or Stilton cheese

- For the vinaigrette, combine the wine vinegar and Dijon mustard in a bowl and mix well. Add the olive oil gradually, whisking until blended. Season with sea salt and pepper.

- For the salad, brown the pecans in the butter in a skillet for 10 minutes or toast in the oven, stirring frequently.

- Combine the endive and romaine in a salad bowl and mix well. Add the cheese, tossing to mix. Drizzle with the vinaigrette and sprinkle with the pecans just before serving.

- May substitute approximately 1 cup good-quality commercially prepared vinaigrette for the homemade version.

Six Servings

CRUNCHY ROMAINE SALAD

Sweet-and-Sour Dressing

1 cup sugar

3/4 cup canola oil

1/2 cup red wine vinegar

1 tablespoon soy sauce, or
   to taste

Salt and pepper to taste

Salad

1 (3-ounce) package ramen
   noodles

1 cup chopped pecans

1/4 cup unsalted butter

1 bunch broccoli, coarsely
   chopped

1 head romaine, torn into
   bite-size pieces

4 green onions, chopped

• For the dressing, combine the sugar, canola oil, wine
  vinegar, soy sauce, salt and pepper in a jar with a
  tightfitting lid. Shake until blended.

• For the salad, break the ramen noodles into small pieces,
  discarding the flavor packet.

• Brown the noodles and pecans in the butter in a skillet.
  Drain on paper towels. Let stand until cool.

• Combine the noodles, pecans, broccoli, romaine and
  green onions in a salad bowl and mix gently. Add 1 cup
  or more of the dressing, tossing to coat.

Ten to Twelve Servings

Caprese is a colorful, classic Italian salad and simple to prepare. Combine 3/4-inch slices fresh mozzarella cheese (made from buffalo milk), plum tomato wedges and fresh basil in a salad bowl. May add strips of roasted red peppers, sliced blanched zucchini and/or slivers of red onion. Toss with a vinaigrette of three parts olive oil to one part vinegar, chopped fresh parsley, oregano, salt, pepper and sugar to taste.

SPINACH SALAD WITH GOAT CHEESE

Dressing

2 tablespoons olive oil

1 tablespoon red wine vinegar or balsamic vinegar

1 teaspoon Dijon mustard

Salt and freshly ground pepper to taste

Salad

1/3 cup pine nuts

Salt to taste

1 bunch spinach, trimmed

1 unpeeled Granny Smith apple, chopped

6 to 8 slices bacon, crisp-fried, crumbled

2 ounces goat cheese, crumbled

- For the dressing, combine the olive oil, wine vinegar, Dijon mustard, salt and pepper in a jar with a tightfitting lid and shake to blend.

- For the salad, spread the pine nuts in a single layer on a foil-lined baking sheet. Spray with butter-flavor nonstick cooking spray and sprinkle with salt.

- Toast in a moderate oven until light brown.

- Tear the spinach leaves into bite-size pieces.

- Combine the spinach, pine nuts, apple, bacon and goat cheese in a salad bowl and toss to mix. Add the dressing just before serving and toss lightly.

Four to Six Servings

SPINACH SALAD WITH STRAWBERRIES AND BANANAS

Dressing

1 1/2 cups sugar

1 1/2 cups salad oil

3/4 cup vinegar

1/3 cup poppy seeds

1/3 cup sesame seeds, toasted

1 1/2 teaspoons paprika

1 1/2 teaspoons Worcestershire sauce

1 1/2 teaspoons minced onion

3/4 teaspoon dry mustard

Salad

1/2 cup nuts

1 pound spinach, torn into bite-size pieces

1 pint strawberries, sliced

4 medium bananas, sliced

- For the dressing, combine the sugar, salad oil, vinegar, poppy seeds, sesame seeds, paprika, Worcestershire sauce, onion and dry mustard in a jar with a tightfitting lid and shake to mix.

- For the salad, spread the nuts on a baking sheet sprayed with nonstick cooking spray.

- Toast the nuts at 250 degrees for 5 minutes.

- Layer the spinach, strawberries, bananas and nuts alternately in a salad bowl until all of the ingredients are used. Pour the desired amount of dressing over the top.

Twelve Servings

WARM SALAD OF PORK AND BLACK-EYED PEAS

2 (15-ounce) cans black-eyed
   peas, drained

1/2 cup sliced celery

1/2 cup sliced fresh
   mushrooms

1/4 cup chopped pimentos

1/4 cup sliced green onions

1/4 cup sliced black olives

2/3 cup Italian salad dressing

2 cloves of garlic, minced

1 pound pork tenderloin, cut
   into thin strips

Fresh spinach leaves

• Combine the black-eyed peas, celery, mushrooms, pimentos, green onions and olives in a bowl and mix well. Add the salad dressing, tossing to coat.

• Heat a skillet sprayed with nonstick cooking spray over medium-high heat until hot. Add the garlic.

• Stir-fry for 30 seconds. Add the pork.

• Stir-fry for 5 minutes or until the pork is cooked through. Remove from heat. Stir in the black-eyed pea mixture and mix well.

• Spoon onto spinach-lined plates. Serve immediately.

Six Servings

When preparing herb-infused oils, always use cold oils, preferably canola or olive oil. Use about one cup fresh herbs for each cup of oil, letting the herb oil stand for eight hours before straining into jars. Store, covered, in the refrigerator for up to one month.

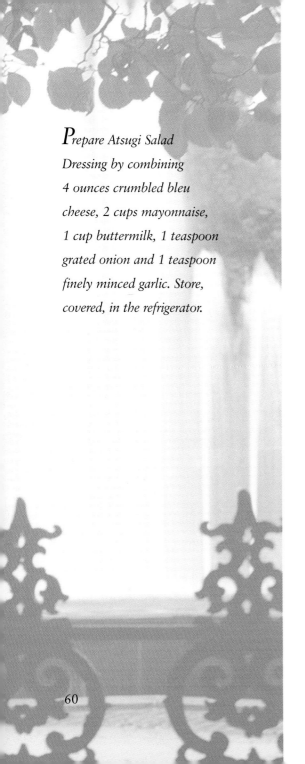

Prepare Atsugi Salad
Dressing by combining
4 ounces crumbled bleu
cheese, 2 cups mayonnaise,
1 cup buttermilk, 1 teaspoon
grated onion and 1 teaspoon
finely minced garlic. Store,
covered, in the refrigerator.

TOMATO ASPIC

The flavor is enhanced if the salad is prepared one day in advance.

1 (28-ounce) can whole
  tomatoes

2 (3-ounce) packages lemon
  gelatin

1/4 cup catsup

2 tablespoons lemon juice

2 tablespoons prepared
  horseradish

1 tablespoon Worcestershire
  sauce

1 teaspoon salt

1/8 teaspoon pepper

1/2 cup finely chopped onion

1/2 cup finely chopped green
  bell pepper

1/2 cup chopped cucumber
  or celery

Sour cream (optional)

10 olive halves (optional)

- Purée the undrained tomatoes in a blender.
- Combine the puréed tomatoes and gelatin in a saucepan and mix well. Bring to a boil, stirring constantly. Boil until the gelatin dissolves, stirring constantly. Remove from heat. Stir in the catsup, lemon juice, horseradish, Worcestershire sauce, salt and pepper and mix well.
- Chill until partially set. Stir in the onion, green pepper and cucumber. Spoon into 10 lightly oiled molds.
- Chill, covered with plastic wrap, until set.
- Invert onto salad plates. Top each aspic with sour cream and an olive half.

Ten Servings

GREEK TORTELLINI SALAD

Vinaigrette Dressing

$1/2$ cup rice vinegar or white
   wine vinegar

$1/2$ cup olive oil or salad oil

3 tablespoons lemon juice

2 tablespoons dry sherry

2 teaspoons dried mint

$1^1/2$ teaspoons seasoned salt

1 teaspoon garlic powder

1 teaspoon black pepper

$1/4$ teaspoon red pepper

Salad

2 (9-ounce) packages fresh
   plain or tricolor cheese
   tortellini, cooked, drained

2 medium red or green bell
   peppers, cut into strips

1 small red onion, thinly
   sliced

$1/4$ cup sliced black olives

$1/2$ cup crumbled feta cheese

- For the vinaigrette, combine the rice vinegar, olive oil, lemon juice, sherry, mint, seasoned salt, garlic powder, black pepper and red pepper in a jar with a tightfitting lid and shake to mix.

- For the salad, combine the pasta, red peppers, onion and olives in a bowl and mix gently. Add the dressing, tossing to coat.

- Chill, covered, for 4 to 24 hours, stirring occasionally. Stir in the feta cheese just before serving. Serve with a slotted spoon.

Twelve to Fourteen Servings

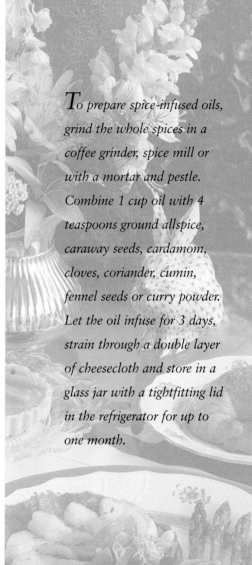

To prepare spice-infused oils, grind the whole spices in a coffee grinder, spice mill or with a mortar and pestle. Combine 1 cup oil with 4 teaspoons ground allspice, caraway seeds, cardamom, cloves, coriander, cumin, fennel seeds or curry powder. Let the oil infuse for 3 days, strain through a double layer of cheesecloth and store in a glass jar with a tightfitting lid in the refrigerator for up to one month.

Stilton Salad With Walnuts

Dijon Vinaigrette

3/4 cup olive oil

1/4 cup red wine vinegar

2 tablespoons water

1 tablespoon minced fresh parsley

1 tablespoon minced onion

1 teaspoon Dijon mustard

1 teaspoon basil

1/2 teaspoon oregano

1 clove of garlic, crushed

Salt and pepper to taste

Salad

3 heads Boston Bibb lettuce, torn into bite-size pieces

3/4 cup chopped walnuts

4 to 6 ounces Stilton cheese, crumbled

- For the vinaigrette, whisk the olive oil, wine vinegar, water, parsley, onion, Dijon mustard, basil, oregano, garlic, salt and pepper in a bowl until mixed.

- Chill, covered, in the refrigerator.

- May be prepared 2 days in advance and stored, covered, in the refrigerator.

- For the salad, bring the Dijon vinaigrette to room temperature.

- Combine the lettuce and walnuts in a bowl and mix well. Sprinkle with the cheese and drizzle with the vinaigrette.

Ten to Twelve Servings

Curried Rice Salad

Great to serve at luncheons. Omit the shrimp and serve with grilled or roasted fillet of beef for dinner.

Curry Dressing

1/2 cup mayonnaise

1 tablespoon soy sauce

1/2 teaspoon fresh lemon juice

1/4 teaspoon curry powder

Salad

2 cups rice, cooked

2 ribs celery, minced

1/2 green bell pepper, chopped

2 green onions tops, minced

3 tablespoons sliced black olives

Slivered almonds

Cooked, peeled, deveined shrimp (optional)

- For the dressing, combine the mayonnaise, soy sauce, lemon juice and curry powder in a bowl and mix well.

- For the salad, combine the rice, celery, green pepper, green onion tops, olives, almonds and shrimp in a bowl and mix well. Stir in the dressing.

Eight to Ten Servings

ORIENTAL WILD RICE SALAD

Orange Dressing

3 tablespoons orange juice

2 tablespoons rice vinegar

1 tablespoon soy sauce

3/4 teaspoon toasted sesame oil

1/2 teaspoon grated gingerroot

1 clove of garlic, minced

Salad

1/4 cup each wild rice and brown rice

1 cup chicken broth

1 (11-ounce) can mandarin oranges, drained

1 (8-ounce) can water chestnuts, drained, chopped

1 small red or green bell pepper, chopped

1 green onion, chopped

1/2 cup frozen peas, thawed

Spinach leaves (optional)

Cashews or peanuts (optional)

- For the dressing, combine the orange juice, rice vinegar, soy sauce, sesame oil, gingerroot and garlic in a jar with a tightfitting lid and shake to mix.

- For the salad, rinse the wild rice under cold water for 1 minute. Combine the wild rice, brown rice and broth in a saucepan and mix well. Bring to a boil; reduce heat.

- Simmer, covered, for 40 minutes or until the rice is tender and the liquid has been absorbed.

- Combine the rice, mandarin oranges, water chestnuts, red pepper and green onion in a bowl and mix well. Stir in the dressing.

- Chill, covered, for 4 to 24 hours. Stir in the peas just before serving.

- Spoon onto spinach-lined salad plates. Sprinkle with cashews or peanuts.

- May substitute white vinegar for the rice vinegar.

Four to Six Servings

SOUPS
SANDWICHES
& BREADS

SOUPS, SANDWICHES & BREADS

BANQUET BY THE WATER

Though the river rushes seaward and the rapids live up to their name, this feast will take time, as it should—for it is a banquet.

Opposite:

White Chocolate Lace Oatmeal Cookies

Muffuletta

Focaccia with Grilled Vegetables and Pesto

Bloody Mary Gazpacho Rimmed with Shrimp

Fresh Dill Dip for Crudités

Roslyn Drive Mint Tea

GOLDSPACHO

Gazpacho is an outstanding summer soup. The great thing is that you can make gazpacho in an array of bright summer colors. Using bright yellow tomatoes, peeling your cucumbers of their dark green skin and using sweet yellow onions like Vidalias, you can make what we like to call Goldspacho. Kristian Niemi, contributor of this recipe and owner of Mr. Friendly's New Southern Cafe, states that Goldspacho should be eaten when the heat index is 98 degrees or above. That means you should enjoy this delightful soup from mid-June to late September in South Carolina.

3 large yellow tomatoes, coarsely chopped

1 yellow or orange bell pepper, coarsely chopped

2 cucumbers, peeled, seeded, chopped

1 medium Vidalia onion or any sweet yellow onion, chopped

1 teaspoon minced garlic

Fresh cilantro to taste

2 cups (about) cold water

3/4 cup (about) cider vinegar

Salt and pepper to taste

- Process the tomatoes, bell pepper, cucumbers, onion, garlic and cilantro in a food processor until chunky or until of the desired consistency.

- Combine the tomato mixture with the desired amount of cold water, desired amount of vinegar, salt and pepper in a bowl and mix well. Amounts of water and vinegar added depend on the consistency desired. Add less liquid for a thicker consistency.

- Chill, covered, until serving time.

- Serve with Charleston benne wafers and peach ice cream for a quick and easy summer supper.

Six to Eight Servings

BLOODY MARY GAZPACHO RIMMED WITH SHRIMP

1 clove of garlic

3 pounds tomatoes, peeled, chopped

2 unpeeled cucumbers, chopped

1/2 cup finely chopped onion

1/2 cup chopped green bell pepper

4 cups tomato juice

1/2 cup olive oil or vegetable oil

3 tablespoons red wine vinegar

1/4 teaspoon cayenne

Salt and black pepper to taste

Peppered vodka

Cooked, peeled, deveined shrimp

- Rub a large bowl with the garlic. Add the tomatoes, cucumbers, onion and green pepper and mix well. Stir in a mixture of the tomato juice, olive oil, wine vinegar, cayenne, salt and black pepper.

- Add the desired amount of vodka and mix well. Chill, covered, thoroughly.

- Rim edge of the bowl with shrimp just before serving.

Ten to Twelve Servings

CHILLED SHRIMP SOUP

1 pound large shrimp, peeled,
  deveined

Salt to taste

1¼ cups fresh orange juice

1 cup fresh lime juice

4 medium tomatoes, seeded,
  chopped

¼ onion, sliced

¼ cup catsup

2 jalapeños, pequin chiles or
  serranos, seeded, minced

2 teaspoons Pickapeppa
  Sauce

Pepper to taste

1 tomato, seeded, chopped

Lime slices

- Cook the shrimp in boiling salted water in a saucepan for 1 minute or until the shrimp turn pink; drain.

- Cut the shrimp lengthwise into halves.

- Combine the orange juice, lime juice, 4 tomatoes, onion, catsup, jalapeños and Pickapeppa sauce in a glass bowl and mix well. Stir in the shrimp.

- Chill, covered, for 8 to 10 hours, stirring occasionally. Season with salt and pepper.

- Ladle into soup bowls. Top with 1 chopped tomato and lime slices.

Four to Six Servings

Bake these Sour Cream Biscuits in miniature muffin cups for your next luncheon or brunch. Combine 2 cups sifted self-rising flour, 1 cup melted margarine and 1 cup sour cream in a bowl. Spoon into buttered miniature muffin cups. Bake at 450 degrees for 10 to 15 minutes or until light brown. May add shredded sharp Cheddar cheese for variety.

HAZELNUT AND ARTICHOKE SOUP

1 cup chopped canned artichoke hearts

1 cup chicken broth

1 cup half-and-half

1/2 cup chopped hazelnuts, roasted

2 tablespoons fresh lemon juice

1/2 teaspoon ground white pepper

- Combine the artichokes, broth, half-and-half, hazelnuts, lemon juice and white pepper in a saucepan and mix well.
- Cook over medium heat until the mixture begins to simmer, stirring frequently; do not boil.
- Process 1 cup of the mixture in a blender until puréed. Return the purée to the saucepan.
- Heat until simmering, stirring frequently; do not boil.
- Ladle into soup bowls.

Three to Four Servings

BLACK BEAN SOUP

1 onion, chopped

2 small cloves of garlic, minced

1 tablespoon olive oil

2 (16-ounce) cans black beans, drained

1 (15-ounce) can stewed tomatoes, drained, chopped

1 (10-ounce) can chicken broth

1/2 cup picante sauce

1/4 cup water

1/4 cup chopped fresh cilantro (optional)

1 teaspoon cumin

2 tablespoons fresh lime juice

- Sauté the onion and garlic in the olive oil in a saucepan until tender. Stir in the black beans, tomatoes, broth, picante sauce, water, cilantro and cumin. Bring to a boil; reduce heat.
- Simmer until of the desired consistency, stirring occasionally. Remove from heat. Stir in the lime juice.
- Ladle into soup bowls.

Four to Six Servings

COLLARD GREEN SOUP

Great for supper on a cold, winter night.

1 pound smoked sausage,
  chopped

4 cups water

2 pounds collard greens,
  shredded

1 (16-ounce) can Great
  Northern beans,
  drained

2 medium potatoes,
  chopped

1 small onion, chopped

1 small green bell pepper,
  chopped

Salt and pepper to taste

- Simmer the sausage in the water in a saucepan for 45 minutes. Stir in the collard greens and beans.
- Cook for 30 minutes, stirring occasionally. Add the potatoes, onion and green pepper. Season with salt and pepper.
- Cook until the potatoes are tender, stirring occasionally.
- Ladle into soup bowls.
- May add chopped jalapeños for a spicier flavor.

Four to Six Servings

CONSOMME ROUGE

Serve hot as a first course with a beef entrée or cold in the summer. The flavor is enhanced if prepared one day in advance.

1 medium onion, cut
  into paper-thin slices

2 small uncooked beets,
  peeled

4 cups chicken stock,
  skimmed

1^1/$_2$ teaspoons red wine

1 teaspoon salt

Sour cream (optional)

- Combine the onion with enough water to cover in a saucepan.
- Cook until tender; drain.
- Process the beets in a food processor until grated.
- Combine the onion, beets, stock, red wine and salt in a saucepan. Bring to a boil; reduce heat.
- Simmer for 25 minutes, stirring occasionally. Strain, discarding the vegetables. Return the clear red broth to the saucepan.
- Cook just until heated through. Ladle into soup bowls. Top each serving with sour cream. Draw a design through the sour cream with a wooden pick if desired.
- May substitute chicken bouillon for the stock, omitting the salt.

Six Servings

CORN AND SAUSAGE BISQUE

Serve Adluh Corn Bread Muffins with that favorite soup or stew for a quick-and-easy Sunday night supper. Prepare the muffins by combining 2 cups Adluh self-rising cornmeal and 1 tablespoon sugar (optional). Stir in a mixture of 1¹/₄ cups milk, 3 tablespoons melted butter and 1 egg. Fill hot greased muffin cups ²/₃ full. Bake at 475 degrees for 15 to 20 minutes or until light brown. May bake in corn stick muffin molds or in a 9x9-inch baking pan.

1 cup chopped onion

3 spring onions, chopped

1 medium red bell pepper, chopped

¹/₂ medium green bell pepper, chopped

1 clove of garlic, minced

2 tablespoons butter

2 cups canned low-sodium chicken broth

1 pound red potatoes, cut into ¹/₂-inch slices

¹/₄ teaspoon cumin

Freshly ground white pepper to taste

1³/₄ cups frozen corn, thawed, puréed

1³/₄ cups frozen corn, thawed

4 ounces cooked kielbasa, cut into ¹/₄-inch slices, cut into halves

¹/₃ cup half-and-half

¹/₃ cup whipping cream

Salt to taste

- Sauté the onion, spring onions, red pepper, green pepper and garlic in the butter in a heavy saucepan for 15 minutes or until the peppers are tender. Stir in the broth, red potatoes, cumin and white pepper. Bring to a boil; reduce heat.

- Simmer for 30 minutes or until the potatoes are tender, stirring occasionally. Stir in the corn, sausage, half-and-half and whipping cream.

- Simmer for 20 minutes or until of the desired consistency, stirring occasionally. Season with salt and white pepper.

- Ladle into soup bowls.

- May be prepared 1 day in advance and stored, covered, in the refrigerator. Reheat over medium heat, adding additional half-and-half as needed for the desired consistency and stirring frequently.

Six Servings

ROASTED GARLIC SOUP

4 heads of garlic

1/4 cup olive oil

4 leeks (white part only), chopped

1 onion, chopped

6 tablespoons unsalted butter

6 tablespoons flour

4 cups chicken stock or low-sodium canned broth, heated

1/3 cup dry sherry

1 cup whipping cream

1 tablespoon fresh lemon juice

Salt and white pepper to taste

2 tablespoons minced fresh chives

- Cut off the top quarter of each garlic head. Arrange the heads in a small baking dish. Drizzle with the olive oil.

- Bake at 350 degrees for 1 hour or until golden brown. Press individual garlic cloves between the thumb and forefinger to release the garlic from the skin. Chop the garlic.

- Sauté the leeks and onion in the butter in a heavy saucepan over medium heat for 10 minutes or until tender. Stir in the garlic. Reduce the heat to low.

- Add the flour and mix well. Cook for 10 minutes, stirring occasionally. Stir in the hot stock and sherry.

- Simmer for 20 minutes, stirring occasionally. Cool the soup slightly.

- Process the soup in batches in a food processor until puréed. May be prepared 1 day in advance to this point. Return the soup to the saucepan. Add the whipping cream and mix well.

- Simmer for 10 minutes or until thickened, stirring frequently. Stir in the lemon juice. Season with salt and white pepper.

- Ladle into soup bowls. Sprinkle with the chives.

Four Servings

Remove the skin from a clove of garlic without mashing it by placing the garlic clove in the microwave and cooking on High power for about ten seconds. Remove the garlic and, holding it at one end, squeeze the clove from the skin. To microwave more than one clove at a time, add two or three seconds to the cooking time.

Indian Soup Of Coconut, Curry And Corn

Try this refreshing summer soup which has been enjoyed by many customers at Saluda's in Columbia.

1 Scotch bonnet chile or habañero

6 tablespoons olive oil

3 tablespoons curry powder

2 tablespoons each chopped gingerroot and garlic

1 cup butter

1/2 cup flour

2 cups chopped onions

1 tablespoon each salt and pepper

3 quarts water

28 ounces coconut milk

1 cup canned stewed tomatoes

1/2 cup each tomato juice and vegetable bouillon

1/4 cup lime juice

1 cup corn

1/2 bunch cilantro

- Process the chile, 4 tablespoons of the olive oil, curry powder, gingerroot and garlic in a food processor until puréed.

- Heat the butter in a skillet until brown. Add the purée and flour, whisking until blended.

- Cook until of roux consistency, stirring constantly.

- Sauté the onions, salt and pepper in the remaining 2 tablespoons olive oil in a saucepan until the onions are tender. Stir in the water, coconut milk, tomatoes, tomato juice, bouillon and lime juice.

- Purée in a food processor. Return the mixture to the saucepan.

- Simmer for 10 minutes, stirring occasionally. Bring to a boil. Whisk in 2 cups of the roux. Remove from heat.

- Stir in the corn and chopped cilantro. Ladle into soup bowls.

Fifteen Servings

Shiitake Mushroom Soup

4 ounces shiitake mushrooms

3 (11-ounce) cans chicken broth

2 tablespoons soy sauce

2 tablespoons cornstarch

2 tablespoons water

Salt and pepper to taste

1/4 cup thinly sliced green onions

- Cut the mushrooms into bite-size pieces, discarding the stems.

- Combine the broth and soy sauce in a saucepan. Bring to a boil.

- Stir in the mushrooms and a mixture of the cornstarch and water.

- Cook until thickened, stirring constantly. Season with salt and pepper.

- Ladle into soup bowls. Sprinkle each serving with 1 tablespoon green onions.

- May substitute 4 cups homemade broth for the canned broth.

Four Servings

PEANUT BUTTER AND VEGETABLE CHICKEN SOUP

4 (10- or 14-ounce) cans
  fat-free chicken broth

2 cups chopped cooked
  chicken

1 cup chopped peeled potato

1 cup chopped carrots

1 cup fresh or canned
  chopped tomatoes

1 cup broccoli florets

1 cup chopped unpeeled
  zucchini

1/2 cup chopped celery

1/2 cup chopped onion

1/2 cup chopped green bell
  pepper

2 cloves of garlic, minced

1 cup smooth peanut butter

1 teaspoon parsley flakes

Salt and pepper to taste

- Combine the broth, chicken, potato and carrots in a stockpot. Bring to a boil; reduce heat.

- Cook over medium heat for 10 minutes or until the vegetables are tender-crisp. Stir in the tomatoes, broccoli, zucchini, celery, onion, green pepper and garlic.

- Simmer for 8 to 10 minutes or until of the desired consistency, stirring occasionally. Add the peanut butter, parsley flakes, salt and pepper and mix well.

- Simmer for 3 minutes longer, stirring frequently. Ladle into soup bowls.

Eight Servings

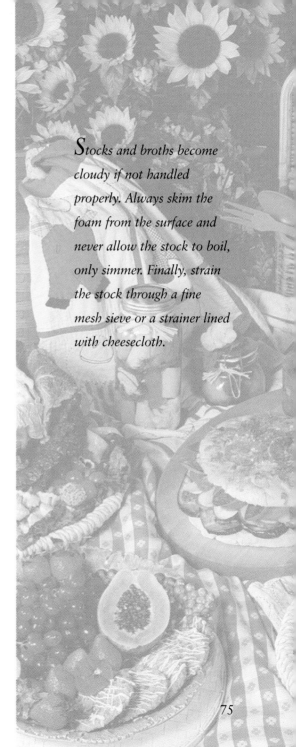

Stocks and broths become cloudy if not handled properly. Always skim the foam from the surface and never allow the stock to boil, only simmer. Finally, strain the stock through a fine mesh sieve or a strainer lined with cheesecloth.

CREAMY RED PEPPER SOUP

Don't throw away those leek tops. Most recipes call for the white and pale green parts only, but the leek tops are great simmered and puréed with other vegetables to produce a soup with a mild onion flavor. Fresh leek tops are also a great addition to vegetable stocks. Combine them with other fresh vegetables such as carrots, celery and onions. Toss in some fresh herbs, whole unpeeled cloves of garlic, a few whole peppercorns and perhaps a half cup or so of dried beans to give the stock some body. Add water just to cover, simmer for about one hour and strain.

Parmesan Butter

1¹/2 ounces Parmesan cheese

6 fresh basil leaves

1 tablespoon chopped fresh parsley

¹/4 cup unsalted butter, softened

Soup

¹/4 cup unsalted butter

4 large red bell peppers, cut into quarters

2 large leek bulbs, sliced

2 teaspoons minced garlic

3 cups canned low-sodium vegetable broth

Salt and pepper to taste

³/4 cup whipping cream

2 tablespoons dry sherry

6 (¹/2-inch-thick) slices French bread

2 tablespoons olive oil

1 clove of garlic

- For the butter, process the cheese in a food processor until finely chopped. Add the basil and parsley.

- Process briefly. Add the butter. Process until smooth.

- For the soup, melt the unsalted butter in a saucepan. Stir in the red peppers, leeks and 2 teaspoons garlic.

- Cook, covered, for 5 minutes, stirring occasionally. Stir in the broth, salt and pepper.

- Simmer, covered, for 30 minutes, stirring occasionally.

- Strain, reserving the vegetables and liquid. Return the liquid to the saucepan.

- Process the reserved vegetables in a food processor or blender until puréed. Add ¹/4 cup of the reserved liquid, processing constantly until blended. Transfer the purée to the saucepan and mix well. Stir in the whipping cream and sherry. Season with salt and pepper.

- Cook the soup over low heat just until heated through, stirring occasionally.

- Sauté the bread slices in the olive oil in a skillet until golden brown on both sides. Drain on paper towels. Cut the clove of garlic into halves. Rub both sides of the bread slices with the garlic halves.

- Ladle the soup into soup bowls. Top each serving with 1 bread slice and a dollop of the Parmesan Butter.

- May substitute roasted red bell peppers or yellow bell peppers for the red bell peppers.

Six Servings

CRAWFORD'S TOMATO BASIL CRAB SOUP

3 (10-ounce) cans
   tomato soup

1 chicken bouillon cube

1 soup can hot water

2 tablespoons chopped
   green onions

1/2 teaspoon basil

1 (7-ounce) can claw
   crab meat, drained,
   flaked

Salt and pepper to taste

Sour cream (optional)

- Pour the soup into a saucepan.

- Dissolve the bouillon cube in the hot water. Stir into the soup. Bring to a boil. Add the green onions and basil and mix well.

- Boil for 5 minutes longer, stirring occasionally. Stir in the crab meat.

- Boil for 3 minutes, stirring occasionally. Season with salt and pepper.

- Ladle into soup bowls. Top each serving with sour cream.

Four Servings

CARROT AND PECAN SANDWICHES

8 ounces cream cheese,
   softened

3 tablespoons
   mayonnaise

4 large carrots, finely
   grated

1/2 cup chopped pecans

1 tablespoon grated
   onion or finely
   minced chives

Salt and pepper to taste

Tabasco sauce to taste

24 slices whole wheat
   bread, crusts trimmed

- Beat the cream cheese and mayonnaise in a mixer bowl until creamy. Stir in the carrots, pecans, onion, salt, pepper and Tabasco sauce.

- Chill, covered, for 8 to 10 hours.

- Spread the cream cheese mixture on 1/2 of the bread slices. Top with the remaining bread slices.

Twelve Sandwiches

FRENCH CLUB SANDWICHES

Wonderful for tailgating and outdoor affairs.

16 ounces cream cheese, softened

1/4 cup mayonnaise

3/4 cup finely chopped celery

1/2 cup shredded Cheddar cheese

1/3 cup chopped fresh parsley

2 tablespoons finely chopped onion

1 tablespoon lemon juice

1 tablespoon Worcestershire sauce

1/4 teaspoon seasoned salt

2 loaves French bread, cut lengthwise into halves

8 to 16 ounces thinly sliced deli ham

Kosher dill pickles, thinly sliced lengthwise

• Beat the cream cheese and mayonnaise in a mixer bowl until creamy. Stir in the celery, Cheddar cheese, parsley, onion, lemon juice, Worcestershire sauce and seasoned salt.

• Spread the cut sides of the bread with the cream cheese mixture. Arrange the ham and 1 layer of pickles on 1/2 of the bread halves. Top with the remaining bread halves. Cut into 1- to 2-inch slices.

Twelve Servings

RAISIN NUT SANDWICH SPREAD

1 egg

3/4 cup sugar

Juice and grated peel of 1 lemon

3/4 cup mayonnaise

1 cup raisins

1 cup chopped nuts

• Whisk the egg in a double boiler. Stir in the sugar, lemon juice and lemon peel.

• Cook for 7 to 8 minutes, stirring constantly. Add the mayonnaise and mix well.

• Cook for 7 minutes longer or until thickened, stirring constantly. Remove from heat.

• Stir in the raisins and nuts. Spread on your favorite bread.

• Store the leftover spread in the refrigerator.

Makes Two to Three Cups

SHRIMP CROISSANTS

Serve with fresh asparagus or a mixed green salad.

1 pound deveined,
   peeled, cooked
   shrimp, chopped

1 cup cubed sharp
   Cheddar cheese

3/4 cup chopped celery

2 tablespoons chopped
   green bell pepper

2 tablespoons minced
   onion

1 teaspoon lemon juice

1/8 teaspoon
   Worcestershire sauce

1/8 teaspoon Tabasco
   sauce

1 cup (about)
   mayonnaise

Salt and pepper to taste

5 croissants, split
   lengthwise

Grated Parmesan cheese

- Combine the shrimp, Cheddar cheese, celery, green pepper, onion, lemon juice, Worcestershire sauce and Tabasco sauce in a bowl and mix well. Add the mayonnaise, stirring until of the desired consistency. Season with salt and pepper.

- Arrange the croissants cut side up on a baking sheet. Broil for 30 seconds or until light brown.

- Spread the shrimp mixture over the cut sides of the croissants. Sprinkle with Parmesan cheese.

- Broil until the Cheddar cheese melts.

Five Servings

SWEET POTATO BISCUITS WITH PINEAPPLE CHUTNEY SPREAD

Pineapple Chutney Spread

1/2 cup butter, softened

2 tablespoons Raggy-O
   Traditions pineapple
   chutney or any flavor
   chutney

2 spring onions, finely
   chopped

Sweet Potato Biscuits

2 cups self-rising flour

1/2 cup vegetable
   shortening

1 1/2 cups mashed cooked
   sweet potatoes

3 tablespoons milk

1 to 2 tablespoons sugar

Thinly sliced smoked
   turkey

- For the spread, combine the butter, chutney and spring onions in a bowl and mix well.

- For the biscuits, combine the flour and shortening and mix well. Stir in the sweet potatoes, milk and sugar. May add additional milk if needed for the desired consistency.

- Roll the dough 1/2 inch thick on a lightly floured surface. Cut with a 1 1/2-inch biscuit cutter. Arrange on an ungreased baking sheet.

- Bake at 425 degrees for 12 minutes or until light brown.

- Split the biscuits into halves. Spread the chutney spread over the bottom halves of the biscuits; layer with the turkey. Top with the biscuit tops. Wrap the biscuits in foil.

- Bake at 350 degrees for 10 minutes.

Eight to Ten Servings

MUFFULETTA

1 1/2 cups chopped green olives

1 cup chopped black olives

2/3 cup olive oil

1/2 cup chopped pimentos

5 tablespoons minced fresh parsley

1 tablespoon chopped fresh oregano

2 teaspoons fresh lemon juice

1 clove of garlic, minced

Pepper to taste

1 large round loaf Italian bread

3/4 cup shredded lettuce

1 cup sliced tomato

4 ounces Italian salami, thinly sliced

4 ounces mozzarella cheese, thinly sliced

4 ounces pepperoni, thinly sliced

- Combine the green olives, black olives, olive oil, pimentos, parsley, oregano, lemon juice, garlic and pepper in a bowl and mix well.

- Marinate, covered, at room temperature for 2 to 4 hours, stirring occasionally.

- Cut the bread horizontally into halves. Remove the soft bread from the bottom half carefully, leaving a 1-inch shell.

- Drain the olive mixture, discarding the marinade. Spoon 1/2 of the olive mixture into the bread shell, spreading to within 3/4 to 1 inch from the side. Layer with the lettuce, tomato, salami, mozzarella cheese and pepperoni. Top with the remaining olive mixture and bread top. Wrap in plastic wrap.

- Place the sandwich on a plate and cover with another plate. Weight the top plate down with a heavy object. This will help to compress the sandwich.

- Chill for 6 hours or longer. Cut into small wedges.

Fifteen Servings

STROMBOLI

1 tablespoon olive oil

1/3 (3-pound) package frozen
   pizza dough, thawed

8 thin slices hard salami

8 thin slices provolone cheese

5 ounces hot Italian sausage,
   cooked, crumbled

1 1/2 teaspoons Dijon mustard

1/4 cup freshly grated
   Parmesan cheese

1/2 teaspoon garlic salt

1/2 teaspoon oregano, crushed

1/2 teaspoon seasoned salt

3/4 cup shredded mozzarella
   cheese

• Brush an 11x17-inch baking sheet with the olive oil.
  Roll the dough out on the prepared baking sheet to
  the edges.

• Arrange the salami lengthwise down the center, leaving a
  1/2-inch border. Layer with the provolone cheese and
  sausage. Spread with the mustard. Sprinkle with the
  Parmesan cheese, garlic salt, oregano and seasoned salt.
  Top with the mozzarella cheese.

• Bring the long sides of the dough together atop the
  filling and brush with water. Pinch and fold over to
  enclose the filling.

• Brush the short ends of the dough with water and pinch
  to enclose.

• Bake at 375 degrees for 25 minutes or until golden
  brown. Serve warm.

• If you do not have time to thaw the dough, use the
  refrigerated pizza dough found in the dairy case.

Four Servings

*Add zip to your sandwiches
by spreading with Murphy's
Mustard. Combine 1 cup dry
mustard and 1 cup white
vinegar in a bowl. Let stand,
covered, at room temperature
for 8 to 10 hours. Beat 1 cup
sugar, 2 beaten eggs and 1/8
teaspoon salt in a mixer bowl
until creamy. Combine with
the mustard mixture in a
saucepan. Cook over medium
heat until bubbly, stirring
constantly. Cool and spoon
into small sterilized jars; seal
with 2-piece lids. Store in
the refrigerator.*

Thai Shrimp Pizza

This recipe is reprinted with permission from Sargento Foods, Inc.

12 ounces uncooked medium shrimp, peeled, deveined

$1^1/2$ teaspoons hot chile oil

$1/4$ cup stir-fry sauce

2 cloves of garlic, minced

1 teaspoon minced gingerroot

1 (12-inch) Italian bread shell or baked pizza crust

$1/3$ cup chopped fresh cilantro

$1^1/2$ cups Sargento 5 Cheese Gourmet Pizza Recipe Blend

2 tablespoons chopped peanuts (optional)

- Thread the shrimp on skewers, allowing the shrimp to touch each other. Brush all sides of the shrimp with the chile oil.

- Grill over medium-high coals (coals will be ash gray) for 2 minutes per side or until the shrimp turn pink. Remove the shrimp from the skewers.

- Combine the stir-fry sauce, garlic and gingerroot in a bowl and mix well. Drizzle over the bread shell. Arrange the shrimp over the top. Sprinkle with the cilantro, Sargento 5 Cheese Gourmet Pizza Recipe Blend and peanuts.

- Transfer to a baking sheet or a sheet of heavy-duty foil. Place on the grill rack.

- Grill for 15 to 18 minutes or until the cheese melts.

- May substitute $1/4$ teaspoon ground ginger for the gingerroot and a mixture of $1^1/2$ teaspoons vegetable oil and $1/2$ teaspoon hot pepper sauce for the hot chile oil.

Four Servings

DONE BUTTERED DILL BISCUITS

Great for after church when time is of the essence, or bake in small muffin cups for a brunch or luncheon.

1/2 cup butter or margarine

1/2 cup sour cream

1/2 cup low-fat cottage cheese

1/4 cup skim milk

1 egg, lightly beaten

2 tablespoons dillweed

2 tablespoons sugar

2 cups reduced-fat baking mix

- Place the butter in a microwave-safe bowl.
- Microwave for 1 minute or until melted. Stir in the sour cream, cottage cheese, skim milk, egg, dillweed and sugar. Add the baking mix, stirring just until moistened. May add additional milk if mixture is too dry.
- Spoon the batter into muffin cups sprayed with nonstick cooking spray.
- Bake at 425 degrees for 10 to 12 minutes or until golden brown. Serve immediately.

Twelve Biscuits

RED PEPPER AND ONION CORN BREAD MUFFINS

This recipe makes eight large muffins. For smaller muffins, use standard muffin cups and reduce the baking time slightly.

1 1/2 cups sifted cake flour

1/2 cup white cornmeal

1 tablespoon baking powder

3/4 cup egg substitute

2/3 cup water

1/3 cup canola oil

1/4 cup chopped fresh cilantro

1/4 cup minced red pepper

3 tablespoons sugar

1 teaspoon salt

1 green onion, minced

- Butter eight 2/3-cup custard cups. Arrange on a baking sheet.
- Heat the custard cups at 350 degrees for 5 minutes.
- Combine the cake flour, cornmeal and baking powder in a bowl and mix well.
- Whisk the egg substitute, water, canola oil, cilantro, red pepper, sugar, salt and green onion in a bowl. Add to the dry ingredients and whisk until mixed. Spoon into the prepared custard cups.
- Bake at 350 degrees for 15 minutes or until a wooden pick inserted in the center comes out clean.
- Cool slightly in the custard cups. Remove to a serving platter. Serve the muffins warm or at room temperature.
- May substitute 3 whole eggs for the egg substitute.

Eight Muffins

CRAB MEAT HUSH PUPPIES

Tim Freeman, executive chef at Richard's, donated this recipe.

8 ounces crab meat

3 uncooked slices bacon, chopped

1/2 cup chopped white onion

1 cup cornmeal

1/2 cup flour

3/4 teaspoon baking powder

Salt and pepper to taste

1 1/2 to 2 cups buttermilk

Vegetable oil for deep-frying

- Combine the crab meat, bacon and onion in a bowl and mix well.

- Combine the cornmeal, flour, baking powder, salt and pepper in a bowl and mix well. Add the crab meat mixture and mix well.

- Add 1/4 cup of the buttermilk and mix well. Continue adding the buttermilk 1/4 cup at a time until the batter is moist but not runny, stirring constantly.

- Heat the oil in a skillet or fryer to 350 degrees. Drop the hush puppy batter by spoonfuls into the hot oil.

- Deep-fry for 2 to 2 1/2 minutes or until golden brown; drain.

Twenty-Four Hush Puppies

CRANBERRY ORANGE MUFFINS

1 cup chopped fresh cranberries

2 tablespoons sugar

2 cups flour

1/3 cup sugar

2 teaspoons baking powder

1 teaspoon grated orange peel

1/2 teaspoon salt

1/2 cup butter

3/4 cup orange juice

1 egg, lightly beaten

1/4 cup melted butter

1/4 cup sugar

1/2 teaspoon cinnamon

- Combine the cranberries and 2 tablespoons sugar in a bowl and mix well.

- Combine the flour, 1/3 cup sugar, baking powder, orange peel and salt in a bowl and mix well. Cut in 1/2 cup butter until crumbly. Add the orange juice and egg, stirring just until moistened. Fold in the cranberry mixture. Spoon into greased muffin cups.

- Bake at 400 degrees for 20 to 25 minutes or until golden brown. Cool in muffin cups for 5 minutes. Remove the muffins.

- Dip the top of each muffin in 1/4 cup melted butter. Sprinkle with a mixture of 1/4 cup sugar and cinnamon.

Twelve Muffins

SEMOLINA BREAD WITH SUN-DRIED TOMATOES

1 cup boiling water

4 to 6 slices sun-dried tomatoes (not oil-pack)

2 cups bread flour or unbleached all-purpose flour

1 cup semolina flour

1/4 cup grated Parmesan cheese

1 1/2 teaspoons salt

1 teaspoon fast-rising yeast

1 1/3 cups water

2 tablespoons minced red bell pepper

2 tablespoons minced green bell pepper

2 tablespoons minced onion

2 tablespoons olive oil

Cornmeal

- Combine boiling water and sun-dried tomatoes in a saucepan. Simmer, covered, over low heat for 5 minutes. Drain and finely chop the tomatoes.

- Pulse the bread flour, semolina flour, cheese, salt and yeast in a food processor fitted with a steel or plastic blade 4 or 5 times. Add 1 1/3 cups water gradually, processing constantly. Process for 90 seconds longer. This step is very important; do not shorten the time. Add the bell peppers, onion and sun-dried tomatoes. Process for 15 to 20 seconds or until the vegetables are mixed with the dough.

- Pour the olive oil into a bowl. Add the dough, turning to coat the surface. Let rise, covered with plastic wrap, for 3 to 4 hours or until doubled in bulk. Punch the dough down. Divide the dough into 2 equal portions.

- Roll 1 portion into a 5x15-inch rectangle on a lightly floured surface. Fold long side over, sealing edge. Roll the dough backward so that the seam is on top. Using the side of your hand in a karate chop motion, press a trench along the length of the dough at the seam. Bring both long sides together above the trench and press along the length to seal. Place seam side down on a baking sheet sprinkled with cornmeal or in baguette pans. Repeat the process with the remaining dough portion.

- Proof for 30 minutes or until the loaves are puffy and almost doubled in bulk. Cut 5 lengthwise diagonal slashes 1/2 inch deep in the top of each loaf. Brush the tops with water. Bake with steam at 425 degrees for 25 minutes or until brown and crusty. Cool completely.

Two Loaves

The crisp crust that is characteristic of French bread is achieved by introducing steam into the oven while it bakes. You can mimic the effect of professional steam-injected ovens by placing a pan of boiling water on the bottom oven rack. First, heat a shallow baking pan on the bottom rack of the oven while the oven is preheating. Bring some water to a boil on the stove. When the loaves have proofed and are ready to bake, place the bread pans on the middle oven rack. Pour the boiling water into the heated baking pan. Close the oven door immediately to trap the steam and continue baking.

GRANDMOTHER'S ROLLS

2 envelopes dry yeast

1 cup lukewarm
  (115-degree) water

1 cup margarine

3/4 cup sugar

2 teaspoons salt

1 cup boiling water

2 eggs, beaten

6 to 7 cups flour

Melted butter

- Dissolve the yeast in the lukewarm water and mix well.
- Combine the margarine, sugar and salt in a bowl. Add the boiling water to the mixture, stirring until blended.
- Let stand until cool. Stir in the eggs. Add the yeast mixture and mix well.
- Add 6 cups of the flour and mix well. Add 1/2 to 1 cup of the remaining flour if the mixture is soupy. The dough should be sticky.
- Chill, covered, for 4 hours or longer. May store in the refrigerator at this point for up to 1 week.
- Roll the dough 1/4 to 1/2 inch thick on a heavily floured surface; cut with a round cutter. Brush with butter. Fold in half and brush with butter again. Arrange in a baking pan.
- Let rise for 1 hour or longer.
- Bake at 400 degrees for 20 minutes.

Thirty-Six to Forty Rolls

HONEY WHOLE WHEAT ROLLS

3/4 cup milk

2 tablespoons butter

1/3 cup honey

1/2 cup cold water

2 cups unbleached
  all-purpose flour

1 cup whole wheat flour

1 envelope dry yeast

1 tablespoon Vital wheat
  gluten

1 teaspoon salt

Cornmeal

Melted butter

- Heat milk and 2 tablespoons butter in a saucepan until butter melts. Remove from heat. Stir in honey. Mix in cold water.
- Process the next 5 ingredients in a food processor container. Add milk mixture gradually, processing constantly for 90 seconds. Place in a lightly oiled bowl, turning to coat the surface.
- Let rise, covered with plastic wrap, for 1 to 2 hours or until doubled in bulk. Punch the dough down. Place on a lightly floured hard surface. Let rise, covered with an inverted bowl, for 15 to 20 minutes to relax the gluten.
- Cut the dough into 18 portions. Shape each portion into a ball. Place the dough balls on a baking sheet sprinkled with cornmeal.
- Let rise, covered, for 45 minutes. Cut a 1/4-inch slash down the center of each roll with a sharp knife. Brush with melted butter.
- Bake on the middle oven rack at 375 degrees for 20 minutes or until light brown.

Eighteen Rolls

HERB FOCACCIA

3 cups bread flour

1¹/₄ teaspoons salt

¹/₂ teaspoon fast-rising yeast

1 cup plus 2 tablespoons
water

1¹/₂ tablespoons olive oil

2¹/₂ tablespoons chopped
fresh rosemary

Olive oil

Cornmeal

Kosher salt

Grated Parmesan cheese

Bell pepper strips

Sliced red onion

Sliced or whole olives

- Combine the flour, salt and yeast in a food processor container fitted with a steel or plastic blade.

- Add the water and 1¹/₂ tablespoons olive oil gradually, processing constantly for 90 seconds. This is a very important step; do not cut the time. Add the rosemary.

- Process for 5 to 10 seconds or until mixed. Place the dough in a 3-quart bowl. Pour a small amount of olive oil over the dough, turning to coat the surface.

- Let rise, covered with plastic wrap, at cool room temperature for 6 to 8 hours. Transfer the dough to a baking sheet sprinkled with cornmeal.

- Starting in the center and working in concentric circles pull the dough outward with left-hand fingers while pulling towards center with right-hand fingers. Your objective is to form an even 12-inch round. Or you may shape the dough into a square or rectangle or a larger round if a thinner bread is desired. Do not use a rolling pin for this step. The indentations left by using your fingertips are characteristic of the bread. The surface of the dough should be oily. Drizzle with additional olive oil if needed. Sprinkle with kosher salt and Parmesan cheese. Arrange bell pepper, onion and olives sparingly over the top. Let rise for 10 minutes or until puffy.

- Bake at 450 degrees for 25 minutes or until brown and crisp. Cool completely before cutting.

- May substitute any fresh herb, a combination of herbs or 2 teaspoons dried herbs for the rosemary.

Six Servings

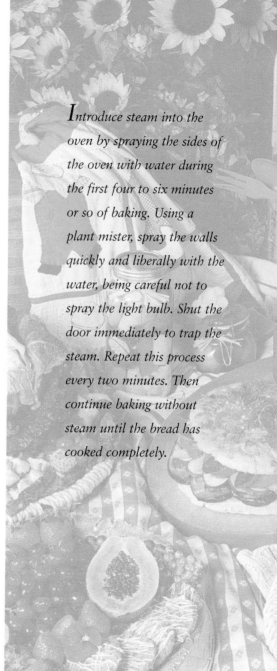

Introduce steam into the oven by spraying the sides of the oven with water during the first four to six minutes or so of baking. Using a plant mister, spray the walls quickly and liberally with the water, being careful not to spray the light bulb. Shut the door immediately to trap the steam. Repeat this process every two minutes. Then continue baking without steam until the bread has cooked completely.

Adluh Biscuits are the perfect addition to any meal, and so easy. Cut 2 to 3 tablespoons shortening into 2 cups sifted Adluh self-rising flour until crumbly. Stir in 3/4 cup milk. Roll to the desired thickness on a lightly floured surface. The secret to good biscuits is to handle the dough as little as possible. Cut with a biscuit cutter. Arrange on a greased baking sheet. Bake at 475 degrees for 8 to 10 minutes or until light brown.

FOCACCIA WITH GRILLED VEGETABLES AND PESTO

2 large yellow or red bell peppers

2 medium zucchini, sliced lengthwise

1 small eggplant, cut horizontally into 1/2-inch slices

1 medium red onion, cut into medium slices

Basil-flavor olive oil or olive oil

Salt to taste

1 focaccia or 1 loaf Italian bread

Pesto or olivada to taste

2 tomatoes, thinly sliced

Fresh basil or arugula

- Grill the bell peppers over hot coals or on a stove-top grill until charred on all sides. Place the bell peppers in a nonrecycled brown paper bag immediately. Let sweat for 15 minutes. Discard the skins and seeds. Cut into large strips.

- Brush the zucchini, eggplant and onion with olive oil. Grill over hot coals until tender, turning and basting with olive oil frequently.

- Arrange the zucchini, eggplant, onion and roasted peppers in a shallow pan. Sprinkle lightly with salt.

- Slice the focaccia horizontally into halves. Grill the cut sides of focaccia until light brown.

- Spread the bottom half with the pesto. Layer the grilled vegetables, tomatoes and basil over the pesto. Top with the remaining focaccia half. Cut into slices.

Four to Six Servings

BED AND BREAKFAST FRENCH TOAST

1 French baguette

4 eggs

1/2 cup vanilla ice cream, softened

1/4 cup fresh orange juice

1 tablespoon vanilla extract

1 tablespoon cinnamon

1/8 teaspoon freshly grated nutmeg

2 tablespoons unsalted butter

- Cut the bread diagonally into twenty-four 3/4-inch slices. Arrange half the bread in a nonreactive dish.

- Beat the eggs, ice cream, orange juice, vanilla, cinnamon and nutmeg in a bowl until blended. Pour half the egg mixture over the bread. Turn over the bread slices.

- Soak for 5 minutes or until saturated.

- Heat 1 tablespoon of the butter in a cast-iron skillet until melted. Arrange the soaked bread slices in a single layer in the skillet.

- Cook over low heat for 2 minutes per side or until golden brown. Transfer to a heated platter to keep warm.

- Repeat the process with the remaining bread slices, egg mixture and butter.

- Serve with heated maple syrup and sliced navel oranges, fresh berries or your favorite fruit.

Eight (Three-Slice) Servings

GRANDMA'S HOMEMADE BREAD PANCAKES

4 slices bread, torn into bite-size pieces

2 cups water

1 cup flour

1 cup milk

1 egg, lightly beaten

1 tablespoon sugar

1/8 teaspoon salt

1/4 cup vegetable oil

Sugar and cinnamon to taste

- Soak the bread in the water in a bowl.

- Combine the flour, milk, egg, sugar and salt in a bowl and mix well.

- Drain the bread. Squeeze the moisture from the bread. Stir bread into the flour mixture.

- Heat the oil in a medium-large skillet until hot. Drop the batter by spoonfuls into the hot skillet.

- Bake for 2 to 3 minutes or until bubbles appear on the surface and the undersides are golden brown. Turn the pancakes.

- Bake for 1 to 1 1/2 minutes longer or until golden brown. Sprinkle each pancake with sugar and cinnamon.

Twelve Pancakes

APPLE SOUR CREAM COFFEE CAKE

2 Granny Smith apples, peeled, chopped

1/2 cup packed brown sugar

4 ounces Raggy-O Traditions apple chutney

1/2 cup water

1 teaspoon vanilla extract

2 cups sugar

1 cup butter, softened

2 eggs

1 cup sour cream

1 teaspoon vanilla extract

2 cups sifted cake flour

1 teaspoon salt

1 teaspoon baking powder

1/2 cup chopped pecans

1/4 cup packed brown sugar

2 teaspoons cinnamon

- Combine the apples, 1/2 cup brown sugar, chutney, water and 1 teaspoon vanilla in a saucepan.

- Cook over medium heat until the apples are tender and most of the liquid has been absorbed, stirring frequently.

- Cream the sugar and butter in a mixer bowl. Beat in the eggs 1 at a time. Fold in the sour cream and 1 teaspoon vanilla. Add a sifted mixture of the cake flour, salt and baking powder and mix well.

- Spoon 1/2 of the batter into a greased and floured 10-inch tube pan. Spread with the apple mixture. Swirl with a spoon to marbleize. Top with the remaining batter. Sprinkle with a mixture of the pecans, 1/4 cup brown sugar and cinnamon.

- Bake at 350 degrees for 55 to 60 minutes or until the coffee cake tests done.

- Cool in the pan on a wire rack.

- May use light butter and nonfat sour cream.

Sixteen Servings

BREAKFAST PIZZA

1 (8-count) can crescent rolls

1 pound hot sausage

Chopped onion to taste (optional)

1 1/2 cups frozen hash brown potatoes

1 1/2 cups shredded sharp Cheddar cheese

8 eggs, beaten

1/2 cup milk

Salt and pepper to taste

- Unroll the crescent roll dough. Pat over the bottom and up the sides of a 9x13-inch baking dish, pressing the edges and the perforations to seal.

- Brown the sausage with the onion in a skillet, stirring until the sausage is crumbly; drain.

- Layer the sausage mixture, hash brown potatoes and cheese in the prepared baking dish.

- Combine the eggs, milk, salt and pepper in a mixer bowl. Beat until blended. Pour over the prepared layers.

- Bake at 325 degrees until set and golden brown.

- May substitute ground beef for the sausage.

Eight to Ten Servings

ORANGE-SCENTED SWEET ROLLS

Filling

Finely grated zest of 1 orange

1/3 cup chopped pecans, toasted

1/3 cup raisins

1/3 cup packed brown sugar

1 teaspoon cinnamon

Rolls

1/2 recipe Grandmother's Rolls (page 86)

Flour

3 tablespoons melted butter

Icing (optional)

3/4 cup confectioners' sugar

1 1/2 tablespoons melted butter

1/8 teaspoon vanilla extract

Hot water

- For the filling, combine the orange zest, pecans, raisins, brown sugar and cinnamon in a bowl and mix well.

- For the rolls, prepare the dough for Grandmother's Rolls at least 4 hours in advance or preferably the night before and store in the refrigerator.

- Pat the dough into a rough rectangle on a lightly floured surface. Let rest, covered, for 20 minutes. Roll the dough into a rectangle 18 inches long and 1/8 inch thick with a lightly floured rolling pin, sprinkling with additional flour as needed to prevent sticking.

- Brush excess flour from the dough. Brush with the melted butter. Sprinkle the filling over the rectangle to within 1 inch of the long sides.

- Roll as for a jelly roll, starting with the long end and pinching the long edge to seal. Cut into 18 slices. Arrange 1 inch apart on a buttered baking sheet, so they will touch slightly when risen. Let rise, covered with a tea towel, for 45 minutes or until doubled in bulk.

- Bake on the middle oven rack at 375 degrees for 20 to 30 minutes or until brown.

- Cool on the baking sheet on a wire rack for 10 to 15 minutes and spread with the icing.

- For the icing, combine the confectioners' sugar, butter and vanilla in a bowl and mix well. Stir in enough hot water to make of a spreading consistency.

- Spread the warm icing over the warm rolls.

Eighteen Rolls

Make a Huffy Puffy or puff pancake a weekend tradition. All you need is an iron skillet, a hot oven, a few basic ingredients and a breakfast companion. For each person, you will need 1 tablespoon butter, 1 egg, 1/4 cup milk, 1/4 cup flour, 1/8 teaspoon salt and freshly grated orange zest to taste. Heat the skillet in a 450-degree oven until hot. Add the butter, swirling the skillet until melted. Pour in a mixture of the egg, milk, flour, salt and orange zest. Bake for 12 to 15 minutes or until puffed and light brown. Serve immediately with warm maple syrup and coffee.

*An easy glide, destination
water lilies. Other flowers,
rare and beautiful, thrive here
as well. Rocky Shoals spider
lilies, an endangered species,
bloom amid polished stones
near the confluence of the
Saluda and Broad rivers.*

EGGS & PASTA

EGGS & PASTA

UPON THE PADS

Nature's bounty supports us in more ways than imagined. Cool water, green pads, and ivory-hued lilies—a naturally elegant setting for fine cuisine.

Opposite:

Crawfish with Sun-Dried Tomato Ravioli

Chile Cheese Fiesta Tart

95

APPLE SAUSAGE QUICHE

Serve for breakfast or brunch.

4 to 8 ounces sausage

1/2 cup mayonnaise

1/2 cup milk

2 tablespoons flour

2 eggs, beaten

8 ounces Swiss or
  Cheddar cheese,
  shredded

1 large apple, peeled,
  chopped

1 (10-inch) deep-dish pie
  shell, partially baked

- Brown the sausage in a skillet, stirring until crumbly; drain.

- Combine the mayonnaise, milk, flour and eggs in a bowl and mix well. Stir in the sausage, cheese and apple. Spoon into the pie shell.

- Bake at 350 degrees for 40 to 45 minutes or until set.

- May bake in two 9-inch pie shells for 20 minutes or until light brown. May use low-fat mayonnaise and cheese. Freeze for future use.

Six Servings

BRUNCH CHEESY EGG CASSEROLE

8 eggs

1 cup milk

1 teaspoon baking
  powder

1 teaspoon sugar

1 teaspoon salt

1 pound Monterey Jack
  cheese, cubed

1 cup cottage cheese

3 ounces cream cheese,
  cubed

6 tablespoons butter,
  sliced

- Whisk the eggs and milk in a bowl until blended.

- Add the baking powder, sugar and salt and mix well. Stir in the Monterey Jack cheese, cottage cheese, cream cheese and butter. Spoon into a 9x11-inch baking dish.

- Bake at 350 degrees for 40 minutes.

Eight Servings

CHILE CHEESE FIESTA TART

3 slices bacon

1/2 cup chopped onion

1/4 cup minced canned green
chiles

1 1/2 cups half-and-half

3 eggs, lightly beaten

1/2 teaspoon seasoned salt

Freshly ground pepper
to taste

2 cups shredded Colby-Jack
cheese

1 green onion, thinly sliced

1 unbaked (9-inch)
homemade pie shell or 1
all ready pie pastry

2 tablespoons finely chopped
red bell pepper

2 tablespoons finely chopped
green bell pepper

Sliced green onions

- Fry the bacon in a skillet until crisp. Drain, reserving the bacon drippings. Crumble the bacon.

- Sauté the onion in the reserved bacon drippings in a skillet until tender. Stir in the chiles.

- Combine the onion mixture and bacon in a bowl. Stir in a mixture of the half-and-half, eggs, seasoned salt and pepper. Add the cheese and 1 green onion and mix well. Spoon into the pie shell.

- Bake at 375 degrees for 10 minutes. Reduce the oven temperature to 350 degrees.

- Bake for 25 minutes longer or until puffed and golden brown.

- Cool on a wire rack for 10 minutes. Sprinkle with the red and green peppers and sliced green onions. Cut into wedges.

- For variety, cut six 5-inch rounds from a recipe for a 2-crust homemade pie pastry or 2 all ready pie pastries. Press the pastry rounds into 1/2-cup tart pans. Spoon the filling into the shells. Bake for 20 minutes or until set and golden brown. Cool in the pans for 5 minutes. Remove to a serving platter. Sprinkle with the red and green peppers and sliced green onions.

Six Servings

To add subtle flavor to scrambled eggs, pierce a peeled clove of garlic with the prongs of the fork that you are using to mix the eggs.

CRAB MEAT AND EGGS NEW ORLEANS-STYLE

1/4 cup butter

3 tablespoons flour

1 1/2 cups milk

3 tablespoons brandy

1/2 teaspoon salt

1/4 teaspoon nutmeg

1/8 teaspoon hot sauce

1 pound fresh crab meat, drained, flaked

1/4 cup melted butter

1/2 teaspoon salt

1/2 teaspoon white pepper

12 eggs, poached

Chopped fresh parsley (optional)

- Heat 1/4 cup butter in a saucepan over low heat until melted. Add the flour, stirring until blended.

- Cook for 1 minute, stirring constantly. Add the milk gradually and mix well.

- Cook over medium heat until thickened and of a sauce consistency, stirring constantly. Stir in the brandy, 1/2 teaspoon salt, nutmeg and hot sauce. Cover to keep warm.

- Sauté the crab meat in 1/4 cup butter in a skillet for 5 minutes, stirring frequently. Stir in 1/2 teaspoon salt and white pepper.

- Spoon 1/2 of the crab meat mixture into 6 ramekins, dividing equally. Top each with 2 poached eggs. Spoon the remaining crab meat mixture over the eggs, dividing equally.

- Top with the brandy sauce. Sprinkle with parsley.

Six Servings

CRUSTLESS CRAB QUICHE

8 ounces fresh mushrooms, sliced

2 tablespoons butter

1 cup sour cream

1 cup small curd cottage cheese

1 cup grated Parmesan cheese

1/4 cup flour

4 eggs

1 teaspoon onion powder

1/4 teaspoon salt

4 drops of Tabasco sauce

6 ounces frozen Alaska King crab meat, thawed, drained

2 cups shredded Monterey Jack cheese

- Sauté the mushrooms in the butter in a skillet. Drain on paper towels.

- Process the sour cream, cottage cheese, Parmesan cheese, flour, eggs, onion powder, salt and Tabasco sauce in a blender until mixed. Pour into a bowl. Fold in the mushrooms, crab meat and Monterey Jack cheese. Spoon into a 10-inch quiche dish.

- Bake at 350 degrees for 45 minutes or until golden brown and a knife inserted in the center comes out clean.

- Let stand for 5 minutes before serving. Cut into wedges.

- May substitute fresh crab meat for the frozen crab meat.

Six Servings

HAM AND SPINACH PIE

1 teaspoon flour

1 all ready pie pastry, at
    room temperature

1 (10-ounce) package frozen
    chopped spinach, thawed

1 medium onion, chopped

1 clove of garlic, minced

3 tablespoons butter

1/2 cup chopped ham

2 tablespoons chopped red
    bell pepper

1/2 teaspoon salt

1/2 teaspoon pepper

1/4 teaspoon nutmeg

15 ounces ricotta cheese

8 ounces mozzarella cheese,
    shredded

1 cup grated Parmesan cheese

3 eggs, beaten

- Sprinkle the flour over 1 side of the pastry. Fit the pastry flour side down into a 9-inch pie plate. Fold the edge under and crimp.

- Squeeze the moisture from the spinach.

- Sauté the onion and garlic in the butter in a skillet over medium heat for 8 minutes or until the onion is tender. Stir in the spinach, ham, red pepper, salt, pepper and nutmeg.

- Sauté for 3 minutes or until all the liquid from the spinach evaporates.

- Combine the ricotta cheese, mozzarella cheese and Parmesan cheese in a bowl and mix well. Stir in the eggs. Add the spinach mixture and mix well. Spoon into the pie shell.

- Bake at 350 degrees for 40 minutes or until set and the top is brown. Let stand for 10 minutes before cutting into wedges.

- May freeze for future use. To reheat, wrap each wedge loosely in foil. Bake at 350 degrees for 30 minutes or until heated through; open the foil packets. Bake for 5 to 10 minutes longer.

Six Servings

Pour water to a depth of 2 inches into a heavy nonstick skillet with sloping sides. Stir in 2 tablespoons white vinegar, 1 teaspoon salt and 1 small bay leaf (optional). Bring to a full boil. Remove from heat and add 2 to 4 eggs to the water. Cover immediately with a tight-fitting lid. Let stand for 4 minutes. Remove the eggs with a slotted spoon. Drain briefly on a slice of dry bread or a folded paper towel. Serve immediately.

PROVENÇAL VEGETABLE CAKE

Provençal Vegetable Cake is a favorite of Francois Fisera of Fleur de Lys.

4 tablespoons olive oil

4 eggs, beaten

Salt and pepper to taste

3 medium tomatoes, thinly sliced

1 large onion, finely chopped

4 eggs, beaten

1 cup shredded Cheddar cheese

1 cup vegetable consommé

1 cup sliced mushrooms

1 clove of elephant garlic, chopped

4 eggs, beaten

1/2 bunch cilantro, chopped

3 cups thinly sliced zucchini

- Coat the bottom and side of a nonstick skillet with 1 tablespoon of the olive oil and blot the excess. Heat until hot. Pour a mixture of 4 eggs, salt and pepper into the prepared skillet, tilting to spread evenly over the bottom.

- Cook for 1 minute or until set. Slide the omelet onto a serving platter. Layer with the tomatoes.

- Sauté the onion in 1 tablespoon of the olive oil until golden brown. Spoon the onion over the tomatoes.

- Coat the bottom and side of a nonstick skillet with 1 tablespoon of the olive oil and blot the excess. Heat until hot. Pour a mixture of 4 eggs, salt and pepper into the prepared skillet, tilting to spread evenly over the bottom. Cook for 1 minute or until set; sprinkle with 1/2 of the cheese. Arrange over the prepared layers.

- Bring consommé to a boil in a saucepan. Add mushrooms and garlic. Simmer until mushrooms are tender. Drain, reserving the mushrooms, garlic and liquid. Spoon the mushrooms and garlic over the prepared layers.

- Coat nonstick skillet with remaining 1 tablespoon olive oil and blot excess. Pour in a mixture of 4 eggs, cilantro, remaining 1/2 cup cheese, salt and pepper. Cook for 1 minute or until set. Arrange over the prepared layers.

- Simmer the zucchini in the reserved liquid until tender-crisp; drain. Decorate the top of the omelet in a fish scale pattern with the zucchini. Cut into wedges.

Six Servings

MARBLEIZED DEVILED EGGS

6 to 12 hard-cooked eggs

Juice of 1 or 2 (16-ounce) cans whole beets

3 to 4 tablespoons sour cream

1 to 2 tablespoons mayonnaise

1 1/2 teaspoons minced onion

1 to 2 teaspoons chopped fresh dillweed

1/4 teaspoon cayenne

Salt and black pepper to taste

- Chill the eggs for 20 minutes. Crack the shells and place the eggs in a bowl.
- Pour the beet juice over the eggs. Add water to cover. The more concentrated the beet juice the brighter red the eggs.
- Chill, uncovered, for 8 to 10 hours. Drain and peel the eggs.
- Cut the eggs lengthwise into halves. Remove the yolks and place in a food processor container fitted with a steel blade. Place the whites on a serving platter.
- Add the sour cream, mayonnaise, onion, dillweed, cayenne, salt and black pepper to the food processor container.
- Process until smooth, scraping the work bowl once or twice.
- Pipe or spoon the egg yolk mixture into the whites. Garnish with sliced stuffed green olives, minced fresh parsley or dillweed and/or paprika.
- Chill thoroughly before serving.

Six to Twelve Servings

To prevent the yolks of hard-cooked eggs from discoloring, insert a sterilized sewing needle about one-fourth inch into the large end of each egg. This lets the air bubble inside the egg escape and prevents the shell from cracking. Next, place the eggs in a single layer in a saucepan and cover with cold water by one inch. Bring to a boil. Remove from heat. Let stand, covered, for seventeen minutes. Plunge into ice water. Let stand for twenty minutes. Prompt chilling of the eggs prevents the discoloring of the yolks, and thorough chilling makes the eggs easier to peel. Store the eggs in a bowl of water in the refrigerator for up to three days.

PASTA GRECO

8 ounces angel hair pasta

Salt to taste

4 ounces feta cheese, crumbled

1/2 cup chopped oil-cured Greek olives

1/4 cup chopped green onions

1/4 cup chopped fresh parsley

8 fresh basil leaves, slivered

1/4 cup virgin olive oil

Pepper to taste

Freshly grated Parmesan cheese

- Cook the pasta in boiling salted water in a saucepan for 5 to 6 minutes or until al dente. Drain; do not rinse.
- Combine the feta cheese, olives, green onions, parsley and basil in a heated pasta bowl and mix well. Add the hot pasta, tossing to mix.
- Add the olive oil and mix well. Add pepper and Parmesan cheese and toss to mix.
- May omit the olive oil.

Four Servings

BOW TIE FIESTA

8 ounces bow tie pasta

1 pound ground beef

1/2 onion, chopped

1/2 green bell pepper, chopped

1 (15-ounce) can tomato sauce

1 tablespoon chili powder

Salt to taste

1 cup sour cream

1 cup salsa

1/2 cup sliced black olives

1/4 cup sliced jalapeños (optional)

1 tomato, chopped

1 cup shredded Cheddar cheese

- Cook the pasta using package directions and cooking for 7 minutes; drain.
- Brown the beef in a skillet, stirring until crumbly; drain. Add the onion and green pepper and mix well.
- Cook until the onion is tender, stirring constantly. Stir in the tomato sauce, chili powder and salt.
- Combine the pasta, ground beef mixture, sour cream, salsa, black olives, jalapeños and tomato in a bowl and mix well. Spoon into a 9x11-inch or 9x9-inch baking dish. Sprinkle with the cheese.
- Bake at 350 degrees for 20 to 30 minutes or until brown and bubbly.

Eight Servings

FETTUCCINI WITH PROSCIUTTO AND SMOKED SALMON

1/2 cup chopped onion

2 tablespoons unsalted butter

1/4 cup dry white wine

1 tablespoon chopped fresh parsley

4 ounces smoked salmon, thinly sliced

4 ounces prosciutto, thinly sliced

1 cup whipping cream

3 eggs, lightly beaten

1/2 cup freshly grated Parmesan cheese

1/4 teaspoon freshly ground white pepper

8 to 16 ounces fettuccini, cooked, drained

- Sauté the onion in the butter in a saucepan until tender. Stir in the wine and parsley.
- Cook until the liquid is reduced by 1/2, stirring constantly. Add the salmon and prosciutto. Remove from heat; toss lightly.
- Bring the whipping cream to a simmer in a saucepan. Stir a small amount of the warm cream into the eggs; stir the eggs into the warm cream. Add the cheese and white pepper and mix well.
- Cook over low heat until thickened, stirring constantly.
- Toss the fettuccini with the salmon mixture in a bowl. Add the cream sauce and toss lightly. Serve immediately.

Four to Six Servings

CAJUN FETTUCCINI

1 boneless skinless chicken breast

1 1/2 cups water

8 ounces peeled medium shrimp

Sliced Cajun or smoked sausage

1/2 cup chopped onion

1 red bell pepper, cut into strips

1 green bell pepper, cut into strips

1 clove of garlic, minced

1 tablespoon olive oil

1/2 cup white wine

1/2 cup chicken broth

1 teaspoon flour

1 cup whipping cream

1 tablespoon Cajun or Creole seasoning

2 tablespoons tomato paste

16 ounces fettuccini, cooked, drained

- Cut the chicken into strips.
- Bring the water to a boil in a saucepan. Add the shrimp.
- Cook for 3 minutes or until the shrimp turn pink.
- Cook the chicken, sausage, onion, bell peppers and garlic in the olive oil in a saucepan until the chicken and sausage are cooked through; drain.
- Bring the white wine to a boil in a saucepan. Whisk in a mixture of the broth and flour.
- Cook until thickened and smooth, stirring constantly. Stir in the whipping cream, Cajun seasoning and tomato paste. Bring to a boil; reduce heat.
- Simmer for 20 minutes, stirring frequently. Stir in the chicken mixture and shrimp. Toss with the warm fettuccini in a bowl.

Six Servings

FETTUCCINI WITH SEAFOOD AND OLIVES

2 scallions, minced

3 cloves of garlic, minced

3/4 cup unsalted butter

1 1/4 cups white bread crumbs

1/2 cup dry marsala or
    sauterne

1/4 cup chopped fresh parsley

1/4 cup grated Parmesan
    cheese

1/2 teaspoon salt

1/8 teaspoon freshly ground
    pepper

8 ounces spinach fettuccini

1/2 cup half-and-half

1/4 cup unsalted butter

12 ounces cooked, peeled,
    deveined medium shrimp

8 ounces scallops, cooked

4 ounces lump crab meat

12 small pimento-stuffed
    green olives

Sprigs of fresh parsley

- Sauté the scallions and garlic in 3/4 cup butter in a skillet for 2 minutes. Stir in the bread crumbs, wine, 1/4 cup parsley, cheese, salt and pepper.

- Sauté for 3 minutes. Remove from heat.

- Cook the fettuccini using package directions until al dente; drain. Toss with the half-and-half and 1/4 cup butter in a bowl. Spoon into a baking dish.

- Spread with 1/2 of the bread crumb mixture. Layer the shrimp, scallops, crab meat and olives over the crumb mixture in the prepared dish; top with the remaining crumb mixture.

- Bake at 375 degrees for 30 minutes. Top with sprigs of fresh parsley just before serving.

Six Servings

FETTUCCINI WITH WINTER SAUCE

1 ounce dried porcini

1/2 medium onion, finely
    chopped

2 slices pancetta, coarsely
    chopped

Chopped leaves of 1 sprig of
    rosemary

2 tablespoons unsalted butter

2 sweet Italian sausages,
    casings removed

1/4 cup dry white wine

1 (28-ounce) can Italian
    tomatoes, drained, seeded,
    crushed

Salt and freshly ground
    pepper to taste

16 ounces fresh fettuccini

1/4 cup freshly grated
    Parmigiano-Reggiano
    cheese

1 tablespoon unsalted butter

- Combine the mushrooms with enough hot water to cover in a bowl.

- Let stand for 20 minutes. Drain, reserving the liquid.

- Rinse the mushrooms and coarsely chop. Strain the reserved liquid.

- Cook the onion, pancetta and rosemary in 2 tablespoons butter in a skillet over medium-low heat for 10 minutes or until the onion is tender and the pancetta has rendered its fat, stirring frequently. Stir in the sausage.

- Cook over medium heat for 5 minutes, stirring constantly with a wooden spoon to break up the sausage. Add the white wine and mix well.

- Cook until the alcohol evaporates, stirring constantly. Add the tomatoes, salt and pepper and mix well.

- Cook for 10 minutes, stirring frequently. Stir in the mushrooms and 3 tablespoons of the reserved liquid.

- Cook for 20 minutes longer, stirring frequently. May add additional reserved liquid as needed if the sauce becomes too dry.

- Cook the fettuccini in boiling salted water in a saucepan until al dente; drain.

- Combine the hot pasta, cheese and 1 tablespoon butter in a bowl and mix well. Add the sausage mixture, tossing to mix. Serve with additional grated Parmigiano-Reggiano cheese.

Six to Eight Servings

FETTUCCINI WITH ZUCCHINI AND MUSHROOM SAUCE

Serve with crusty rolls and sliced fresh fruit.

8 ounces mushrooms, thinly sliced

1/8 teaspoon garlic salt

1/4 cup butter

1 1/2 pounds zucchini, julienned

16 ounces fettuccini, cooked, drained

1 cup half-and-half

1 cup grated Parmesan cheese

1/2 cup chopped fresh parsley

1 egg, lightly beaten

1/2 teaspoon salt

- Cook the mushrooms and garlic salt in the butter in a skillet for 2 minutes, stirring frequently. Stir in the zucchini.

- Cook for 8 minutes longer, stirring frequently.

- Combine the mushroom mixture and hot pasta in a bowl, tossing to mix. Stir in a mixture of the half-and-half, cheese, parsley, egg and salt.

- To avoid raw eggs that may carry salmonella, we suggest using an equivalent amount of commercial egg substitute.

Eight Servings

SHRIMP AND FETTUCCINI

1/2 onion, chopped

12 fresh mushrooms, sliced

1/2 cup chopped green onions

1/4 cup chopped, seeded, peeled fresh tomato

2 cloves of garlic, minced

4 teaspoons minced fresh parsley

2 teaspoons Creole seasoning

1/4 cup unsalted butter

1/4 cup shrimp stock

12 ounces fettuccini, cooked, drained

24 medium shrimp, peeled, deveined

1/2 cup dry white wine

1/4 cup unsalted butter

- Sauté the onion, mushrooms, green onions, tomato, garlic, parsley and Creole seasoning in 1/4 cup butter in a saucepan for 30 seconds. Stir in the stock; reduce heat.

- Simmer until the onions are tender, stirring frequently. Add the fettuccini, shrimp and white wine.

- Simmer until most of the liquid has evaporated, stirring frequently. Remove from heat. Add 1/4 cup butter, stirring until mixed. Serve immediately.

- May substitute bottled clam juice for the shrimp stock.

Four Servings

Black Bean Lasagna

8 ounces lasagna noodles

1 (16-ounce) can black beans

1 each red and green bell pepper

Olive oil to taste

1 (28-ounce) can crushed tomatoes

1 (16-ounce) can corn, drained

1 (4-ounce) can jalapeños, drained, chopped

1 small onion, chopped

1/4 cup chopped fresh cilantro

4 cloves of garlic, chopped

1 tablespoon chili powder

2 teaspoons each oregano and cumin

Salt and pepper to taste

2 cups cottage cheese

8 ounces Cheddar cheese, shredded

1 cup grated Parmesan cheese

1 cup shredded mozzarella cheese

- Cook the noodles using package directions; drain.
- Rinse and drain the black beans.
- Brush the red pepper and green pepper with olive oil. Place on a baking sheet.
- Broil on the top oven rack until the skins are blistered and charred on all sides, turning frequently. Place in a nonrecycled brown paper bag immediately. Let stand until cool. Peel, seed and chop the peppers.
- Combine the roasted peppers, undrained tomatoes, black beans, corn, jalapeños, onion, cilantro, garlic, chili powder, oregano, cumin, salt and pepper in a saucepan and mix well.
- Simmer for 15 minutes, stirring occasionally.
- Mix the cottage cheese and Cheddar cheese in a bowl.
- Layer the black bean mixture, noodles, cottage cheese mixture and Parmesan cheese 1/2 at a time in a 9x13-inch baking dish. Sprinkle with the mozzarella cheese.
- Bake, covered with foil, at 350 degrees for 1 hour. Remove the foil.
- Bake for 10 minutes longer.

Eight to Ten Servings

BOLOGNESE LASAGNA

For the Béchamel Sauce, bring 3 cups milk to a simmer in a saucepan over medium-low heat. Heat 6 tablespoons butter in a sauce-pan over low heat until melted. Stir in 4 1/2 table-spoons flour. Cook for 2 minutes, whisking constantly; do not brown. Stir in the hot milk gradually. Cook until of the consistency of sour cream, stirring constantly. Mix in 1/4 teaspoon salt. Remove from heat. If prepared in advance, cover the surface with plastic wrap to prevent a film from forming.

Meat Sauce

2/3 cup each chopped celery
   and chopped carrot

1/2 cup chopped onion

3 tablespoons butter

1 tablespoon vegetable oil

12 ounces ground chuck

1/4 teaspoon each salt and
   freshly ground pepper

1/8 teaspoon ground nutmeg

1 cup milk

1 cup dry white wine

1 1/2 cups canned whole
   Italian plum tomatoes,
   chopped

Lasagna

Béchamel Sauce (at left)

2 tablespoons butter

12 lasagna noodles, cooked,
   drained

2/3 cup freshly grated
   Parmigiano-Reggiano
   cheese

- For the meat sauce, cook the celery, carrot and onion in a mixture of the butter and oil in a saucepan over medium heat for 5 minutes or until the vegetables are tender, stirring frequently. Add the ground chuck, salt, pepper and nutmeg.

- Cook until the ground chuck is no longer red, stirring constantly; drain. Stir in the milk.

- Simmer until the milk is absorbed, stirring occasionally. Stir in the wine. Cook until the wine is absorbed, stirring constantly. Stir in the undrained tomatoes.

- Simmer for 1 to 3 hours or until of the desired consistency, stirring occasionally and adding 1/2 cup of water at a time as needed if sauce becomes too dry. Skim the fat and adjust the seasonings as desired. Set aside or store, covered, in the refrigerator.

- For the lasagna, combine the meat sauce and Béchamel Sauce in a bowl and mix well.

- Spread the bottom and sides of a 9x12-inch baking with 1 tablespoon of the butter. Layer 3 noodles, 1 1/4 cups of the meat sauce mixture and 2 tablespoons of the cheese in the prepared baking dish. Repeat the layers twice. Layer with the remaining 3 noodles, remaining meat sauce mixture and sprinkle with the remaining cheese. Dot with the remaining 1 tablespoon butter.

- Bake at 350 degrees for 30 minutes or until brown and bubbly. Increase the oven temperature to 400 degrees. Bake for 5 to 10 minutes longer if the top is not brown. Let stand for 10 to 15 minutes before serving.

Six to Nine Servings

VEGETARIAN LASAGNA

1 (15-ounce) can tomatoes

1 (15-ounce) can tomato
   sauce

1 teaspoon oregano, crushed

1 teaspoon basil, crushed

1/8 teaspoon pepper

1 large onion, chopped

1 1/2 teaspoons minced garlic

2 tablespoons olive oil

2 small zucchini, chopped

8 ounces mushrooms, sliced

1 large carrot, chopped

1 green bell pepper, chopped

2 cups ricotta cheese

1 cup grated Parmesan cheese

1 cup shredded mozzarella
   cheese

8 ounces lasagna noodles,
   cooked, rinsed, drained

1 (4-ounce) can sliced black
   olives, drained

- Combine the undrained tomatoes, tomato sauce, oregano, basil and pepper in a saucepan and mix well.

- Simmer over low heat until of the desired consistency, stirring occasionally.

- Sauté the onion and garlic in the olive oil in a skillet over medium heat until the onion is golden brown. Stir in the zucchini, mushrooms, carrot and green pepper.

- Cook for 5 to 10 minutes or until the vegetables are tender, stirring occasionally. Stir the vegetables into the tomato mixture.

- Simmer for 15 minutes, stirring occasionally.

- Combine the ricotta cheese, Parmesan cheese and mozzarella cheese in a bowl and mix well.

- Spoon 1 cup of the tomato mixture into an 8x12-inch baking dish. Layer with 1/2 of the noodles, 1/2 of the cheese mixture and 1/2 of the remaining tomato mixture. Top with the remaining noodles, remaining cheese mixture and remaining tomato mixture. Sprinkle with the black olives.

- Bake at 350 degrees for 30 to 45 minutes or until bubbly.

- Let stand for 10 minutes before serving.

Six to Eight Servings

Like all pasta, the best lasagna noodles are fresh. Homemade lasagna noodles are delicate and delicious, giving a whole new texture and flavor to any recipe. If you do not have the equipment, time or inclination to make your own pasta, fresh pasta is available in many supermarkets. Dried lasagna noodles are thick and tough compared with fresh, but if you are using dried noodles look for the imported brands that contain approximately twenty pieces per pound. The "no-boil" noodles are also thin and delicate, but always boil them before using unless you are following the recipe on the package.

Linguini With Yellow Tomatoes And Goat Cheese

1¹/2 pounds yellow tomatoes

5 tablespoons extra-virgin olive oil

3 tablespoons minced capers

2 cloves of garlic, finely minced

¹/4 teaspoon red pepper flakes

Salt to taste

16 ounces tomato linguini

¹/3 cup packed fresh basil

4 ounces goat cheese, crumbled

- Peel, seed and thinly slice the tomatoes. Place the slices in a serving bowl.

- Drizzle the tomatoes with a mixture of the olive oil, capers, garlic, red pepper flakes and salt.

- Cook the pasta in boiling salted water in a saucepan until al dente; drain.

- Tear the basil into bite-size pieces. Stir the basil and goat cheese into the tomato mixture. Add the pasta, tossing to mix.

- Spoon onto heated dinner plates. Serve immediately.

- May use any type of firm creamy goat cheese.

- May substitute red tomatoes or a combination of red and yellow tomatoes for the yellow tomatoes.

Four Servings

Chick's Seafood Linguini

2 cloves of garlic, minced

¹/2 cup butter

Flour

4 cups whipping cream

Salt and pepper to taste

1 pint oysters with liquor

1 pound shrimp, peeled, deveined

Sherry to taste

16 ounces linguini, cooked, drained

- Sauté the garlic in the butter in a saucepan until light brown. Discard the garlic, reserving the pan drippings.

- Combine the reserved pan drippings with enough flour to make a roux and mix well. Add the whipping cream gradually, stirring constantly.

- Cook until thickened, stirring constantly. Season with salt and pepper. Stir in the oysters with liquor and shrimp.

- Cook for 8 to 10 minutes or until the edges of the oysters begin to curl and the shrimp turn pink. Stir in the sherry.

- Spoon over hot cooked linguini on a serving platter.

Six to Eight Servings

MACARONI WITH THREE CHEESES

16 ounces macaroni

1 cup freshly grated Parmesan cheese

1/2 cup ricotta cheese

1/2 cup shredded mozzarella cheese

3 tablespoons butter

1 1/2 cups whipping cream

1/8 teaspoon nutmeg

1/8 teaspoon seasoned salt

1/8 teaspoon freshly ground white pepper

1/8 teaspoon cayenne

- Cook the pasta using package directions until al dente. Drain, rinse with cold water and drain again.

- Combine the pasta, Parmesan cheese, ricotta cheese, mozzarella cheese and butter in a bowl and mix well. Stir in a mixture of the whipping cream, nutmeg, seasoned salt, white pepper and cayenne. Spoon into a buttered baking dish.

- Bake at 400 degrees for 20 minutes or until brown and bubbly.

- May substitute penne for the macaroni.

Six to Eight Servings

LEMON DILL ORZO WITH GRUYERE

1 to 2 tablespoons butter

2 teaspoons freshly grated lemon zest

16 ounces orzo

Salt to taste

1/2 cup finely chopped shallots

1/2 cup finely chopped celery

2 tablespoons unsalted butter

2 tablespoons olive oil

3 tablespoons flour

2 cups chicken broth

1 teaspoon freshly grated lemon zest

Pepper to taste

2 cups coarsely grated Gruyère cheese

1/4 cup minced fresh dillweed

- Spread 1 to 2 tablespoons butter over the bottom and side of a 2-quart gratin dish or shallow baking dish. Sprinkle with 2 teaspoons lemon zest.

- Cook the orzo in boiling salted water in a saucepan for 6 minutes or until al dente; drain.

- Cook the shallots and celery in 2 tablespoons butter and olive oil in a saucepan over medium heat until the celery is tender, stirring constantly. Add the flour and mix well.

- Cook for 3 minutes, stirring constantly. Add the broth in a fine stream, whisking constantly. Bring to a boil, whisking constantly. Stir in 1 teaspoon zest, salt and pepper.

- Simmer for 3 minutes or until thickened, whisking constantly. Combine with the pasta, Gruyère cheese and dillweed in a bowl and mix well. Spoon into the prepared gratin dish.

- Bake at 400 degrees for 30 minutes or until bubbly.

Six to Eight Servings

CRAWFISH WITH SUN-DRIED TOMATO RAVIOLI

Susan Fuller Slack serves this dish with a chilled mixed green salad and crusty French baguette.

1 shallot, minced

1 clove of garlic, minced

2 tablespoons unsalted butter

1 cup whipping cream

1 cup chopped, seeded, peeled plum tomatoes

8 to 12 ounces peeled cooked crawfish tails, chopped

1/4 cup minced oil-pack sun-dried tomatoes

1 tablespoon minced fresh basil

Salt and freshly ground pepper to taste

8 to 10 ounces fresh sun-dried tomato ravioli

1/4 cup sliced imported black olives

1 green onion, sliced

- Sauté the shallot and garlic in the butter in a saucepan over medium heat for 30 seconds, stirring constantly. Stir in the whipping cream and plum tomatoes.

- Simmer over medium-low heat for 8 to 10 minutes, stirring frequently. Stir in the crawfish, sun-dried tomatoes, basil, salt and pepper.

- Simmer for 1 minute longer, stirring occasionally. Remove from heat. Cover to keep warm.

- Cook the ravioli in boiling salted water in a saucepan for 4 to 6 minutes or until tender; drain.

- Combine the ravioli with the crawfish mixture in a heated bowl, tossing to mix. Sprinkle with the black olives and green onion. Serve immediately.

- May substitute shrimp for the crawfish and any type of ravioli for the sun-dried tomato ravioli.

Four Servings

MUSHROOM STROGANOFF

1 pound medium to large
   mushrooms

2 tablespoons butter or
   vegetable oil

1 large red onion, finely
   chopped

Pepper to taste

1 teaspoon paprika

Salt to taste

1/2 cup sour cream or
   whipping cream

12 ounces noodles, cooked,
   drained

- Wipe the mushrooms with a damp paper towel. Let stand at room temperature in a dry environment for 8 to 10 hours. Cut into 1/8-inch slices.

- Heat the butter in a skillet until melted. Add the onion and mix well.

- Cook until tender, stirring frequently. Transfer the onion to a bowl with a slotted spoon, reserving the pan drippings. Increase the heat to high. Stir 1/3 of the mushrooms and pepper into the reserved pan drippings.

- Cook until brown but not soft, stirring constantly. Remove the mushrooms with a slotted spoon to a bowl. Repeat the process twice with the remaining mushrooms and pepper.

- Decrease the heat to medium. Return the mushrooms to the skillet. Stir in the onion, paprika and salt. Add the sour cream and mix well.

- Cook just until heated through, stirring constantly. Spoon over the noodles on a serving platter.

- If you do not have time to let the mushrooms stand at room temperature for 8 to 10 hours, be sure to cook until all the liquid has evaporated.

Four Servings

Wash a large quantity of mushrooms in a hurry by plunging the mushrooms into a mixture of 2 quarts water, 1/2 cup vinegar and 1/4 cup salt. Quickly swirl the mushrooms around to loosen the dirt, then remove the mushrooms. The slightly acidic saline solution dislodges the dirt almost instantly, and the vinegar helps to preserve the mushrooms' whiteness.

CHICKEN AND ARTICHOKE-STUFFED SHELLS

1 pound boneless skinless chicken breasts

1 (15-ounce) can diced tomatoes, drained

8 ounces fresh mushrooms, sliced

1 (8-ounce) jar artichokes, drained, minced

1 (8-ounce) can sliced black olives, drained

1/4 cup chopped fresh basil

2 cloves of garlic, finely chopped

3 tablespoons olive oil

1 egg, lightly beaten

12 ounces jumbo pasta shells, cooked, drained

1 (26-ounce) jar marinara sauce

Freshly grated Parmesan cheese

- Combine the chicken with enough water to cover in a saucepan. Bring to a boil; reduce heat.

- Simmer for 1 hour or until the chicken is cooked through; drain. Cut into bite-size pieces.

- Combine the tomatoes, mushrooms, artichokes, black olives, basil and garlic in a bowl and mix well. Cook the artichoke mixture in the olive oil in a skillet until tender and thickened, stirring frequently. Stir in the chicken and egg.

- Cook for 5 minutes or until heated through, stirring occasionally. Remove from heat. Stuff equal portions of the artichoke mixture into the pasta shells. Arrange in a 9x15-inch baking pan. Pour the marinara sauce over the shells.

- Bake, covered, at 350 degrees for 30 minutes or until bubbly. Sprinkle with Parmesan cheese just before serving.

- May substitute 2 tablespoons dried basil for the fresh basil.

Six Servings

BORDELAISE SHRIMP SPAGHETTI

1 cup butter

1 cup olive oil

1 cup minced shallots

1/2 cup minced garlic

5 pounds shrimp, peeled, deveined

1 1/2 cups oyster water

1 tablespoon Tabasco sauce

Salt and pepper to taste

1 cup minced fresh parsley

16 ounces spaghetti, cooked, drained

1/2 cup freshly grated Parmesan cheese

1/2 cup freshly grated Romano cheese

- Heat the butter in a cast-iron skillet until melted. Stir in the olive oil. Bring to a simmer. Stir in the shallots and garlic.

- Sauté over medium heat for 5 minutes. Add the shrimp and mix well.

- Cook for 5 minutes or until the shrimp turn pink, stirring frequently. Remove from heat. Stir in the oyster water, Tabasco sauce, salt and pepper. Pour into a bowl.

- Marinate, covered, in the refrigerator for 1 hour or longer, stirring occasionally.

- Bring the shrimp mixture to a simmer in a saucepan just before serving. Stir in the parsley. Spoon the shrimp mixture over the spaghetti on dinner plates. Sprinkle with the Parmesan cheese and Romano cheese.

- May substitute chicken broth for oyster water.

Eight Servings

PASTA JAMBALAYA

1/2 cup each chopped red onion, green bell pepper and celery

4 cloves of garlic, chopped

6 tablespoons corn oil

1 (16-ounce) can diced tomatoes

1 (11-ounce) can tomato purée

1 cup chicken stock

2 teaspoons Tabasco sauce

1 teaspoon black pepper

1/4 teaspoon cayenne

8 ounces andouille sausage, sliced

1/4 cup cubed tasso ham

8 ounces boneless skinless chicken breasts

24 ounces fusilli, cooked, drained

1 cup each shredded provolone and smoked Gouda cheese

Finely chopped green onions

- Sauté the onion, green pepper, celery and garlic in 4 tablespoons of the corn oil in a stockpot until tender.
- Add the undrained tomatoes, tomato purée, stock, Tabasco sauce, black pepper and cayenne and mix well. Stir in the sausage and ham.
- Simmer for 30 minutes, stirring occasionally.
- Cut the chicken into bite-size pieces.
- Sauté in the remaining 1 to 2 tablespoons corn oil in a skillet until cooked through; drain. Stir into the tomato mixture.
- Simmer just until heated through, stirring frequently.
- Spoon the sauce over the pasta on 4 dinner plates.
- Sprinkle with a mixture of the provolone cheese and Gouda cheese. Top with the green onions.

Four Servings

Pasta Jambalaya is a favorite entrée of many customers of Stellinis, an Italian restaurant in northeast Columbia.

MAIN EVENTS

MAIN EVENTS

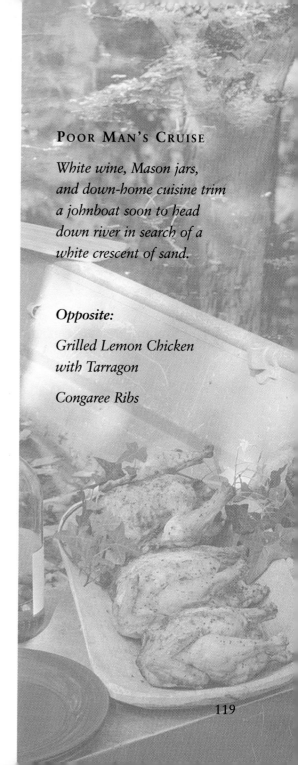

POOR MAN'S CRUISE

White wine, Mason jars, and down-home cuisine trim a johnboat soon to head down river in search of a white crescent of sand.

Opposite:

Grilled Lemon Chicken with Tarragon

Congaree Ribs

BEEF TENDERLOIN STUFFED WITH LOBSTER

Try this versatile Pork or Beef Marinade. Mix 1/2 cup olive oil, 1/2 cup dry red wine, 1/4 cup soy sauce, 1/4 cup catsup, 1 teaspoon minced garlic, 1/2 teaspoon hot curry powder, 1/2 teaspoon onion powder, 1/4 teaspoon ginger powder and Tabasco sauce to taste. Pour over pork or beef tenderloin. Marinate in the refrigerator for 8 to 10 hours, turning occasionally. Bake pork tenderloin at 350 degrees for approximately 45 minutes or until cooked through. Bake beef tenderloin until of the desired degree of doneness. May thicken the marinade with flour to make gravy.

2 (4-ounce) lobster tails

Salt to taste

1 (3- to 4-pound) whole beef tenderloin, butterflied

1 tablespoon melted butter

1 tablespoon lemon juice

6 slices bacon, partially cooked

1/2 cup sliced green onions

1/2 cup butter

1/2 cup dry white wine

1/8 teaspoon garlic salt

- Combine the lobster tails and salt with enough water to cover in a stockpot. Bring to a boil; reduce heat.

- Simmer, covered, for 5 to 6 minutes or until the lobster meat is opaque; drain.

- Cut the tails lengthwise into halves. Remove the lobster meat and chop into bite-size pieces. Arrange the lobster meat down the center of the tenderloin. Drizzle the lobster meat with a mixture of 1 tablespoon butter and lemon juice. Secure the tenderloin at 1-inch intervals with heavy kitchen twine to enclose the lobster meat. Place the tenderloin on a rack in a shallow roasting pan.

- Roast at 425 degrees for 45 minutes for rare, 1 hour for well done or until of the desired degree of doneness. Lay the bacon on top of the tenderloin.

- Roast for 5 minutes longer.

- Cook the green onions in 1/2 cup butter in a saucepan over low heat until tender, stirring occasionally. Stir in the white wine and garlic salt.

- Bring to a boil, stirring constantly. Remove from heat.

- Slice the tenderloin and arrange on a serving platter. Drizzle with the wine sauce.

Eight Servings

Filets Mignons With Clemson Bleu Cheese Sauce

Clemson Bleu Cheese Sauce

3/4 cup madeira

2 tablespoons minced
  shallots

1 clove of garlic, minced

1 cup whipping cream

1/2 cup demi-glace or brown
  stock

1/2 cup butter, softened

6 ounces Stilton, Gorgonzola
  or other bleu cheese,
  crumbled, softened

Cayenne to taste

Seasoned salt to taste

Filets Mignons

4 (6- to 8-ounce) filets
  mignons

Seasoned salt and freshly
  ground pepper to taste

3 tablespoons butter, softened

- For the sauce, combine the wine, shallots and garlic in a saucepan and mix well.

- Cook over medium-high heat until reduced to 2 tablespoons, stirring constantly. Stir in the whipping cream and demi-glace.

- Cook the sauce over high heat until reduced to 1 cup, stirring constantly.

- Beat the butter and cheese in a bowl until smooth. Whisk into the wine sauce gradually.

- Simmer for 3 minutes, stirring frequently. Strain into a bowl. Season with cayenne and seasoned salt. Cover to keep warm.

- For the filets, sprinkle both sides of the beef with seasoned salt and pepper. Rub with the butter.

- Grill over hot coals until of the desired degree of doneness.

- Serve immediately with the sauce and hot cooked rice or noodles.

Four Servings

Rob Patterson at Saluda's in Columbia serves Mango and Crab Meat Fruits de Mer on Filets Mignons and Catfish Roulades. Prepare this sauce by first making a roux using 2 cups butter, 4 cups flour and 1 tablespoon blackening seasoning. Bring 2 quarts whipping cream, 1 quart clam juice and 1 quart white wine to a boil in a saucepan. Whisk in 1/2 cup of the roux. Remove from heat. Whisk in 2 tablespoons salt and pepper blend, 1 teaspoon Dijon mustard and 1 teaspoon chipotle purée. Stir in 1 1/2 cups mango chutney and 1 pound crab meat.

CONGAREE VISTA STEAK

The three basic elements essential to successful sautéing are the correct pan, high heat and the right fat. Use a pan wide enough to accommodate all the ingredients in a single layer. The pan sides may be sloping or straight but must be low enough that the liquid evaporates quickly. Always use a heavy-bottomed pan for even heat. High heat is essential for sautéing. Since butter burns at a high temperature, blend the butter with oil to get the flavor of butter when sautéing. Once the pan and the fat are hot, add the ingredients. A crust will form on the food, preventing sticking and allowing for caramelization.

4 (10-ounce) boneless rib eye
    steaks, 1 inch thick

5 teaspoons Creole seasoning

1/4 cup olive oil

8 cups sliced assorted fresh
    wild mushrooms

1/2 cup chopped onion

1/2 cup chopped green onions

2 tablespoons minced garlic

1 teaspoon salt

Freshly ground pepper
    to taste

1/2 cup unsalted butter,
    chopped

- Sprinkle both sides of each steak with 1 teaspoon of the Creole seasoning. Pound the seasoning into the steak with the side of a knife or the palm of your hand once or twice.
- Heat the olive oil in a skillet over high heat until hot. Add the steaks.
- Sauté for 4 minutes; turn the steaks.
- Sauté for 2 minutes. Stir in the mushrooms, onion, green onions, garlic, salt, pepper and remaining 1 teaspoon Creole seasoning.
- Sauté for 2 minutes. Turn the steaks. Dot the steaks with the butter.
- Cook, covered, for 1 minute. Remove from heat.
- Arrange each steak on a dinner plate. Cover with 3/4 cup of the mushroom mixture.

Four Servings

BARBECUE BEEF

Serve with Slaw for Barbecue on page 53.

4 cups beef stew meat

2 onions, sliced

1¹/₂ cups water

¹/₄ cup vinegar

¹/₄ cup sugar

¹/₄ cup butter

4 teaspoons prepared
    mustard

1 tablespoon salt

¹/₄ teaspoon black pepper

¹/₄ teaspoon cayenne

2 thick slices lemon

1 cup catsup

3 tablespoons
    Worcestershire sauce

Hamburger buns

- Combine the stew meat, onions, water, vinegar, sugar, butter, mustard, salt, black pepper, cayenne and lemon slices in a large saucepan and mix well. Bring to a boil; reduce heat.
- Simmer for 1 hour or until of the desired consistency, stirring occasionally. Stir in the catsup and Worcestershire sauce.
- Cook just until heated through, stirring occasionally.
- Spoon onto heated buns.

Eight to Ten Servings

BURGUNDY BEEF

2 pounds beef stew meat

2 teaspoons salt

¹/₂ teaspoon freshly
    ground pepper

2 tablespoons vegetable
    oil

1 medium onion,
    chopped

1 cup sour cream or
    whipping cream

1 cup shredded medium
    Cheddar cheese

¹/₂ cup burgundy

1 clove of garlic, minced

³/₄ teaspoon chopped
    fresh thyme

³/₄ teaspoon chopped
    fresh marjoram

³/₄ teaspoon chopped
    fresh basil

1 (10-ounce) can cream
    of mushroom soup

1¹/₂ cups long grain rice,
    cooked

- Season the beef with the salt and pepper.
- Heat the oil in a skillet over medium-high heat until hot. Add the beef.
- Cook until brown on all sides, turning frequently. Stir in the onion.
- Cook until the onion is tender; drain. Combine the beef mixture, sour cream, cheese, burgundy, garlic, thyme, marjoram and basil in a bowl and mix well. Spoon into a 3-quart baking dish.
- Bake, covered, at 325 degrees for 2 hours or until the beef is cooked through. Stir in the soup.
- Bake, covered, for 20 minutes longer. Serve over the hot cooked rice.

Six to Eight Servings

OLD-FASHIONED BEEF STEW

4 pounds boneless beef round

1 cup vegetable oil

2 large onions, chopped

3 ribs celery, sliced

6 carrots, peeled, cut into
    1-inch slices

1 teaspoon minced garlic

1 teaspoon each salt and
    celery salt

3/4 cup flour

1 tablespoon paprika

1 teaspoon basil

1/2 teaspoon oregano

4 cups beef bouillon

1 1/2 cups burgundy

1 cup water

1 bay leaf

12 peppercorns

1 (16-ounce) can chopped
    tomatoes

4 medium potatoes

1 (16-ounce) jar small
    onions, drained

- Cut the beef into 1 1/2-inch cubes.

- Heat the oil in a heavy stockpot over medium-high heat until hot. Add the beef.

- Cook until brown on all sides, turning frequently. Stir in the chopped onions, celery, carrots, garlic, salt and celery salt.

- Cook over medium heat for 10 minutes, stirring frequently. Reduce heat to low.

- Add a mixture of the flour, paprika, basil and oregano gradually, stirring constantly until mixed. Stir in the bouillon, wine and water. Bring to a gentle boil.

- Tie the bay leaf and peppercorns in cheesecloth. Add the seasoning bag to the stockpot. Stir in the undrained tomatoes. Bring to a boil; reduce heat.

- Simmer, covered, for 1 1/2 hours, stirring occasionally. Peel and coarsely chop the potatoes. Add the potatoes and small onions to the stew and mix well. Bring to a boil; reduce heat.

- Cook, covered, for 40 minutes or until the potatoes are tender, stirring occasionally. Discard the seasoning bag. Ladle the stew into bowls.

- May substitute beef shoulder roast for the beef round.

Twelve Servings

EGGPLANT PARMESAN WITH BEEF

1 medium eggplant

1 teaspoon salt

9 tablespoons butter or
  margarine

1 pound ground beef

1 medium onion, chopped

1/3 cup chopped green bell
  pepper

1 (28-ounce) can tomatoes,
  coarsely chopped

1 (6-ounce) can tomato paste

1 teaspoon salt

1/2 teaspoon whole oregano

1/2 teaspoon each basil,
  whole marjoram and
  pepper

2 eggs, beaten

3/4 cup dry bread crumbs

2 cups shredded mozzarella
  cheese

3/4 cup grated Parmesan
  cheese

Green bell pepper rings

Sprigs of fresh parsley

- Cut the eggplant into 1/4-inch slices. Sprinkle with 1 teaspoon salt. Let stand for 1 hour.

- Heat 1 tablespoon of the butter in a skillet until melted. Add the ground beef, onion and 1/3 cup green pepper.

- Cook until the ground beef is brown and crumbly, stirring constantly; drain. Mix in the undrained tomatoes and the next 6 ingredients. Bring to a boil; reduce heat.

- Simmer for 30 minutes, stirring occasionally.

- Dip the eggplant slices in the eggs; coat with the bread crumbs.

- Heat 4 tablespoons of the butter in a heavy skillet. Arrange the eggplant slices in a single layer in the skillet.

- Cook until brown on both sides, turning once or twice. Drain on paper towels. Repeat the process with the remaining eggplant slices and remaining 4 tablespoons butter, adding additional butter if needed.

- Layer 1/3 of the ground beef mixture, 1/2 of the eggplant slices, 1/2 of the mozzarella cheese and 1/4 cup of the Parmesan cheese in a lightly greased 9x13-inch baking dish. Repeat the layers. Top with the remaining ground beef mixture and sprinkle with the remaining 1/4 cup Parmesan cheese.

- Bake at 350 degrees for 30 to 35 minutes. Top with the green pepper rings and parsley sprigs.

- Let stand for 10 to 15 minutes before serving.

Eight to Ten Servings

MEAT LOAF WITH BROWN SUGAR GLAZE

For the Brown Sugar Glaze, combine 1/2 cup catsup, 1/4 cup packed brown sugar and 4 teaspoons cider vinegar or white vinegar in a bowl and mix well.

1 medium onion, chopped

2 cloves of garlic, minced

2 teaspoons vegetable oil

1 pound ground chuck

8 ounces ground pork

8 ounces ground veal

1/2 cup milk or plain yogurt

2 eggs, lightly beaten

2 teaspoons Dijon mustard

2 teaspoons Worcestershire sauce

1 teaspoon salt

1/2 teaspoon thyme

1/2 teaspoon freshly ground pepper

1/4 teaspoon hot pepper sauce

1 1/3 cups fresh bread crumbs

1/3 cup minced fresh parsley

Brown Sugar Glaze (at left)

6 to 8 thin slices bacon

- Sauté the onion and garlic in the oil in a skillet for 5 minutes or until tender; drain. Let stand until cool.

- Combine the ground chuck, ground pork and ground veal in a bowl and mix well.

- Combine the milk, eggs, Dijon mustard, Worcestershire sauce, salt, thyme, pepper and hot pepper sauce in a bowl and mix well. Add to the ground chuck mixture and mix well. Add the bread crumbs, parsley and onion mixture, stirring with a fork until the mixture no longer sticks to the bowl. Add additional milk 2 tablespoons at a time if needed until the mixture no longer sticks to the side of the bowl.

- Pat the mixture with moistened hands into a 5x9-inch loaf on a hard surface. Arrange in a foil-lined baking pan.

- Brush with half the Brown Sugar Glaze. Place the bacon crosswise over the loaf, overlapping slightly and tucking the bacon ends under the loaf.

- Bake at 350 degrees for 1 hour or until a meat thermometer registers 160 degrees.

- Cool in the pan on a wire rack for 20 minutes or longer.

- Simmer the remaining Brown Sugar Glaze in a saucepan over medium heat until slightly thickened, stirring frequently.

- Slice the meat loaf and serve with the warm glaze.

Eight to Ten Servings

Zucchini Moussaka

3 small zucchini, cut into 1/4-inch slices

1 large onion, sliced

2 tablespoons vegetable oil

1 pound lean ground beef

1 (8-ounce) can tomato sauce

1 clove of garlic, minced

1/2 teaspoon salt

1/4 teaspoon cinnamon

1 cup cottage cheese

1 egg, lightly beaten

1/4 cup grated Parmesan cheese

- Brown the zucchini and onion in the oil in a skillet. Transfer with a slotted spoon to a shallow 2-quart baking dish.
- Brown the ground beef in the skillet, stirring until crumbly; drain. Stir in the tomato sauce, garlic, salt and cinnamon.
- Simmer for 10 to 15 minutes, stirring occasionally. Spread over the zucchini mixture.
- Combine the cottage cheese and egg in a bowl and mix well. Spread the cheese mixture over the prepared layers. Sprinkle with the Parmesan cheese.
- Bake at 350 degrees for 30 minutes.

Four to Six Servings

Grilled Leg Of Lamb

1 cup white wine

1/2 cup olive oil

2 onions, thinly sliced

2 cloves of garlic, minced

2 tablespoons chopped fresh parsley

2 teaspoons oregano

1/2 teaspoon salt

1/2 teaspoon pepper

1 bay leaf

1/2 leg of lamb, boned, butterflied

- Place 1 large sealable plastic bag within another large sealable plastic bag to make a double thickness. Pour the white wine, olive oil, onions, garlic, parsley, oregano, salt, pepper and bay leaf into the inner bag. Add the lamb and seal tightly.
- Marinate in the refrigerator for 8 to 10 hours or longer, turning occasionally. Drain, reserving the marinade.
- Add mesquite chips to the hot coals just before placing the lamb on the grill rack.
- Grill the lamb over hot coals for 15 to 20 minutes, basting with the reserved marinade occasionally. Turn the lamb.
- Grill for 15 to 20 minutes longer or until of the desired degree of doneness, basting with the reserved marinade occasionally.
- Let stand for 5 minutes before slicing.

Five to Six Servings

MUSTARD MARINADE

Combine 2 tablespoons Dijon mustard or other good-quality mustard, 2 tablespoons fresh lemon juice, 1 tablespoon chopped fresh rosemary, 1/2 teaspoon salt and 2 cloves of chopped garlic. Whisk in 1/4 cup olive oil. Pour over pork or lamb in a nonreactive bowl or sealable plastic bag. Marinate in the refrigerator for 4 hours or up to 2 days. Grill or broil as desired.

BRAISED LAMB SHANKS

6 (1-pound) lamb shanks

Salt and pepper to taste

1/2 cup flour

6 tablespoons vegetable oil

5 cups chopped purple onions

4 cups beef stock or canned broth

2 (12-ounce) bottles good quality stout

4 carrots, peeled, cut into 1-inch slices

2 to 3 pounds red potatoes, peeled, cut into 1-inch pieces

- Season the lamb with salt and pepper. Coat with the flour. Shake off the excess flour and reserve the flour.

- Heat the oil in a heavy saucepan over high heat until hot. Add the lamb in batches.

- Cook until brown on all sides. Transfer the lamb to a bowl with a slotted spoon, reserving the pan drippings. Add the onions to the reserved pan drippings and mix well.

- Sauté over medium heat for 5 minutes or until tender, loosening any browned bits of food. Stir in the reserved flour.

- Cook for 1 minute, stirring constantly. Return the lamb and any accumulated juices to the saucepan. Stir in the stock and stout. Cover and bring to a boil; reduce heat.

- Simmer for 1 hour or until the lamb is almost tender, stirring occasionally. Add the carrots and red potatoes.

- Simmer for 40 minutes or until the vegetables and lamb are tender and the mixture is slightly thickened, stirring occasionally. Skim the fat from the surface of the stew.

- May be prepared 1 day in advance and stored, covered, in the refrigerator. Reheat over low heat before serving.

Six Servings

CURRIED LAMB STEW

3 pounds lean leg of lamb

2 cups chopped onions

1/4 cup butter

2 bay leaves, crushed

1 clove of garlic, minced

2 tablespoons curry powder

1 tablespoon salt

1/4 teaspoon thyme

4 cups canned beef broth

2 tablespoons tomato sauce

1 green apple

1/4 cup chutney

2 tablespoons flaked coconut

1/3 cup cold water

2 1/2 tablespoons cornstarch

1/2 cup light cream

12 small white onions

12 ounces fresh mushrooms

1 (16-ounce) can whole
  carrots, drained

1 (10-ounce) package frozen
  Fordhook lima beans,
  thawed

- Cut the lamb into bite-size pieces.

- Sauté 2 cups chopped onions in the butter in a heavy saucepan until golden brown. Stir in the lamb, bay leaves, garlic, curry powder, salt and thyme. Add the broth and tomato sauce and mix well. Bring to a boil; reduce heat.

- Simmer, covered, for 1 1/2 hours or until the lamb is tender, stirring occasionally. Peel and finely chop the green apple. Stir the apple, chutney and coconut into the lamb mixture.

- Cook, covered, for 15 minutes, stirring occasionally. Add a mixture of the cold water and cornstarch and mix well.

- Cook until thickened, stirring constantly. May cool and store, covered, in the refrigerator for 1 day or freeze for future use at this point.

- Stir the light cream into the mixture 30 minutes before serving. Bring to a simmer, stirring frequently. Add 12 small onions.

- Cook for 20 minutes, stirring occasionally. Slice the mushrooms. Stir the carrots, mushrooms and lima beans into the lamb mixture.

- Cook for 5 minutes or until heated through, stirring occasionally. Serve over hot cooked noodles tossed with butter and poppy seeds.

Ten Servings

To truss the pork loin, place the pork on a work surface with the short end toward you. Cut a piece of kitchen twine ten times the length of the pork. Tie one end around the far end. Hold the length of twine in your left hand about four inches from the pork. With your right hand, make a loop and slip it over the end of the pork and position it about one inch below the first loop; pull gently to secure. Repeat until the pork is completely trussed, keeping the twine snug between the loops. At the end of the process bring the twine up the length of the pork, slipping the twine through each loop to secure. Tie the ends together at the top.

Roasted Vegetable Stuffing

5 cups cut assorted fresh
  vegetables (white
  mushroom quarters,
  julienned red or yellow
  bell peppers, sliced yellow
  squash, thinly sliced
  carrots, 2-inch lengths
  of scallions)

2 tablespoons chopped,
  mixed, fresh herbs
  (parsley, thyme, rosemary
  and oregano)

1 tablespoon chopped
  shallots

1 teaspoon chopped garlic

Salt and pepper to taste

4 tablespoons olive oil

Pork Loin

1 (2- to 2 1/2-pound) boneless
  pork loin, butterflied

Salt and pepper to taste

Greek seasoning

Dale's steak seasoning

- For the stuffing, combine the assorted vegetables, herbs, shallots, garlic, salt, pepper and 3 tablespoons of the olive oil in a bowl and mix well. Let stand at room temperature for 30 minutes.

- Sauté the vegetable mixture in the remaining olive oil in a skillet over high heat for 2 to 3 minutes. Spread the vegetables on a baking sheet.

- Bake at 400 degrees for 5 to 10 minutes or until tender. Let stand until cool.

- Lay a double thickness of plastic wrap on a hard surface. Spoon the vegetable stuffing down the center to a length equal to that of the pork loin. Fold over 1 side of the plastic wrap and shape the mixture into a log. Wrap the log completely in the plastic wrap. Twist the ends to seal. Tie both ends with kitchen twine. Freeze until firm.

- For the pork, season the pork with salt and pepper. Sprinkle heavily with Greek seasoning. Place in a large sealable plastic bag. Pour enough steak seasoning over the pork to cover by 1/4 to 1/2 inch when laid on side.

- Marinate in the refrigerator for 24 hours; drain.

- Lay the pork loin flat on a hard surface, spreading open like a book. Remove the plastic wrap from the stuffing log. Place in the center of the pork loin. Bring the long ends together in the center, overlapping slightly to enclose the stuffing and truss. Arrange on a baking sheet.

- Bake at 350 degrees until a meat thermometer inserted in the thickest portion of the loin registers 170 degrees.

Six to Eight Servings

HOISIN GINGER PORK WITH MANGOES

3/4 cup hoisin sauce

1/4 cup rice wine vinegar

1/4 cup olive oil

1/4 cup minced fresh cilantro

3 tablespoons soy sauce

1 1/2 tablespoons minced
  gingerroot

3 cloves of garlic, minced

2 pounds pork loin, cubed

3 ripe mangoes, coarsely
  chopped

Toasted sesame seeds

Hot Pepper Mango
  Mayonnaise (at right)

- Combine the hoisin sauce, rice wine vinegar, olive oil, cilantro, soy sauce, gingerroot and garlic in a bowl and mix well. Add the pork, tossing to coat.

- Marinate, covered, in the refrigerator for 2 to 10 hours, turning occasionally. Drain, discarding the marinade.

- Thread 2 cubes of the pork and 1 piece of the mango on each of 50 skewers. Cover the ends of the skewers with foil. Arrange on a broiler rack.

- Broil 4 inches from the heat source for 4 minutes per side or until the pork is cooked through. Sprinkle with sesame seeds.

- Serve immediately with Hot Pepper Mango Mayonnaise.

- May be frozen for future use.

Fifty Servings

Prepare Hot Pepper Mango Mayonnaise by processing 1 egg, 1 1/2 teaspoons Dijon mustard, 1 tablespoon lemon juice and salt to taste in a food processor for 30 seconds. Add 1/2 cup vegetable oil and 1/2 cup olive oil gradually, processing constantly until blended. Season with 1/2 teaspoon Tabasco sauce and salt to taste. Add 1/4 cup Major Grey's mango chutney. Process for 30 seconds. To avoid raw eggs that may carry salmonella, bring 2 inches of water to a boil in a small saucepan. Remove from heat. Lower the egg into the hot water and let stand for 1 minute. Remove the egg carefully. Cool slightly before removing the shell.

PORK ROAST WITH APRICOT SAUCE

Apricot Sauce

1 (10-ounce) jar apricot
  preserves

2 tablespoons sherry

1 tablespoon soy sauce

Pork Roast

1 tablespoon flour

4 pounds boneless pork loin

1/2 cup sherry

1/2 cup soy sauce

2 tablespoons dry mustard

2 teaspoons thyme

1 teaspoon ground ginger

2 cloves of garlic, minced

- For the sauce, combine the preserves, sherry and soy sauce in a saucepan and mix well.

- Cook over low heat until the preserves melt, stirring frequently. Remove from heat. Cover to keep warm.

- For the pork, add the flour to an oven-cooking bag and shake. Place the pork in the bag.

- Combine the sherry, soy sauce, dry mustard, thyme, ginger and garlic in a bowl and mix well. Pour over the pork in the bag and seal tightly. Rotate the bag several times to coat the pork. Place on a baking sheet. Cut 6 slits in the top of the bag.

- Bake at 350 degrees for 2 hours. Remove the pork from the bag and place on a serving platter; drizzle with some of the warm sauce.

- Slice and serve with the remaining warm sauce.

Eight Servings

GINGER ALE PORK CHOPS

4 (1-inch-thick) loin pork chops

$1/2$ teaspoon ground ginger

1 tablespoon unsalted butter

$3/4$ cup ginger ale

$1/4$ cup minced fresh gingerroot

$1/4$ cup slivered crystallized ginger

$1/4$ cup coarsely chopped walnuts

$1/4$ cup golden raisins

$1/2$ cup whipping cream

- Sprinkle the pork chops on all sides with the ginger.

- Heat the butter in a skillet over medium-high heat until melted. Add the pork chops.

- Cook for 2 to 3 minutes per side or until brown. Arrange the pork chops in a baking pan, reserving the pan drippings.

- Add the ginger ale, gingerroot and crystallized ginger to the pan drippings and mix well.

- Cook over high heat for 2 to 3 minutes, stirring constantly. Pour over the pork chops.

- Bake at 350 degrees for 30 minutes. Sprinkle with the walnuts and golden raisins.

- Bake for 15 minutes longer. Remove the pork chops to a serving platter. Cover to keep warm. Stir the whipping cream into the pan drippings in the baking pan.

- Cook over high heat for 2 minutes or until thickened and slightly reduced, stirring constantly to loosen browned bits of food. Pour over the pork chops. Serve immediately.

Four Servings

CURRY LIME MARINADE

Enjoy the unusual flavor of this Curry Lime Marinade the next time you grill pork chops or pork tenderloin. Combine 2 tablespoons vegetable oil, 2 tablespoons lime juice, 1 tablespoon curry powder, 1 teaspoon finely grated lime peel, 1 teaspoon sugar or honey, 1 teaspoon soy sauce, $1/2$ teaspoon ground red pepper and 3 cloves of minced garlic. Pour over the pork, turning to coat. Marinate, covered, in the refrigerator for 2 hours or longer, turning occasionally. May also use on turkey, chicken or beef.

Pork Cutlets With Paprika In Sour Cream

8 slices boneless pork

Salt and pepper to taste

1 teaspoon paprika

2 tablespoons butter

1/4 cup finely chopped onion

1/2 cup dry white wine

1/2 cup chicken broth

1/2 to 3/4 cup sour cream

Finely chopped fresh parsley

- Pound the pork between sheets of waxed paper with a meat mallet until flattened. Sprinkle with salt and pepper. Shake the paprika through a sieve over the pork.

- Heat the butter in a nonstick skillet over high heat until melted. Arrange the pork in a single layer in the skillet.

- Cook for 3 to 4 minutes per side or until brown. Remove the pork to a serving platter. Cover to keep warm. Discard the fat. Add the onion to the skillet.

- Cook until tender, stirring frequently. Deglaze the skillet with the white wine. Stir in the broth.

- Simmer for 5 minutes, stirring occasionally. Remove from heat. Stir in the sour cream. Spoon over the pork chops. Sprinkle with parsley.

Eight Servings

Congaree Ribs

2 (28-ounce) cans chopped tomatoes

1/3 cup cider vinegar

1 medium onion, minced

2 tablespoons brown sugar

1 1/2 tablespoons Worcestershire sauce

1 tablespoon honey

2 teaspoons dry mustard

2 lemon slices

1/8 teaspoon hot Chinese chili oil

Sichuan chile flakes to taste

4 pounds country-style pork ribs

Salt and freshly ground pepper to taste

- Bring the undrained tomatoes and the next 9 ingredients to a boil in a saucepan over medium-high heat; reduce heat.

- Simmer for 30 minutes, stirring occasionally.

- Sprinkle the ribs with salt and pepper. Arrange on a baking sheet lined with foil.

- Bake on the center oven rack at 450 degrees for 8 to 10 minutes or until brown on all sides, turning once or twice. Let stand until cool.

- Place the ribs in a shallow baking dish. Pour the tomato mixture over the ribs, turning to coat.

- Marinate, covered, in the refrigerator for 8 to 10 hours, turning occasionally. Drain, reserving the marinade.

- Grill the ribs 4 inches above hot coals for 25 to 35 minutes or until cooked through, turning and basting frequently with the reserved marinade.

Four Servings

Sweet And Spicy Glazed Ham

1 (14- to 18-pound) whole
  smoked ham, with bone
  and rind

1/2 cup bourbon or apple
  cider

2 to 3 tablespoons whole
  cloves

Spice Glaze (at right)

1 cup packed light brown
  sugar

3/4 cup packed dark brown
  sugar

- Rinse the ham and pat dry. Let stand at room
  temperature for 2 hours.

- Place the ham in a roasting pan lined with foil. Pour the
  bourbon over the ham.

- Bake on the bottom oven rack at 350 degrees for 2
  hours or until a meat thermometer registers 140 degrees.
  Cool for 30 minutes.

- Trim the rind and excess fat from the ham, leaving
  approximately a 1/4-inch fat covering. Score the
  remaining fat on top into a pattern of 2-inch diamonds
  1/4 inch deep. Insert the whole cloves at the intersection
  of each diamond. Drizzle with some of the Spice Glaze.

- Combine 1 cup light brown sugar and 3/4 cup dark
  brown sugar in a bowl and mix well. Pack the sugar
  mixture over the top of the ham.

- Bake for 20 minutes; baste with 1/2 of the remaining
  glaze. Bake for 40 minutes longer, basting with the
  remaining glaze after 20 minutes. The ham will be dark
  brown and crusty.

- Let stand for 30 minutes before carving.

- Do not use 100 proof bourbon.

Twenty-Five to Thirty Servings

For the Spice Glaze, toast 1/4 cup yellow mustard seeds, 2 tablespoons whole or crushed cardamom pods and 1 tablespoon whole or crushed fennel seeds in a heavy skillet over medium-low heat for 3 to 4 minutes. Grind the spices until the cardamom is broken up. Mix the spice mixture, 3/4 cup prepared mustard, 3 tablespoons light corn syrup, 2 tablespoons molasses, 2 tablespoons light brown sugar, 1 tablespoon ground ginger and 2 teaspoons cinnamon in a bowl.

VEAL IN CREAM SAUCE

2 pounds veal steak,
   1/2 inch thick

1 teaspoon salt

Ground pepper to taste

2 tablespoons butter

1/4 cup dry white wine

1 1/2 cups whipping
   cream

1 (4-ounce) can
   mushrooms, drained

2 tablespoons brandy

1 tablespoon butter

Toast points

- Cut the veal into large julienne strips. Pat dry. Season with the salt and pepper.

- Heat an electric frying skillet to 350 degrees. Add 2 tablespoons butter. Heat until the butter foams and begins to subside and add the veal.

- Sauté for 8 minutes or until brown on all sides. Remove the veal to a serving platter with a slotted spoon. Cover to keep warm. Stir in the white wine.

- Cook until slightly reduced, stirring frequently. Add the whipping cream and mix well. Stir in the mushrooms.

- Simmer for 5 minutes or until slightly thickened, stirring frequently. Add the veal, brandy and 1 tablespoon butter.

- Simmer just until heated through, stirring frequently. Serve over toast points.

- May substitute veal scallopini for the veal steak and fresh mushrooms for the canned mushrooms.

Four to Six Servings

RUTLEDGE-STYLE DOVE

12 dove breasts

1/2 teaspoon salt

1/2 teaspoon pepper

1/4 cup butter or
   margarine

1 small onion, sliced

1 1/2 cups water

1 cup Durkee sauce

- Rinse the dove and pat dry. Season with the salt and pepper.

- Sauté the dove in the butter in a skillet for 10 minutes, turning frequently. Add the onion.

- Sauté for 5 minutes or until the onion is tender. Stir in the water and Durkee sauce. Bring to a boil; reduce heat.

- Cook, covered, over low heat for 40 minutes, stirring occasionally. May add additional water if needed.

Four Servings

SOUTHERN-FRIED MARSH HENS

10 marsh hens, cleaned,
  cut into halves

Salt to taste

Vinegar

Pepper to taste

Garlic powder to taste

Worcestershire sauce
  to taste

Milk

Eggs

Flour

Vegetable oil for
  deep-frying

- Rinse the hens. Soak in a mixture of water, salt and vinegar for 8 to 10 hours; drain. Rinse and pat dry.

- Season the birds with salt, pepper, garlic powder and Worcestershire sauce. Dip in a mixture of milk and eggs; coat with flour.

- Deep-fry in oil in a fryer until golden brown; drain.

- May simmer fried hens in onion gravy for 1 hour.

Ten Servings

GRILLED QUAIL

Serve with jalapeño cheese grits, grilled portobellos and Crunchy Romaine Salad, page 57.

Quail, cleaned

Melted butter

Salt and pepper to taste

Greek seasoning to taste

- Brush the quail with melted butter. Season with salt and pepper. Sprinkle heavily with Greek seasoning.

- Grill the quail over medium-low coals for 3 to 5 minutes per side or until the juices are no longer pink, basting with melted butter occasionally.

- May substitute Butter Buds for the butter.

Variable Servings

Smothered Pheasant

1 pheasant breast

Butter

1 (10-ounce) can cream
of mushroom soup

1 cup sour cream

1/2 cup vegetable oil

1/2 cup chopped celery

1/2 cup chopped onion

1/3 cup sherry

1 (3-ounce) can
mushrooms

- Rinse the pheasant and pat dry.
  Cut into 1-inch pieces.
- Brown the pheasant in butter
  in a skillet, stirring frequently.
  Arrange in a lightly buttered
  9x12-inch baking dish.
- Combine the soup, sour cream,
  oil, celery, onion, sherry and
  undrained mushrooms in a
  bowl and mix well. Pour over
  the pheasant.
- Bake, covered, at 350 degrees for
  1 to 1 1/2 hours, removing the
  cover 30 minutes before the end
  of the cooking process.
- Serve over hot cooked rice
  or noodles.

Six Servings

Wild Pork Pilau

1 (8-pound) female hog
shoulder roast

Salt and pepper to taste

Sage to taste

Celery salt to taste

Garlic powder to taste

Onion powder to taste

2 onions, chopped

4 cups water

1/4 cup cooking sherry

2 cups converted rice

- Season the pork with salt,
  pepper, sage, celery salt, garlic
  powder and onion powder.
- Combine the pork, onions, water
  and sherry in a stockpot.
- Parboil for 2 hours or until the
  pork is tender. Remove the pork
  to a platter and shred, reserving
  the stock. Discard the bones.
- Combine the reserved stock,
  shredded pork and rice in
  a saucepan.
- Simmer until the rice is tender,
  stirring occasionally.

Variable Servings

Tad's Turkey

1 wild turkey

2 teaspoons sage

2 teaspoons salt

1 teaspoon garlic powder

1 teaspoon pepper

2 onions, chopped

Sections of 1 orange, seeded, chopped

1 apple, chopped

2 ribs celery, chopped

1/2 green bell pepper, chopped

4 slices lean bacon

6 tablespoons cooking sherry

3/4 cup unsweetened grapefruit juice

- Rinse the turkey and pat dry. Rub the turkey inside and outside with the sage, salt, garlic powder and pepper.

- Combine the onions, orange, apple, celery and green pepper in a bowl and mix well. Spoon into the turkey cavity. Lay the bacon across the breast of the turkey. Place breast side up in an oven-cooking bag. Pour the sherry and grapefruit juice into the turkey cavity. Seal the bag.

- Bake at 300 to 325 degrees for 3 hours or until the turkey is cooked through.

Variable Servings

Tadpole's Marinated Venison Loin

Try this marinade on beef tenderloin, London broil, flank steak and/or pork tenderloin. You will not be disappointed.

1 whole venison loin

6 tablespoons Worcestershire sauce

1/4 cup cooking sherry

2 tablespoons lemon juice

2 teaspoons garlic powder

1 teaspoon crushed red pepper

1 teaspoon salt

1 teaspoon oregano

- Place the venison in a large sealable plastic bag.

- Combine the Worcestershire sauce, sherry, lemon juice, garlic powder, red pepper, salt and oregano in a bowl and mix well. Pour over the venison and seal the bag tightly. Rotate the bag to coat the venison.

- Marinate the venison in the refrigerator for 4 to 24 hours, turning occasionally; drain.

- Grill with lid down over medium-hot coals for 1 hour or until cooked through, turning several times.

Variable Servings

SAVORY VENISON POTPIE

To prepare the Potpie Pastry, mix 1½ cups flour and ¼ teaspoon salt in a bowl. Cut in ½ cup vegetable shortening until crumbly. Sprinkle 1 tablespoon of water over a portion of the mixture and toss gently with a fork until moistened. Push that portion to the side of the bowl. Repeat the process until all of the pastry is moistened. Shape the pastry into a ball on a lightly floured surface. Roll into a ⅛-inch-thick circle 1 inch larger in circumference than a round 1½-quart baking dish.

1½ pounds (1½-inch-thick) boneless venison, cut into 2-inch strips

3 tablespoons flour

¾ teaspoon salt

½ teaspoon pepper

3 tablespoons vegetable oil

2 medium onions, thinly sliced

2 medium potatoes, cut into bite-size chunks

1 medium carrot, thinly sliced

1 cup beer

½ cup beef broth

½ cup tomato paste

1 bay leaf

½ teaspoon thyme, crushed

¼ cup beer

1 tablespoon flour

Potpie Pastry (at left)

1 to 2 tablespoons milk

- Coat the venison with a mixture of 3 tablespoons flour, salt and pepper.

- Brown ⅓ of the venison in 1 tablespoon of the oil in a heavy saucepan. Repeat the process with the remaining venison and remaining oil. Transfer the venison to a bowl with a slotted spoon, reserving the pan drippings. Add the onions to the pan drippings.

- Cook until tender; drain. Return the venison to the saucepan. Add the potatoes, carrot, 1 cup beer, broth, tomato paste, bay leaf and thyme. Bring to a boil; reduce heat.

- Simmer for 1 hour or until the venison is tender, stirring occasionally; do not overcook. Discard the bay leaf. Stir in a mixture of ¼ cup beer and 1 tablespoon flour.

- Cook until thickened, stirring constantly. Spoon into a 1½-quart baking dish. Top with the Potpie Pastry. Turn the pastry edge under and crimp to seal. Cut vents in the top of the pastry. Brush with the milk. Place on a baking sheet.

- Bake at 450 degrees for 15 to 20 minutes or until brown.

- May substitute 1 all ready pie pastry for the homemade pastry.

Six Servings

Venison Spaghetti

1/4 cup olive oil

1/4 cup butter

1 cup finely chopped onion

2 pounds ground venison

1 pound sweet Italian sausage

4 cloves of garlic, finely chopped

1 tablespoon salt

Black pepper to taste

1 teaspoon crushed red pepper

Chopped fresh parsley

Chopped fresh basil

Chopped fresh oregano

6 ounces beer

1 (28-ounce) can chopped tomatoes

1 bell pepper, chopped

1 cup tomato purée

2 tablespoons tomato paste

Hot cooked spaghetti

- Heat the olive oil in a heavy saucepan over low heat. Add the butter. Heat until melted. Add the onion and mix well.

- Sauté until the onion is golden brown. Stir in the venison and sausage.

- Cook until brown, stirring until the venison and sausage are crumbly; drain. Stir in the garlic, salt, black pepper, red pepper, parsley, basil and oregano.

- Cook over low heat for 10 minutes, stirring occasionally. Add the beer and mix well.

- Steam, covered, for several more minutes, stirring occasionally. Add the undrained tomatoes, bell pepper, tomato purée and tomato paste and mix well. Bring to a boil; reduce heat.

- Cook, covered, over low heat for 1 hour, adding additional parsley, basil and oregano near the end of the cooking process. Serve over hot cooked spaghetti.

- Add Tabasco sauce to taste for a spicier flavor.

- May substitute canned spaghetti sauce for the tomato purée. May freeze for future use.

Six to Eight Servings

Rob Patterson of Saluda's Restaurant in Columbia, serves Orange Chipotle Vinaigrette with Smoked or Grilled Duck Breast. Try this for a special treat at your next game dinner. Process 1 quart frozen orange juice concentrate, 2 cups water, 2 tablespoons Dijon mustard, 2 tablespoons chipotle purée and 2 tablespoons salt and pepper blend in a blender until puréed. Drizzle over warm duck.

Here is a simple guideline for determining the temperature of your charcoal fire. Hold your hand, palm side down, five inches above the cooking grate. If you can stand the heat for only two to three seconds, the fire is medium-hot. If you can keep your hand in place for four to five seconds, the fire is medium-low. Regardless of the temperature of the fire, always allow the cooking grate to heat thoroughly before placing the food on the grill. This sears the surface of the food, allowing for a moister product, beautiful caramelization and those gorgeous grill marks.

GRILLED LEMON CHICKEN WITH TARRAGON

Lemon Butter

1 cup unsalted butter, softened

1/4 cup dry white wine

1/4 cup half-and-half

1/4 cup fresh lemon juice

2 tablespoons grated lemon zest

Chicken

2 ounces cream cheese, softened

2 ounces fresh mild goat cheese, softened

1 to 2 tablespoons chopped fresh tarragon

1 teaspoon chopped fresh parsley

Salt and freshly ground pepper to taste

1 (5-pound) roasting chicken

- For the lemon butter, combine the butter, white wine, half-and-half, lemon juice and lemon zest in a blender or food processor container.

- Process until smooth.

- For the chicken, combine the cream cheese, goat cheese, tarragon and parsley in a mixer bowl or food processor container.

- Beat until smooth, scraping the bowl occasionally. Season with salt and pepper.

- Loosen the skin over the breast of the chicken. Stuff the cream cheese mixture between the skin and breast meat, patting until evenly distributed. Pull the skin back over the cream cheese mixture. Truss the chicken. Brush generously with some of the Lemon Butter.

- Place the chicken on a grill rack 4 to 6 inches from the heat source.

- Grill over hot mesquite coals for 45 minutes or until the chicken is cooked through, turning and basting with the remaining Lemon Butter every 10 minutes.

Six to Eight Servings

CHICKEN AND ONIONS

1 (3-pound) chicken, cut into
    8 pieces

Salt and pepper to taste

Paprika to taste

1¹/₂ tablespoons butter

2 large onions, sliced

³/₄ cup dry white wine

1 large bay leaf

1 (15-ounce) can chicken
    broth

3 tablespoons flour

3 tablespoons water

¹/₃ cup whipping cream

¹/₈ teaspoon nutmeg

- Season the chicken with salt and pepper. Sprinkle heavily with paprika.

- Brown the chicken in the butter in a skillet for 10 minutes, turning occasionally. Transfer the chicken to a platter with a slotted spoon, reserving the pan drippings. Add the onions to the reserved pan drippings and stir to loosen any browned bits; reduce heat.

- Cook, covered, over low heat for 15 minutes or until the onions are tender, stirring occasionally. Remove the onions to a sieve and press with the back of a spoon to express as much of the fat as possible. Return the onions to the skillet. Place the chicken in a single layer on top of the onions. Add the wine and bay leaf. Bring to a boil.

- Boil for 8 minutes or until most of the wine evaporates and the mixture is of a syrupy consistency. Add the broth. Bring to a boil; reduce heat.

- Simmer, covered, for 30 minutes or until the chicken is cooked through, turning the chicken occasionally. Transfer the chicken to a platter with tongs, reserving the onion mixture. Cover the chicken to keep warm.

- Stir a mixture of the flour and water into the onion mixture. Add the whipping cream and nutmeg and mix well. Bring to a boil. Boil for 8 minutes or until thickened and of a sauce consistency, stirring occasionally. Return the chicken to the skillet.

- Simmer until heated through, stirring occasionally. Discard the bay leaf. Adjust the seasonings as desired.

Four Servings

Marinate chicken breasts or pork chops in this unusual Pineapple Ginger Marinade. Prepare by combining 2 tablespoons olive oil, 2 tablespoons soy sauce, 2 tablespoons pineapple juice, 1 tablespoon rice vinegar, 1 tablespoon honey and 1/4 teaspoon ground ginger. Pour over chicken or pork. Marinate in the refrigerator for 6 to 8 hours. Grill until cooked through.

CHICKEN WITH CHAMPAGNE SAUCE

6 boneless chicken breast halves

Flour

Salt and pepper to taste

12 ounces (or more) fresh mushrooms, cut into quarters

2 tablespoons butter

Juice of 1/2 lemon

1/4 cup butter

1 tablespoon vegetable oil

3/4 cup whipping cream

1/4 cup Champagne

- Pound the chicken between sheets of waxed paper with a meat mallet until flattened.

- Coat with a mixture of flour, salt and pepper.

- Cook the mushrooms in a mixture of 2 tablespoons butter and lemon juice in a skillet, stirring frequently. Remove with a slotted spoon to a bowl, reserving the pan drippings. Add 1/4 cup butter and oil to the pan drippings.

- Heat until the butter melts, stirring frequently. Add the chicken.

- Cook until the chicken is brown on both sides, turning occasionally. Stir in the mushrooms, whipping cream and Champagne.

- Simmer, covered, for 7 minutes or until the chicken is cooked through, stirring occasionally.

Six Servings

CRUSTY HERBED CHICKEN WITH CREMINI SHALLOT SAUCE

6 ounces cremini caps, coarsely chopped

3 tablespoons olive oil

1/3 cup fine dry bread crumbs

2 tablespoons minced fresh parsley

1 tablespoon minced fresh thyme

Salt to taste

1/2 cup flour

Ground pepper to taste

4 medium boneless skinless chicken breast halves

1 egg, lightly beaten

1 tablespoon unsalted butter

1/2 cup chopped shallots

6 ounces cremini caps, coarsely chopped

1 tablespoon chopped fresh rosemary

1/4 cup dry sherry

1 tablespoon vinegar

1/2 cup whipping cream

- Sauté 6 ounces mushrooms in 1 tablespoon of the olive oil in a cast-iron skillet over high heat until light brown but not tender. Remove the mushrooms to a cutting board with a slotted spoon and mince.

- Mix the minced mushrooms, bread crumbs, parsley, thyme and salt in a shallow dish. Mix the flour, salt and pepper in a shallow dish.

- Coat the chicken with the flour mixture; dip in the egg. Coat with the bread crumb mixture. May be prepared to this point and stored in the refrigerator for up to 2 hours in advance of cooking.

- Sauté the chicken in the remaining 2 tablespoons olive oil in the cast-iron skillet for 1 minute per side or until brown. Bake at 450 degrees for 10 minutes or until the chicken is cooked through. Remove the chicken with a slotted spoon to a platter, reserving the pan drippings. Tent with foil to keep warm. Heat the butter and pan drippings until hot. Stir in the shallots.

- Cook until tender, stirring constantly to loosen any browned bits. Stir in 6 ounces mushrooms, rosemary, salt and pepper. Sauté over medium-high heat until the mushrooms are light brown and tender. Stir in a mixture of the sherry and vinegar. Bring to a boil. Boil until the liquid evaporates. Stir in the whipping cream.

- Boil for 1 minute or until slightly thickened. Drizzle over the chicken. Serve immediately.

Four Servings

GINGERED CHICKEN PEARS AND WALNUTS

1 (16-ounce) can pear
  halves

2 whole chicken breasts,
  split

1/4 teaspoon salt

3 tablespoons margarine

3/4 cup ginger ale

1/4 cup packed brown
  sugar

3 tablespoons soy sauce

1/4 cup water

2 teaspoons cornstarch

1/4 teaspoon ginger
  powder

1/4 cup chopped walnuts

- Drain the pears, reserving the juice. Combine the reserved juice with enough water to measure 3/4 cup. Cut the pears into wedges.

- Sprinkle the chicken with the salt.

- Cook the chicken in the margarine in a skillet for 10 minutes or until brown.

- Pour a mixture of the pear juice mixture, ginger ale, brown sugar and soy sauce over the chicken.

- Cook, covered, over medium heat for 25 minutes. Transfer the chicken with a slotted spoon to a greased 8x8-inch baking dish and arrange in a single layer, reserving the pan drippings. Arrange the pears around the chicken.

- Stir a mixture of the water, cornstarch and ginger powder into the pan drippings.

- Cook until thickened, stirring constantly. Pour over the chicken and pears. Sprinkle with the walnuts.

- Bake at 350 degrees for 10 minutes.

Four Servings

GRECIAN CHICKEN BREASTS

Serve over hot cooked white or wild rice.

6 boneless skinless
  chicken breast halves

Salt and pepper to taste

1 (10-ounce) package
  frozen chopped
  spinach, thawed

8 ounces feta cheese,
  crumbled

1/2 cup mayonnaise

1 clove of garlic, minced

1/4 cup flour

1/2 teaspoon paprika

12 slices bacon

- Make a vertical cut to but not through the surface in the side of each chicken breast to form a pocket. Season with salt and pepper.

- Squeeze the moisture from the spinach. Combine with the feta cheese, mayonnaise and garlic in a bowl and mix well. Stuff into each pocket.

- Coat the chicken lightly with a mixture of the flour and paprika. Wrap each half with 2 slices of bacon. Arrange on a rack in a baking pan.

- Bake at 325 degrees for 1 hour or until the chicken is cooked through.

- Reduce the amount of fat grams by using fat-free mayonnaise and turkey bacon.

Six Servings

Italian Chicken And Rice

2 1/2 tablespoons honey

5 tablespoons wine vinegar

4 or 5 whole boneless skinless chicken breasts

1 teaspoon Italian seasoning

Salt and pepper to taste

2 tablespoons olive oil

3/4 cup chopped onion

1 (16-ounce) can pasta-ready tomatoes

1 1/4 teaspoons cinnamon

Hot cooked rice

- Dissolve the honey in the wine vinegar in a bowl and mix well.
- Cut the chicken into halves or thirds. Season with the Italian seasoning, salt and pepper.
- Heat the oil in a large skillet over medium-high heat. Add the chicken.
- Cook for 5 minutes or until brown; turn the chicken. Stir in the onion.
- Cook for 1 minute, stirring constantly. Add the undrained tomatoes, honey mixture and cinnamon and mix well.
- Cook for 5 minutes, stirring occasionally; reduce heat.
- Simmer, loosely covered, for 45 to 60 minutes or until the chicken is cooked through, stirring occasionally. Spoon over hot cooked rice.

Eight to Ten Servings

Grilled Lemon Chicken With Basil

4 boneless skinless chicken breast halves

1/2 cup olive oil

1/4 cup lemon juice

2 tablespoons white wine vinegar

2 tablespoons chopped fresh basil

1 teaspoon lemon zest

2 cloves of garlic, crushed

Salt and freshly ground pepper to taste

- Arrange the chicken in a single layer in a 9x13-inch dish.
- Combine the olive oil, lemon juice, wine vinegar, basil, lemon zest, garlic, salt and pepper in a bowl and mix well. Pour over the chicken, turning to coat.
- Marinate, covered, in the refrigerator for 45 minutes, turning once; drain.
- Grill the chicken over hot coals for 20 minutes or until cooked through, turning occasionally. May bake, covered, at 350 degrees for 45 minutes.

Four Servings

LEMON CHICKEN SCALLOPINI

4 boneless skinless
   chicken breast halves

1/4 cup flour

Salt and pepper to taste

2 tablespoons butter

1 tablespoon vegetable
   oil

1 clove of garlic, minced

1 cup chicken broth

1/4 cup white wine

1/4 teaspoon marjoram

1 (15-ounce) can
   artichoke hearts,
   drained, cut into
   quarters

3 tablespoons lemon
   juice

3 tablespoons capers

- Coat the chicken with a mixture
  of the flour, salt and pepper.

- Cook the chicken in a mixture of
  the butter and oil in a skillet over
  medium-high heat for 4 minutes
  per side or until light brown.

- Transfer the chicken to a platter
  with a slotted spoon, reserving
  the pan drippings. Tent the
  chicken with foil to keep warm.

- Cook the garlic in the pan
  drippings for 1 minute or until
  tender, stirring constantly. Stir in
  the broth, wine and marjoram.
  Bring to a boil, stirring constantly.
  Add the chicken and artichokes.

- Simmer, covered, for 10 to 15
  minutes or until the chicken is
  cooked through and the sauce is
  slightly thickened, stirring
  frequently. Stir in the lemon juice
  and capers.

- Arrange the chicken on a serving
  platter. Spoon the sauce and
  artichokes over the chicken.

  Four Servings

QUICK PAELLA

1 (4-ounce) bag Success
   brown rice or white
   rice

12 ounces boneless
   skinless chicken
   breasts, cubed

1 tablespoon olive oil

1 (15-ounce) can no-salt-
   added stewed
   tomatoes

1 envelope onion soup
   mix

1/2 cup white wine or
   water

1 cup frozen artichoke
   hearts, thawed

1 cup frozen peas,
   thawed

- Prepare the brown rice using
  package directions.

- Sauté the chicken in the olive oil
  in a saucepan until light brown.
  Add the undrained tomatoes,
  soup mix and white wine and
  mix well.

- Simmer for 5 minutes, stirring
  occasionally. Stir in the
  artichokes and peas.

- Simmer for 10 minutes, stirring
  occasionally. Add the brown rice
  and mix well.

- Cook just until heated through,
  stirring constantly.

  Four to Six Servings

ROSEMARY-SPRIGGED BREASTS OF CHICKEN

1/4 cup soy sauce

Juice of 1 lime

1 clove of garlic, crushed

4 boneless skinless chicken breast halves

1/2 cup flour

Salt and pepper to taste

1 to 2 tablespoons vegetable oil

1 tablespoon butter

4 (3- to 4-inch) sprigs of fresh rosemary

- Pour a mixture of the soy sauce, lime juice and garlic over the chicken in a nonreactive bowl or sealable plastic bag.

- Marinate in the refrigerator for 30 minutes, turning once or twice. Drain and pat dry with paper towels.

- Coat the chicken with a mixture of the flour, salt and pepper and shake to remove the excess.

- Sauté the chicken in a hot mixture of the oil and butter in a skillet for 4 to 5 minutes or until brown, shaking the pan from time to time so that a crust forms on the bottom. Place 1 sprig of the rosemary on top of each chicken breast. Hold the rosemary in place with tongs and turn.

- Cook for 4 to 5 minutes longer or until brown and cooked through. Serve immediately.

Four Servings

WHITE CHILI

1 pound dried large white beans

6 cups chicken broth

1 medium onion, chopped

2 cloves of garlic, minced

1 medium onion, chopped

1 tablespoon vegetable oil

2 (4-ounce) cans chopped green chiles, drained

2 teaspoons cumin

1 1/2 teaspoons oregano

1/4 teaspoon ground cloves

1/4 teaspoon cayenne

4 cups chopped cooked chicken breast

3 cups shredded Monterey Jack cheese

- Sort and rinse the beans. Combine the beans, broth, 1 onion and garlic in a stockpot and mix well. Bring to a boil; reduce heat.

- Simmer for 3 hours or until the beans are tender, stirring occasionally. May add additional broth if needed for desired consistency.

- Sauté 1 onion in the oil in a skillet until tender. Add the chiles, cumin, oregano, cloves and cayenne and mix well. Stir into the bean mixture. Add the chicken and mix well.

- Simmer the chili for 1 hour, stirring occasionally.

- Ladle into chili bowls. Sprinkle with the cheese.

- Guacamole, crushed tortilla chips, chopped tomatoes, chopped fresh parsley or chopped black olives make great accompaniments.

Eight to Ten Servings

ROASTED CORNISH GAME HENS

High-temperature roasting and the self-basting action of the lemons in the birds' cavities ensure a crispy skin and moist meat.

1 to 2 tablespoons vegetable oil

1 tablespoon butter

2 Cornish game hens

Kosher salt to taste

Freshly ground pepper to taste

2 small lemons

4 to 8 cloves of garlic, crushed

Mixed chopped fresh herbs (optional)

1 small onion, cut into quarters

1 rib celery with leaves, coarsely chopped

- Heat the oil and butter in a cast-iron skillet or ovenproof skillet until the butter melts.

- Sprinkle the cavities of the game hens with salt and pepper.

- Roll the lemons on a hard surface until softened. Prick on all sides with a fork.

- Place 1 lemon, 2 to 4 cloves of garlic and fresh herbs in the cavity of each hen. Roll the hens in the oil mixture. Sprinkle liberally on all sides with salt and pepper.

- Place the hens breast side up in the prepared skillet. Sprinkle with the onion and celery.

- Roast at 475 degrees for 10 minutes. Turn the hens on their side. Roast for 10 minutes. Turn the hens on the opposite side.

- Roast for 10 minutes. Turn the hens breast side down.

- Roast for 20 to 30 minutes longer or until the game hens are cooked through.

- Discard the lemons and place the game hens on a serving platter.

- May baste the hens with heated apricot preserves during the last 10 minutes of the cooking process.

Two to Four Servings

*F*or Grilled Soy Chicken, pour a mixture of 5 table-spoons plus 1 teaspoon butter, 2/3 bottle of soy sauce, 2 tablespoons prepared mustard, 2 tablespoons grated onion and Tabasco sauce to taste over 3 pounds of chicken pieces, turning to coat. Marinate, covered, in the refrigerator for several hours, turning occasionally. Grill over hot coals until cooked through, turning and basting with the soy sauce mixture frequently. May cook over low heat for 1 hour or until cooked through.

Carolina Deep-Fried Turkey

For safety reasons, this recipe should be prepared outdoors.

1 tablespoon thyme

1 tablespoon oregano

2 teaspoons garlic powder

1¹/2 teaspoons whole black
    peppercorns

3 tablespoons Konriko hot
    Creole seasoning

1 (15-pound) fresh turkey

4 gallons peanut oil

- Combine the thyme, oregano, garlic powder, peppercorns and Creole seasoning in a bowl and mix well.

- Rub the seasoning mixture over the outside of the turkey, under the skin and inside the cavity.

- Marinate, covered, in the refrigerator for 8 to 10 hours or for up to 24 hours.

- Using a single long length of heavy cotton butcher's twine, tie together the wings, then the legs, then run the twine through the cavity, making a large long loop. Make a sturdy knot. This loop will be used to lower the turkey into the hot oil.

- Heat the peanut oil in a large cauldron to 350 degrees. Lower the turkey into the hot oil.

- Fry for 4 minutes per pound or until golden brown. Remove the turkey from the oil by lifting the twine.

- Place on a wire rack to drain. Let stand for 15 minutes before serving.

Ten to Twelve Servings

Grilled Turkey Tenderloin and Veggies

Great for a summer cookout. Arrange the turkey and vegetables on one large platter and let your guests serve themselves.

1/4 cup soy sauce

1 pound turkey tenderloin

Chopped garlic

8 to 12 small zucchini, sliced lengthwise

8 to 12 small yellow squash, sliced lengthwise

1 small eggplant, sliced lengthwise

Salt to taste

4 small onions

4 portobello mushrooms

Extra-virgin olive oil

Pepper to taste

Balsamic vinegar

- Pour the soy sauce over the turkey in a nonreactive dish. Sprinkle with garlic.

- Marinate, covered, in the refrigerator for 2 to 4 hours, turning occasionally.

- Place the zucchini, yellow squash and eggplant in a colander. Sprinkle with salt.

- Let stand for 2 to 4 hours. Rinse and pat dry.

- Place the zucchini, yellow squash, eggplant, onions and mushrooms on a platter. Drizzle with olive oil; sprinkle with salt, pepper and garlic. Wrap the onions in foil.

- Place the onions on a grill rack. Arrange the remaining vegetables on the grill rack.

- Grill until of the desired degree of crispness and grill marks appear, turning once. Remove to a serving platter. Drizzle with balsamic vinegar.

- Drain the turkey. Grill until cooked through.

- Slice the tenderloin. Arrange around the vegetables.

Four Servings

FRIED CATFISH DIJON

Serve with Creole Tartar Sauce (at right) and Black Beans and Rice, page 173.

4 boneless catfish fillets

2 tablespoons olive oil

1 tablespoon fresh lemon
juice

1 tablespoon Dijon mustard

1/4 teaspoon lemon pepper

1 cup stone-ground yellow
cornmeal

1/4 teaspoon salt

1/4 teaspoon garlic powder

3/4 cup safflower oil

Lemon wedges

- Arrange the fillets in a nonreactive dish.

- Combine the olive oil, lemon juice, Dijon mustard and
lemon pepper in a bowl and mix well. Pour over the
fish, turning to coat.

- Marinate at room temperature for 30 minutes, turning
occasionally; drain.

- Combine the cornmeal, salt and garlic powder in a
shallow dish and mix well. Coat the fillets with the
cornmeal mixture.

- Heat the safflower oil in a heavy skillet over medium-
high heat until hot. Add the fillets.

- Fry until crisp and brown on both sides, turning once or
twice; drain. Serve immediately with lemon wedges.

Four Servings

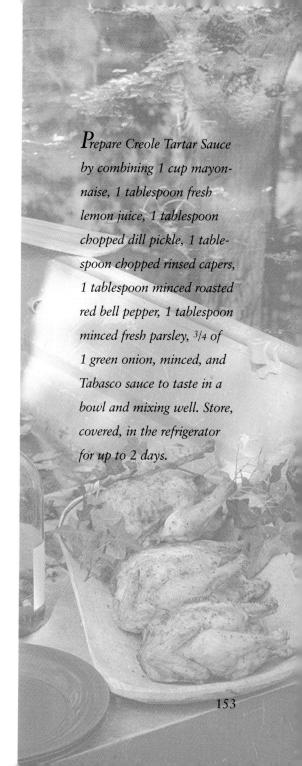

Prepare Creole Tartar Sauce by combining 1 cup mayonnaise, 1 tablespoon fresh lemon juice, 1 tablespoon chopped dill pickle, 1 tablespoon chopped rinsed capers, 1 tablespoon minced roasted red bell pepper, 1 tablespoon minced fresh parsley, 3/4 of 1 green onion, minced, and Tabasco sauce to taste in a bowl and mixing well. Store, covered, in the refrigerator for up to 2 days.

Grilled Grouper With Basil And Mint

Bill Goulding, a Florida restaurateur, serves this recipe at his restaurant. This is an old Italian way of preparing fish, using the freshest of ingredients and a minimum of time for preparation.

4 (8-ounce) grouper or red snapper fillets

2 tablespoons melted butter or margarine

3 cups Italian bread crumbs

2 plum tomatoes, cut into 1/2-inch pieces

12 basil leaves, coarsely chopped

6 mint leaves, coarsely chopped

1/4 cup olive oil

Salt and pepper to taste

- Brush both sides of the fillets with the butter. Coat with the bread crumbs.
- Combine the tomatoes, basil, mint, olive oil, salt and pepper in a bowl and mix well.
- Place the fillets on a lightly oiled grill rack.
- Grill over hot coals until the fish flakes easily, turning 3 times.
- Remove the fillets to a serving platter. Top each fillet with some of the tomato mixture.
- Serve immediately with roasted red potatoes or your favorite rice dish.

Four Servings

Grouper Piccata

Andy Marchant, owner and chef of the Restaurant at Cinnamon Hill, states that this is a quick and easy way to prepare a popular South Carolina seafood. Serve with a crisp sauvignon blanc.

4 (6-ounce) grouper fillets

Flour

2 eggs, beaten

3 tablespoons butter

1/2 cup dry white wine

1/4 cup lemon juice

2 ounces capers (optional)

1 lemon, sliced

1 ounce chopped fresh parsley

3 tablespoons roux

- Coat the fillets in flour. Dip in the eggs.
- Heat a large sauté pan over high heat until hot. Add the butter.
- Cook until the butter melts. Add the fillets. Reduce the heat to medium-high.
- Cook for 4 minutes per side or until brown. Add the white wine and lemon juice.
- Simmer for several minutes. Stir in the capers, lemon slices and parsley. Add the roux and mix well.
- Cook just until thickened, stirring frequently.
- To make the roux, combine equal portions of butter and flour and cook until thickened.

Four Servings

GROUPER ST. CHARLES

Pierce Culliton, chef at Frank's Restaurant & Bar, located on Pawleys Island, shares one of his favorite recipes.

1 cup milk

4 (7-ounce) black grouper fillets

2 cups flour

Salt and pepper to taste

$1/4$ cup vegetable oil

12 shrimp, peeled, deveined (26 to 30 count)

$1/4$ cup Fish Fumet (at right)

2 tablespoons white wine

$1/2$ tomato, chopped

2 green onions, chopped

8 mushrooms, sliced

1 shallot, minced

1 clove of garlic, minced

2 tablespoons butter, slightly softened

- Pour the milk over the fillets in a shallow dish. Drain, shaking off the excess milk. Coat lightly with a mixture of the flour, salt and pepper and shake off excess. Reserve the remaining flour mixture.

- Heat the oil in a large ovenproof sauté pan until hot but not smoking. Add the fillets.

- Cook until brown; turn the fillets carefully. Add the shrimp.

- Bake at 500 degrees for 4 to 5 minutes or until the fillets flake easily. Remove the fillets to 4 heated dinner plates; top with the shrimp. Stir the Fish Fumet and white wine into the pan drippings.

- Cook until slightly reduced, stirring frequently. Add the tomato, green onions, mushrooms, shallot and garlic and mix well.

- Simmer until of the desired consistency, stirring frequently. Coat the butter in the reserved flour mixture. Add to the tomato mixture, swirling the pan until mixed.

- Cook until slightly thickened, stirring constantly. Pour over the fillets. Serve immediately.

Four Servings

FISH FUMET

Cook 1 chopped medium onion in 1 tablespoon butter in a saucepan over low heat until tender. Stir in $1^1/2$ to 2 pounds of fish bones of a mild-flavor fish, 1 quart water, 1 cup dry white wine, 8 to 10 peppercorns, 1 bay leaf, 3 sprigs of fresh parsley and 2 sprigs of fresh thyme. Bring to a boil and skim; reduce heat. Simmer for 20 minutes; strain. Cool slightly and store in the refrigerator for up to 1 day or freeze for future use.

Sesame Glazed Salmon

3 tablespoons dark
  brown sugar

4 teaspoons Dijon
  mustard

1 tablespoon soy sauce

2 (7- to 8-ounce) salmon
  steaks, 3/4 inch thick

1 teaspoon rice vinegar

1/4 teaspoon sesame oil

1 teaspoon sesame seeds,
  roasted

1 green onion, minced

- Whisk brown sugar, Dijon mustard and soy sauce in a bowl until mixed. Reserve 1 tablespoon of the glaze.

- Brush 1 side of the salmon steaks with 1/2 of the remaining glaze. Arrange glaze side down on grill rack.

- Grill over hot coals for 4 minutes or until slightly charred. Brush with the remaining glaze. Turn the salmon.

- Grill for 5 minutes longer or until slightly charred and the steaks flake easily. Remove to a serving platter.

- Drizzle with a mixture of the reserved 1 tablespoon glaze, rice vinegar and sesame oil. Sprinkle with the sesame seeds and green onion.

Two Servings

Herb Grilled Salmon

Stellinis, of Columbia, was most gracious to share this recipe.

4 salmon fillets

1/4 cup horseradish
  mustard or Dijon
  mustard

2 tablespoons chopped
  fresh thyme

1 tablespoon pepper

1 tablespoon chopped
  fresh chives

4 teaspoons chopped
  fresh cilantro

2 teaspoons chopped
  fresh rosemary

- Coat the fillets with the horseradish mustard. Roll in a mixture of the thyme, pepper, chives, cilantro and rosemary.

- Grill the salmon over hot coals for 4 to 5 minutes per side or until the fillets flake easily, turning only once.

Four Servings

Northwest Grilled Salmon Fillets

Don't be alarmed by the brown sugar in the marinade. It is wonderful paired with the flavor of fresh grilled salmon. Serve with wilted spinach salad, wild rice, asparagus and honey wheat rolls.

4 (6-ounce) salmon fillets

2 tablespoons Worcestershire sauce

2 tablespoons fresh lemon juice

1 tablespoon brown sugar

1 tablespoon vegetable oil

Lemon wedges

- Place the fillets in a glass dish or sealable plastic bag.

- Combine the Worcestershire sauce, lemon juice, brown sugar and oil in a bowl and mix well. Pour over the fillets, turning to coat.

- Marinate in the refrigerator for 30 to 60 minutes, turning occasionally. Drain, reserving the marinade.

- Cover the grill rack with heavy-duty foil and pierce. Place the fillets skin side down on the foil.

- Grill with the cover down over medium-high coals for 7 to 10 minutes or until the fillets flake easily, basting twice with the reserved marinade. Remove the fillets from the grill by sliding a large spatula just between the skin and the flesh, leaving the skin on the foil.

- Arrange the salmon on a serving platter. Top with lemon wedges.

Four Servings

Salmon steaks and fillets are done when a creamy white liquid appears on the surface of the fish.

Fish fillets are convenient to use, but once fish has been removed from the bone it spoils quickly. If possible, buy fresh whole fish and have it filleted at the market. Look for fish that have bright clear eyes, firm flesh, mild odor and bright pink or red gills. Whether you have your fish filleted at the market or prefer to do it yourself, always save and freeze the head and bones for making stock.

Poached Salmon With Cucumber Dill Raita

Cucumber Dill Raita

2 cups plain yogurt

1/4 cup sour cream

2 tablespoons chopped red onion

1 small cucumber, peeled, seeded, chopped

1 to 2 tablespoons minced fresh dillweed

1/2 teaspoon salt

1/2 teaspoon sugar

1/4 teaspoon white pepper

Salmon

6 cups water

2 1/2 cups dry white wine

1/2 onion, sliced

10 peppercorns

6 (7- to 8-ounce) center-cut salmon fillets, skinned

- For the raita, combine the yogurt, sour cream, red onion, cucumber, dillweed, salt, sugar and white pepper in a bowl and mix well.

- Chill, covered, for 1 to 10 hours. May be served as a salad dressing or as a sauce on various types of seafood.

- For the salmon, combine 3 cups of the water, 1 1/4 cups of the white wine, 1/2 of the onion and 1/2 of the peppercorns in a large skillet. Bring to a boil. Remove from heat. Add 3 of the salmon fillets.

- Let stand for 6 minutes; turn the fillets.

- Let stand for 5 minutes longer. Bring the liquid to a simmer.

- Cook just until the salmon is cooked through. Transfer with a slotted spoon to a platter.

- Repeat the process with the remaining salmon fillets, remaining white wine, remaining onion and remaining peppercorns.

- Chill, covered, for 3 to 10 hours.

- Let the salmon stand at room temperature for 1 hour before serving. Top with the raita.

Six Servings

GRILLED MARINATED SWORDFISH

1/2 cup soy sauce

1/2 cup sherry

1/4 cup vegetable oil

1 tablespoon lemon juice

1 clove of garlic, crushed

6 swordfish fillets,
  1/2 inch thick

Julienned scallions

Lime twists

- Combine the soy sauce, sherry, oil, lemon juice and garlic in a bowl and mix well. Pour over the fillets in a shallow dish, turning to coat.

- Marinate, covered, in the refrigerator for no longer than 3 hours, turning occasionally; drain. Arrange the fillets on a grill rack brushed lightly with oil.

- Grill for 5 to 8 minutes per side or until the fillets flake easily. Remove to a serving platter. Top with scallions and lime twists.

- May also use this marinade on large-mouth bass fillets.

Six Servings

BARBECUED MARINATED YELLOWFIN TUNA

David Williamson, of the Cellars Restaurant in northeast Columbia, suggests serving the tuna with rice and grilled vegetables.

2 cups fresh orange juice

1 cup red wine vinegar

1 (6-ounce) can tomato paste

1/2 cup soy sauce

1/2 cup sugar

1/2 cup olive oil

1 small yellow onion, chopped

4 cloves of garlic, minced

1 1/2 tablespoons whole pickling spice

1 tablespoon cumin

1 teaspoon hot pepper flakes

1 teaspoon black pepper

6 (8-ounce) yellowfin tuna steaks, 3/4 to 1 inch thick

- Combine the orange juice, wine vinegar, tomato paste, soy sauce, sugar, olive oil, onion, garlic, pickling spice, cumin, hot pepper flakes and black pepper in a bowl and mix well. Pour over the tuna in a shallow dish, turning to coat.

- Marinate, covered, in the refrigerator for 3 to 24 hours, turning occasionally; drain.

- Grill the tuna over medium-high coals for 3 to 5 minutes per side for medium-rare or until done to taste.

Six Servings

LOW COUNTRY CRAB CAKES WITH TOMATO BASIL TARTAR SAUCE

To prepare Tomato Basil Tartar Sauce, mix 2 chopped, seeded, peeled tomatoes, 1/4 cup finely chopped Vidalia onion or other sweet onion, 1 finely chopped seeded fresh jalapeño, 2 tablespoons chopped sweet pickle, 2 tablespoons chopped fresh basil and 1 tablespoon finely chopped capers in a bowl. Stir in 2 cups mayonnaise and 1 to 2 tablespoons fresh lemon juice. Chill, covered, for 1 hour. May be stored, covered, in the refrigerator for up to 3 months.

6 tablespoons unsalted butter

3/4 cup flour

2 cups milk, scalded

Salt and freshly ground black pepper to taste

3 cups bread crumbs

Cayenne to taste

1 pound fresh lump crab meat

1 red bell pepper, finely chopped

1/2 medium yellow bell pepper, finely chopped

4 green onions, minced

1/4 cup vegetable oil

Tomato Basil Tartar Sauce (at left)

- Heat the butter in a skillet over medium heat until melted; reduce heat. Stir in the flour.

- Cook for 3 minutes, stirring constantly. Add the scalded milk gradually, stirring constantly until blended. Season with salt and black pepper.

- Simmer over low heat for 10 minutes or until thickened and of a sauce consistency, stirring constantly. Remove from heat.

- Combine the bread crumbs, cayenne, salt and black pepper in a bowl and mix well.

- Combine the crab meat, red pepper, yellow pepper and green onions in a bowl and mix well. Stir in 1/2 of the seasoned bread crumbs. Fold in the white sauce. Add some of the remaining seasoned bread crumbs, stirring until the mixture adheres and is no longer sticky. Shape into 8 patties. Coat the patties with the remaining seasoned bread crumbs.

- Fry the crab cakes in the oil in a skillet for 2 minutes per side or until golden brown; drain.

- Place 2 crab cakes on each of 4 heated dinner plates; top with the Tomato Basil Tartar Sauce.

Four Servings

Carolina Oyster Casserole

1/2 cup butter or margarine

1/2 cup flour

1 1/2 teaspoons paprika

1/2 teaspoon salt

1/4 teaspoon black pepper

1/8 teaspoon cayenne

1 onion, finely chopped

1/2 green bell pepper, finely chopped

1/2 clove of garlic, minced

1 tablespoon Worcestershire sauce

1 teaspoon lemon juice

1 quart oysters with liquor, heated

1/4 cup cracker crumbs

- Heat the butter in a saucepan until melted. Stir in the flour.
- Cook for 4 minutes or until light brown, stirring constantly. Add the paprika, salt, black pepper and cayenne.
- Cook for 3 minutes, stirring constantly. Add the onion, green pepper and garlic and mix well.
- Cook over low heat for 5 minutes, stirring frequently. Remove from heat. Stir in the Worcestershire sauce, lemon juice and undrained oysters. Spoon into a baking dish. Sprinkle with the cracker crumbs.
- Bake at 400 degrees for 30 minutes.

Eight Servings

Scallop Seviche

The action of the acid in the lime juice "cooks" the scallops.

1 1/2 pounds bay scallops

1 1/4 cups fresh lime juice

1/2 red onion, minced

2 jalapeños, minced

2 cloves of garlic, minced

1 bunch cilantro, minced

Salt and pepper to taste

5 heads endive, separated into spears

- Combine the scallops, lime juice, onion, jalapeños, garlic, cilantro, salt and pepper in a bowl and mix gently.
- Marinate, covered, in the refrigerator for 1 to 10 hours, turning occasionally.
- Place a small spoonful of the mixture at the base of each endive spear. Arrange on a serving platter
- Separate the endive into spears 30 minutes before serving. A longer time frame can result in the spears turning brown.
- It is recommended that pregnant women not consume raw protein.

Fifty Servings

BARBECUE SHRIMP

4 pounds fresh shrimp
   with heads (16 to
   20 count)

1¹/2 cups butter

¹/4 cup Creole seasoning

1 tablespoon freshly
   ground pepper

1 tablespoon rosemary

1 tablespoon
   Worcestershire sauce

2¹/2 cloves of garlic,
   minced

1¹/2 cups beer

- Sauté the shrimp in ¹/2 cup of the butter in a heavy skillet until well coated. Stir in the Creole seasoning, pepper, rosemary, Worcestershire sauce and garlic.

- Sauté until the shrimp begin to curl slightly and turn pink; reduce heat. Add the remaining 1 cup butter in small batches, swirling the skillet constantly until the butter melts. Do not allow to boil. Stir in the beer.

- Serve with hot cooked rice and crusty French bread.

Eight to Ten Servings

SHRIMP ETOUFFEE

6 tablespoons butter

3 tablespoons flour

1 cup chopped onion

6 green onions with tops,
   chopped

¹/2 cup chopped green
   bell pepper

¹/2 cup chopped celery

3 pounds shrimp, peeled,
   deveined

2 cups water

¹/4 cup chopped fresh
   parsley

Salt and pepper to taste

1 small bay leaf

Tabasco sauce to taste

Hot cooked rice

- Heat the butter in a skillet until melted. Stir in the flour.

- Cook until brown in color, stirring constantly. Add the onion, green onions, green pepper and celery.

- Cook until the vegetables are tender, stirring frequently. Stir in the shrimp, water, parsley, salt, pepper, bay leaf and Tabasco sauce.

- Simmer for 20 minutes or until the shrimp turn pink, stirring occasionally. Discard the bay leaf.

- Serve over hot cooked rice.

Four to Six Servings

LIME CILANTRO SHRIMP WITH KIWIFRUIT

3/4 cup extra-virgin olive oil

2 1/2 tablespoons fresh lime juice

2 1/2 tablespoons rice vinegar

1 teaspoon grated lime zest

1/8 teaspoon Tabasco sauce, or to taste

2 tablespoons minced green onions

2 tablespoons minced fresh cilantro

Salt and freshly ground pepper to taste

1 1/2 pounds peeled cooked shrimp with tails

Lettuce leaves

2 kiwifruit, peeled, sliced

- Whisk the olive oil, lime juice, rice vinegar, lime zest and Tabasco sauce in a bowl. Stir in the green onions, cilantro, salt and pepper. Add the shrimp and mix well.

- Marinate, covered, in the refrigerator for 1 to 10 hours, stirring occasionally; drain.

- Spoon onto a lettuce-lined serving platter. Top with the kiwifruit.

Four to Six Servings

PICKLED SHRIMP

Serve with grits on Christmas morning or on a bed of Bibb lettuce for a luncheon.

3 pounds shrimp

1 medium onion, sliced, separated into rings

3 bay leaves

3/4 cup cider vinegar

1 tablespoon pickling spice

1 teaspoon salt

1 teaspoon celery salt

- Combine the shrimp with enough water to cover in a stockpot. Bring to a boil.

- Boil until the shrimp turn pink. Drain, reserving 1/2 cup of the liquid.

- Layer the shrimp, onion and bay leaves 1/3 at a time in a bowl.

- Combine the vinegar, pickling spice, salt, celery salt and reserved cooking liquid in a bowl and mix well. Pour over the prepared layers.

- Marinate, covered, in the refrigerator for 3 hours or longer before serving. Discard the bay leaves.

- May add lemon juice, Tabasco sauce, 1 tablespoon vegetable oil, garlic and/or Worcestershire sauce to the marinade for variety.

- May be prepared 1 day in advance.

Six to Eight Servings

UNDER THE SEA

To improve the texture and flavor of frozen shrimp, try defrosting them in a cold brine solution. For two pounds of frozen shrimp, prepare the following solution. Combine 2 cups kosher salt and 2 cups boiling water in a bowl, stirring until the salt is almost dissolved. Add 3 1/2 quarts of ice water, stirring until the salt is completely dissolved. Add the shrimp. Let stand for 45 minutes. Drain and rinse with cold water. If time is of the essence, increase the amount of salt to 3 cups and let stand for 20 minutes. The results are almost the same.

1 1/2 pounds red snapper or flounder

12 ounces scallops

1 pound large shrimp, peeled, deveined

8 ounces crab meat

3 (10-ounce) cans cream of shrimp soup

1/4 cup butter or margarine

1/4 cup chablis or any white wine

2 tablespoons Worcestershire sauce

4 cloves of garlic, crushed

4 ounces saltine crackers, crushed

Paprika to taste

- Arrange the red snapper in the center of a 9x13-inch baking dish. Place the scallops and shrimp on and around the fish. Sprinkle with the crab meat.
- Combine the soup, butter, white wine, Worcestershire sauce and garlic in a saucepan and mix well.
- Cook over medium heat until blended, stirring frequently. Pour over the seafood. Top with the crackers and sprinkle heavily with paprika.
- Bake at 350 degrees for 45 minutes.

Twelve Servings

SEAFOOD-STUFFED EGGPLANT

Seafood-Stuffed Eggplant is a customer favorite at Stellinis located in Columbia.

4 medium eggplant

Salt to taste

2 cups water

1 teaspoon salt

1/4 cup whipping cream

1 small onion, minced

2 ribs celery, chopped

2 tablespoons butter

1 pound medium shrimp,
    peeled, deveined

8 ounces crab meat

1/4 cup dry sherry

2 cups Italian bread crumbs

1/2 teaspoon salt

1/2 teaspoon black pepper

1/4 teaspoon cayenne

1/4 cup grated Parmesan
    cheese

2 tablespoons butter, softened

- Cut the eggplant horizontally into halves. Scoop out the pulp, leaving a 1/2-inch shell.

- Soak the eggplant shells and pulp in salted ice water in separate bowls for 20 minutes; drain.

- Combine the eggplant pulp, 2 cups water and 1 teaspoon salt in a saucepan. Bring to a boil; reduce heat.

- Simmer for 10 minutes, stirring occasionally; drain. Stir in the whipping cream.

- Cook until reduced, stirring constantly.

- Sauté the onion and celery in 2 tablespoons butter in a skillet until tender. Stir in the shrimp and crab meat.

- Sauté for 2 minutes; the shrimp will be slightly undercooked. Add the sherry and mix well.

- Simmer for 1 minute, stirring frequently.

- Combine the shrimp mixture, eggplant pulp mixture, 1 1/2 cups of the bread crumbs, 1/2 teaspoon salt, black pepper and cayenne in a bowl and mix well. Spoon into the eggplant shells. Arrange on a baking sheet. Sprinkle with a mixture of the remaining 1/2 cup bread crumbs, 1/4 cup cheese and 2 tablespoons butter.

- Bake at 350 degrees for 20 minutes or until the eggplant shells are tender.

Eight Servings

Try this Spicy Citrus Marinade the next time you grill shrimp or chicken. Combine 1/3 cup lime juice, 1/3 cup olive oil, 2 tablespoons chopped fresh cilantro, 2 tablespoons orange juice, 1 clove of crushed garlic, 1 chopped seeded jalapeño and salt and pepper to taste. Add the shrimp or chicken, turning to coat. Marinate at room temperature for 30 minutes. Drain, reserving the marinade. Grill over hot coals until cooked through, basting with the reserved marinade frequently.

SHRIMP AND ARTICHOKE CASSEROLE

1 (14-ounce) can artichoke hearts

1½ to 2 pounds shrimp, cooked, peeled, deveined

8 ounces mushrooms

2 tablespoons butter

¼ teaspoon flour

4½ tablespoons butter

4½ tablespoons flour

1 cup whipping cream

½ cup half-and-half

Salt and pepper to taste

¼ cup dry sherry

1 tablespoon Worcestershire sauce

¼ cup grated Parmesan cheese

Paprika to taste

- Drain the artichokes and cut into halves. Arrange over the bottom of a baking dish. Top with the shrimp.

- Sauté the mushrooms in 2 tablespoons butter in a skillet. Sprinkle with ¼ teaspoon flour and stir. Spoon over the prepared layers.

- Heat 4½ tablespoons butter in a saucepan until melted. Add 4½ tablespoons flour, stirring until blended. Stir in the whipping cream and half-and-half.

- Cook until thickened, stirring constantly. Season with salt and pepper. Remove from heat. Stir in the sherry and Worcestershire sauce. Pour over the prepared layers. Sprinkle with the cheese and paprika.

- Bake at 375 degrees for 20 minutes.

Six Servings

SHRIMP AND CRAB CASSEROLE

2 pounds peeled cooked shrimp

2 pounds crab meat

2 medium onions, finely chopped

2 medium green bell peppers, finely chopped

1 large rib celery, finely chopped

3 cups mayonnaise

1 bottle Durkee sauce

Salt and pepper to taste

Tabasco sauce to taste

Toasted bread crumbs

- Combine the shrimp, crab meat, onions, green peppers and celery in a bowl and mix well. Stir in the mayonnaise, Durkee sauce, salt, pepper and Tabasco sauce.

- Spoon into a 9x13-inch baking dish. Sprinkle with bread crumbs.

- Bake at 400 degrees for 20 minutes.

Eight Servings

SHRIMP CAKES WITH CREAMY YELLOW GRITS AND TASSO GRAVY

Tim Freeman, executive chef at Richard's in downtown Columbia, shares one of his recipes.

6 ounces chopped shrimp

1/2 cup chopped andouille sausage

1/4 cup chopped onion

1/4 cup chopped red bell pepper

1/4 cup chopped scallions (green part only)

1 1/2 teaspoons blackening seasoning

1/4 teaspoon cayenne

1/8 teaspoon salt

1/8 teaspoon white pepper

1/2 cup mayonnaise

1 egg, beaten

1 cup bread crumbs

Olive oil

Creamy Yellow Grits (page 192)

Tasso Gravy (at right)

Freshly grated Parmesan cheese

- Combine the shrimp, sausage, onion, red pepper, scallion tops, blackening seasoning, cayenne, salt and white pepper in a bowl and mix well. Stir in the mayonnaise. Add the egg and mix well. Stir in the bread crumbs. Shape into 4 cakes.

- Heat a medium sauté pan until hot. Add cold olive oil. Heat until hot. Add the shrimp cakes.

- Cook for 30 seconds and turn. Cook for 30 to 45 seconds longer. Transfer the cakes to a baking dish.

- Bake at 450 degrees for 5 minutes or until golden brown and firm to the touch.

- Spoon the desired amount of Creamy Yellow Grits onto 2 dinner plates. Top each serving with 2 shrimp cakes. Drizzle with the desired amount of Tasso Gravy. Sprinkle with the cheese.

Two Servings

Prepare Tasso Gravy by sautéing 2 cups finely chopped tasso ham and 1 cup chopped onion in hot vegetable oil in a sauté pan until the onion is tender. Stir in 1 tablespoon minced garlic, 1/8 teaspoon blackening seasoning and 3 dashes of Tabasco sauce. Cook for 1 minute, stirring constantly. Deglaze the pan with 1 cup sherry. Cook for 3 minutes or until the liquid has been reduced by 1/4. Stir in 2 cups whipping cream. Cook for 3 minutes, stirring constantly. Stir in 1 cup grated Parmesan cheese. Season with salt and white pepper to taste.

SIDE DISHES

SIDE DISHES

THE ANGLER'S HARVEST

Catfish from the lower Saluda River corridor, finely filleted and fried golden brown. Since bass, perch, bream, and trout also thrive here, this unique river has surrendered many a fish to the frying pan.

Opposite:

Fried Catfish Dijon with Creole Tartar Sauce

Herb Focaccia

Broccoli Timbales

Zucchini Stuffed with Corn Confetti

Black Beans and Rice

Asparagus With Pignolas

3 tablespoons pignolas

3 quarts water

Salt to taste

1 pound asparagus, trimmed

$1/2$ to 1 teaspoon minced garlic

3 tablespoons unsalted butter

$1/4$ cup chopped Virginia ham or Canadian bacon

2 tablespoons grated Parmesan cheese

1 teaspoon chopped fresh basil

Freshly ground pepper to taste

2 tablespoons grated Parmesan cheese

- Spread the pignolas on a foil-lined baking sheet. Toast at 350 degrees for 3 to 5 minutes.
- Bring the water and salt to a boil in a saucepan. Add the asparagus.
- Boil for 6 to 8 minutes or until tender-crisp; drain. Rinse with cold water. Arrange the asparagus in a baking dish.
- Sauté the garlic in the butter in a saucepan for 1 to 2 minutes. Add the ham and mix well.
- Sauté for 2 minutes.
- Combine the pignolas, 2 tablespoons cheese, basil and pepper in a bowl and mix well. Stir in the ham mixture. Spread over the asparagus. Sprinkle with 2 tablespoons cheese.
- Broil for 2 minutes or until the cheese is almost melted.
- May substitute $1/2$ teaspoon dried basil for the fresh basil.

Four Servings

Marinated Asparagus

1 pound fresh asparagus, trimmed

6 tablespoons olive oil

$1/4$ cup capers

3 tablespoons white wine vinegar

2 tablespoons chopped scallions

Salt and pepper to taste

Crumbled feta cheese

- Cook the asparagus in boiling water in a saucepan for 1 minute and 40 seconds; drain. Arrange in a dish.
- Combine the olive oil, capers, wine vinegar, scallions, salt and pepper in a bowl and mix well. Pour over the asparagus, turning to coat.
- Marinate at room temperature for several hours, turning occasionally; drain.
- Arrange the asparagus on a serving platter. Top with feta cheese.
- May chill for 2 hours before serving. If the marinade thickens, bring to room temperature before serving.

Four Servings

Marinated Sesame Asparagus

Delicious for lunch or served as an appetizer. Oriental sesame oil is toasted and has a distinctive taste. A few drops adds a lot of flavor. Do not substitute with untoasted oil from Middle Eastern markets.

1 pound medium fresh
   asparagus

Salt to taste

1/4 cup safflower oil

2 tablespoons rice
   vinegar

1/2 teaspoon Oriental
   sesame seed oil

Salt and freshly ground
   pepper to taste

1 teaspoon sesame seeds,
   toasted (optional)

- Discard the tough stems of the asparagus. Trim the ends to an even length.

- Parboil the asparagus in boiling salted water in a saucepan for 3 minutes. Drain and rinse in ice water. Drain and pat dry. Arrange the asparagus in a dish.

- Whisk the safflower oil, rice vinegar, sesame seed oil, salt and pepper in a bowl. Pour over the asparagus, turning to coat.

- Marinate, covered, in the refrigerator for 30 minutes or longer; drain.

- Arrange the asparagus on a serving platter. Sprinkle with the sesame seeds.

Four Servings

Black Beans And Rice

2 cups chicken broth

1 cup long grain rice

1/2 teaspoon salt

1 (15-ounce) can black
   beans, drained, rinsed

3/4 cup finely chopped
   ham

3 green onions, thinly
   sliced

2 tablespoons butter

- Bring the broth, rice and salt to a boil in a saucepan; reduce heat.

- Simmer, covered, for 15 minutes or until the rice is tender. Remove from heat.

- Let stand for 10 minutes. Stir in the beans. Cover to keep warm.

- Sauté the ham and green onions in the butter in a skillet for 1 minute. Stir into the rice mixture. Serve warm.

Five to Six Servings

GREEN BEANS WITH GARLIC AND BASIL

2 pounds fresh green
   beans

3 cloves of garlic,
   crushed

Salt and pepper to taste

Chopped fresh basil
   to taste

1 to 2 tablespoons olive
   oil

1/4 cup grated Parmesan
   cheese (optional)

- Trim and remove the strings from the beans. Combine the beans with enough water to cover in a saucepan. Bring to a boil; reduce heat.

- Simmer, covered, for 6 to 8 minutes or until tender-crisp; drain. Plunge the beans into ice water; drain.

- Sauté the garlic, salt, pepper and basil in the olive oil in a skillet. Add the beans and mix well.

- Sauté until heated through. Spoon onto a serving platter. Sprinkle with the cheese.

- May add 1 cup sliced fresh mushrooms, 1/3 cup chopped onion and/or 8 ounces sliced water chestnuts for variety.

- The beans may be blanched early in the day and stored in the refrigerator until just before preparation time.

Six to Eight Servings

NELL'S GREEN BEANS

1 1/4 quarts water

2 pounds fresh green
   beans, trimmed

6 tablespoons butter or
   margarine

2 tablespoons fresh
   lemon juice

2 teaspoons seasoned salt

1 teaspoon onion salt

1/4 teaspoon pepper

1/4 cup grated Parmesan
   cheese

- Bring the water to a boil in a 2 1/2-quart saucepan. Add the green beans.

- Cook for 20 to 25 minutes or until the desired degree of crispness; drain. Cover to keep warm. The beans should be slightly crunchy; do not overcook.

- Combine the butter, lemon juice, seasoned salt, onion salt and pepper in a microwave-safe dish.

- Microwave until the butter melts and mix well. Stir in the cheese.

- Spoon the beans into a serving bowl. Add the butter mixture, tossing to coat. Serve immediately.

Four to Six Servings

RED BEANS AND RICE

1 pound dried red beans

1 cup chopped onion

1 cup chopped green bell
   pepper

1 cup chopped celery

1/2 cup chopped green onions

3 tablespoons minced garlic

2 tablespoons vegetable oil or
   bacon drippings

2 cups chopped smoked ham

8 ounces sliced smoked
   sausage

1 teaspoon salt

1 teaspoon thyme

1/2 teaspoon pepper

4 bay leaves

8 to 10 cups water

Hot cooked rice

- Sort and rinse the beans. Combine the beans with enough water to cover in a bowl.

- Let stand for 8 to 10 hours; drain.

- Sauté the onion, green pepper, celery, green onions and garlic in the oil in a heavy saucepan for 5 minutes. Stir in the ham, sausage, salt, thyme, pepper and bay leaves. Add the beans and 8 to 10 cups water and mix well.

- Bring to a boil; reduce heat to medium.

- Simmer for 2 hours or until the beans are tender, stirring occasionally. Add additional water as needed for desired consistency. Discard the bay leaves.

- Spoon the beans over the hot cooked rice in a bowl.

Eight Servings

STIR-FRIED BROCCOLI AND MUSHROOMS

Serve Butter Pecan Sauce over steamed broccoli, steamed asparagus or your favorite vegetable. Heat $1/2$ cup butter, $1/4$ cup fresh lemon juice, $1/4$ cup chopped pecans, 2 tablespoons chopped fresh chives, $1/2$ teaspoon salt, $1/4$ teaspoon pepper and $1/4$ teaspoon marjoram in a saucepan until bubbly. Drizzle over desired vegetables.

2 pounds broccoli

2 large cloves of garlic, cut into halves

$1/4$ cup olive oil

12 ounces fresh mushrooms of choice, sliced

4 to 5 tablespoons sunflower kernels, lightly toasted

$3/4$ teaspoon seasoned salt

Freshly grated pepper to taste

1 tablespoon freshly grated asiago cheese

- Cut the broccoli florets from the stems. Cut the florets into bite-size pieces. Cut the stems horizontally into halves. Slice the halves into $1^{1/2}$-inch strips.

- Sauté the garlic in the olive oil in a skillet over medium heat until golden brown. Discard the garlic. Add the broccoli strips.

- Sauté for 4 to 5 minutes or until tender-crisp. Add the florets and mix well.

- Sauté for 3 minutes. Stir in the mushrooms and sunflower kernels.

- Sauté for 2 minutes. Add the seasoned salt and pepper and mix well.

- Spoon the broccoli mixture onto a heated serving platter. Sprinkle with the cheese. Serve immediately.

Six to Eight Servings

BROCCOLI TIMBALES

4 cups chopped broccoli
 florets

1/3 cup chopped onion

2 tablespoons minced red bell
 pepper

1 tablespoon butter

1/4 cup whipping cream

3 eggs

1 tablespoon minced fresh
 parsley

1/4 teaspoon salt

1/8 teaspoon pepper

1/16 teaspoon grated nutmeg

1 cup shredded Swiss cheese

Red bell pepper strips

- Butter 6 timbale molds or custard cups.

- Blanch the broccoli in boiling water in a saucepan for 1 minute; drain.

- Sauté the onion and red pepper in 1 tablespoon butter in a skillet for 1 minute. Stir in the broccoli.

- Cook for 3 minutes, stirring constantly. Cool slightly.

- Whisk the whipping cream, eggs, parsley, salt, pepper, nutmeg and cheese in a bowl. Add the broccoli mixture and mix gently. Spoon into the prepared molds, dividing equally. Place the molds on a baking sheet.

- Bake at 350 degrees for 25 minutes or until set. Cool for 5 minutes.

- Loosen the timbales from the molds with a sharp knife. Invert onto a serving platter or 6 dinner plates. Top with red bell pepper strips. Serve immediately.

Six Servings

Sweet-And-Sour Red Cabbage

1 large head red cabbage, julienned

2 large onions, thinly sliced

1 tart apple, peeled, chopped

1 cup red wine vinegar

1/2 cup sugar

1 tablespoon caraway seeds

1 1/2 teaspoons salt

1/4 teaspoon pepper

1 bay leaf

1/4 cup vegetable oil

- Combine the cabbage, onions and apple in a bowl and mix well. Add a mixture of the wine vinegar, sugar, caraway seeds, salt, pepper and bay leaf and mix well.

- Heat the oil in a heavy skillet over medium heat. Add the cabbage mixture; reduce heat.

- Simmer, covered, for 1 hour or until the cabbage is tender, stirring occasionally. Discard the bay leaf.

- Serve hot or cold.

Ten to Twelve Servings

Baked Corn

2 cups milk

2 tablespoons cornstarch

2 cups (heaping) fresh corn kernels with milk

2 tablespoons melted butter

2 tablespoons sugar

2 eggs, beaten

1/2 to 3/4 teaspoon seasoned salt

1/2 teaspoon pepper

Paprika to taste

- Combine the milk and cornstarch in a bowl, stirring until the cornstarch dissolves. Stir in the corn, butter, sugar, eggs, seasoned salt and pepper. Spoon into a buttered 1 1/2-quart baking dish. Sprinkle with paprika.

- Bake at 375 degrees for 1 hour or until set. Serve immediately.

- It is very important to scrape the milk from the corncob after cutting the kernels from the cob. Mix the milk with the other ingredients.

Four to Six Servings

Eggplant With Chevre

1 large eggplant

1 to 2 tablespoons olive oil

Salt and pepper to taste

3 ounces chèvre or other soft goat cheese

4 or 5 Roma tomatoes, sliced

Chopped fresh basil or oregano

- Cut the eggplant into $^{1}/_{2}$- to $^{3}/_{4}$-inch slices. Brush with olive oil and sprinkle with salt and pepper. Arrange in a single layer on a baking sheet.

- Bake at 350 degrees for 20 to 30 minutes or until tender. Spread the cheese on the slices. Top with enough tomato slices to cover each eggplant round. Sprinkle with basil or oregano.

- Broil for 5 minutes or until the cheese melts.

Four to Six Servings

Imam Bayildi

$1^{1}/_{2}$ cups water

$^{1}/_{4}$ cup olive oil

$^{3}/_{4}$ cup minced onion

$^{1}/_{4}$ cup rice

$^{1}/_{2}$ teaspoon salt

1 large eggplant, chopped, cooked, drained

$1^{1}/_{2}$ cups chopped canned tomatoes

$^{1}/_{2}$ cup chopped green bell pepper

$^{1}/_{2}$ cup chopped fresh parsley

$^{1}/_{4}$ cup minced fresh mint

$^{1}/_{2}$ cup seedless raisins

$^{1}/_{2}$ cup slivered almonds

1 clove of garlic, minced

Salt and pepper to taste

- Bring the water, olive oil, onion, rice and $^{1}/_{2}$ teaspoon salt to a boil in a saucepan; reduce heat.

- Simmer, covered, until the rice is tender; drain.

- Stir in the eggplant, tomatoes, green pepper, parsley, mint, raisins, almonds, garlic, salt to taste and pepper. Spoon into a greased baking dish.

- Bake at 350 degrees for 1 hour.

Four Servings

Okra And Tomato Casserole

To peel tomatoes easily, blanch in boiling water for approximately ten seconds. Remove with a slotted spoon. Cool slightly and peel. May blanch tomatoes in advance, but do not peel until just before needed. The tomatoes will stay fresher this way. To seed tomatoes, first blanch and peel. Cut the tomatoes horizontally into halves. Hold the tomato halves in the palm of your hand and squeeze the pulp and seeds into a bowl. Remove any remaining pulp with a small spoon. For tomato juice, squeeze the pulp into a small strainer over a bowl.

Great way to use your garden supply of okra and tomatoes.

6 tablespoons chopped onion

2 tablespoons vegetable oil or bacon drippings

1 pound fresh okra, sliced

1 quart fresh or canned tomatoes, peeled, chopped

1½ teaspoons salt

1 teaspoon sugar

¼ teaspoon curry powder

¼ teaspoon paprika

⅛ teaspoon crushed red pepper

2½ tablespoons grated Parmesan cheese

8 butter crackers, crushed

- Sauté the onion in the oil in a skillet. Add the okra and mix well.
- Cook until the okra is tender, stirring constantly. Add the tomatoes, salt, sugar, curry powder, paprika and red pepper and mix well.
- Cook for 5 minutes, stirring frequently. Spoon into a greased 9x13-inch baking dish. Sprinkle with the cheese and cracker crumbs.
- Bake at 350 degrees for 35 minutes.

Eight Servings

GRILLED ONION PACKAGES

4 small Vidalia onions

4 beef bouillon cubes

4 teaspoons butter or
 olive oil

Salt and pepper to taste

4 sprigs of fresh thyme or
 dried thyme to taste

Balsamic vinegar to taste

• Peel the onions and remove the cores. Place each onion on a sheet of heavy-duty foil large enough to enclose the onion.

• Place 1 bouillon cube in the center of each onion. Spread the butter over the bouillon cube. Sprinkle with salt and pepper and top with the thyme. Drizzle with balsamic vinegar. Wrap tightly to seal.

• Grill over hot coals for 20 minutes or until tender, turning occasionally.

Four Servings

ONION TART

This tart is rich, creamy and slightly sweet—a comfort food like no other! It can be prepared one or two days in advance and stored in the refrigerator. Serve hot or at room temperature.

1 all ready pie pastry

2 tablespoons butter

1 tablespoon extra-virgin
 olive oil

3 onions, minced

2/3 cup half-and-half

2 eggs

1 teaspoon salt

1/8 teaspoon nutmeg

1 ounce Gruyère cheese,
 thinly sliced

2 ounces Gruyère cheese,
 shredded

• Fit the pie pastry into a greased and floured 10-inch quiche pan or 8-inch springform pan. Prick the bottom with a fork.

• Bake at 400 degrees for 7 to 10 minutes. Cool on a wire rack.

• Heat the butter and olive oil in a skillet over medium heat. Add the onions.

• Cook over low heat for 40 minutes or until the onions are soft and creamy, stirring occasionally.

• Beat the half-and-half, eggs, salt and nutmeg in a mixer bowl. Stir in the onions.

• Arrange the sliced cheese over the bottom of the baked layer. Pour the onion mixture over the cheese. Sprinkle with the shredded cheese.

• Bake at 375 degrees for 25 to 30 minutes or until brown and set.

Six to Eight Servings

Vidalia Onion Casserole

4 cups sliced Vidalia
    onions

$1/4$ cup butter

$1/3$ cup sherry

2 tablespoons cornstarch

2 tablespoons butter

$2/3$ cup chicken broth

$1/2$ cup bread crumbs

$1/2$ cup grated Parmesan
    cheese

- Sauté the onions in $1/4$ cup butter in a skillet until tender. Spoon into a $1^1/_2$-quart baking dish.

- Combine the sherry and cornstarch in a bowl, stirring until the cornstarch is dissolved.

- Heat 2 tablespoons butter in a saucepan until melted. Add the sherry mixture, stirring until blended. Stir in the chicken broth.

- Cook until thickened, stirring constantly. Pour over the onions. Sprinkle with the bread crumbs and cheese.

- Bake at 350 degrees for 30 minutes.

Four to Six Servings

New Potatoes With Spring Onion Vinaigrette

$3/4$ cup vegetable oil

$1/2$ cup white wine
    vinegar

1 tablespoon (rounded)
    Dijon mustard

2 spring onions (light
    green part only),
    finely chopped

Salt and white pepper to
    taste

12 medium new potatoes

- Whisk the oil, wine vinegar, Dijon mustard, spring onions, salt and white pepper in a bowl until mixed.

- Peel a strip around the center of each new potato, leaving the skin on the top and lower portions of the potatoes.

- Combine the potatoes with enough water to cover in a saucepan. Bring to a boil.

- Boil until tender; drain. Toss the potatoes with the vinaigrette in a bowl. Serve at room temperature.

Six Servings

MASHED POTATO PIE

2 to 3 tablespoons fresh
   bread crumbs

3 tablespoons grated
   Parmesan cheese or
   Romano cheese

3 tablespoons chopped fresh
   parsley

4 medium baking potatoes

1 cup ricotta cheese

1/4 cup half-and-half

2 eggs

1 to 2 tablespoons chopped
   fresh chives

1/4 cup grated Parmesan
   cheese

5 tablespoons grated
   Parmesan cheese

- Combine the bread crumbs, 3 tablespoons Parmesan cheese and parsley in a bowl and mix well. Sprinkle over the bottom and up the side of a generously buttered 8- or 9-inch pie plate or quiche pan. Shake out excess crumbs. Chill in the refrigerator.

- Bake the potatoes on the center oven rack at 450 degrees for 1 to 1 1/2 hours or until very tender. Cut the potatoes horizontally into halves. Scoop the pulp into a mixer bowl. Discard the potato skins or reserve for toasting.

- Add the ricotta cheese and half-and-half to the hot potato pulp, beating until smooth. Add the eggs 1 at a time, beating well after each addition. Beat in the chives and 1/4 cup Parmesan cheese until mixed. Spoon into the prepared pie plate. Sprinkle with 5 tablespoons Parmesan cheese.

- Bake on the center oven rack at 350 degrees for 35 to 45 minutes or until puffy and light brown. Serve warm or at room temperature.

- May prepare and bake the pie 1 day in advance and store in the refrigerator or may prepare 1 day in advance and bake just before serving.

- May substitute a mixture of the Parmesan cheese and Romano cheese for either cheese and 2 cups instant or leftover mashed potatoes for the baking potatoes.

Six Servings

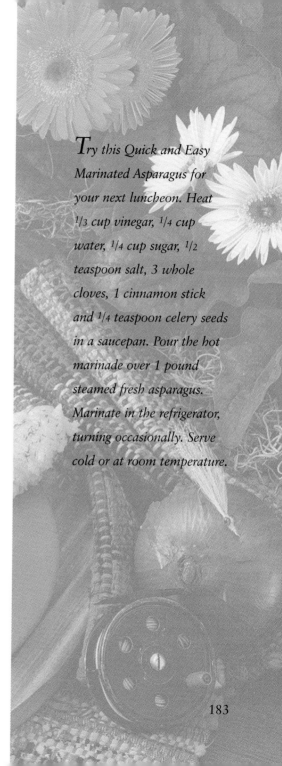

Try this Quick and Easy Marinated Asparagus for your next luncheon. Heat 1/3 cup vinegar, 1/4 cup water, 1/4 cup sugar, 1/2 teaspoon salt, 3 whole cloves, 1 cinnamon stick and 1/4 teaspoon celery seeds in a saucepan. Pour the hot marinade over 1 pound steamed fresh asparagus. Marinate in the refrigerator, turning occasionally. Serve cold or at room temperature.

SWEET POTATO SOUFFLE

Use leftover sweet potatoes to make sweet potato biscuits or a soufflé. Or try baking a sweet potato twice. Store leftover sweet potatoes in the refrigerator. Reheat at 425 degrees until the skin puffs. The sweet potato will be extra sweet.

A family reunion must!

3¹/₂ cups mashed cooked
   sweet potatoes
1 cup whipping cream
¹/₂ cup sugar
¹/₄ cup butter, softened
2 eggs, lightly beaten
1 teaspoon vanilla extract
¹/₂ cup packed brown sugar
¹/₃ cup flour
¹/₄ cup melted butter
1 cup chopped pecans

- Combine the sweet potatoes, whipping cream, sugar, softened butter, eggs and vanilla in a bowl and mix well. Spoon into a baking dish.
- Combine the brown sugar, flour and melted butter in a bowl and mix well. Stir in the pecans. Spread over the sweet potatoes. May be prepared to this point 1 day in advance and stored, covered, in the refrigerator.
- Bake, covered, at 275 degrees for 40 minutes; remove the cover.
- Bake for 10 minutes longer.
- May substitute two 15-ounce cans sweet potatoes for the homemade sweet potatoes and may increase the sugar to ³/₄ cup for a sweeter version.

Ten Servings

Sweet Potatoes Topped With Maple Cream

8 medium sweet potatoes

1 cup sour cream

1/4 cup maple syrup

1/2 teaspoon salt

1/2 teaspoon ginger

1/4 teaspoon nutmeg

1/2 cup chopped pecans, toasted

- Bake the sweet potatoes on a baking sheet at 375 degrees for 1 hour. Cut the sweet potatoes horizontally into halves. Place on a serving platter.
- Combine the sour cream, maple syrup, salt, ginger and nutmeg in a bowl and mix well. Spread over the sweet potatoes. Sprinkle with the pecans.

Eight Servings

For luscious baked sweet potatoes with tender, edible skins, follow a few simple guidelines. First, preheat the oven to 400 degrees. Line a baking sheet with foil. Scrub each sweet potato, pierce the skin on one side with a fork or the tip of a paring knife and brush with vegetable oil. Place the sweet potatoes pierced sides up on a baking sheet. Bake without turning for 50 to 60 minutes or until tender.

Spinach Souffle

1 tablespoon butter

Grated Parmesan cheese
    to taste

3 tablespoons butter

3 tablespoons flour

1 cup boiling milk

1/2 teaspoon salt

1/8 teaspoon black pepper

1/8 teaspoon cayenne

1/8 teaspoon nutmeg

4 egg yolks, beaten

1 (10-ounce) package frozen
    spinach, thawed, drained

2 tablespoons minced green
    onions

2 tablespoons butter

1/4 teaspoon salt

4 egg whites

1/8 teaspoon salt

1/2 cup shredded Swiss cheese

- Preheat the oven to 400 degrees. Rub 1 tablespoon butter over the bottom and up the side of a soufflé dish. Sprinkle heavily with Parmesan cheese.

- Heat 3 tablespoons butter in a saucepan until melted. Add the flour, stirring until smooth. Remove from heat. Whisk in the boiling milk until blended. Stir in 1/2 teaspoon salt, black pepper, cayenne and nutmeg.

- Cook over medium heat until thickened, stirring constantly. Remove from heat.

- Whisk a small amount of the hot mixture into the egg yolks. Add the egg yolks 1/4 at a time to the hot mixture, whisking well after each addition.

- Squeeze the moisture from the spinach. Sauté the green onions in 2 tablespoons butter in a skillet. Stir in the spinach and 1/4 teaspoon salt.

- Cook over medium heat for several minutes to allow any excess water to evaporate, stirring frequently. Stir into the egg yolk sauce.

- Beat the egg whites and 1/8 teaspoon salt in a mixer bowl until fluffy or of the consistency of meringue. Fold 1/2 of the egg whites and all but 1 tablespoon of the Swiss cheese into the spinach mixture. Fold in the remaining egg whites. Spoon into the prepared soufflé dish. Sprinkle with the remaining 1 tablespoon Swiss cheese.

- Decrease the oven temperature to 375 degrees. Bake on the middle oven rack for 25 to 30 minutes. Serve immediately.

Four to Six Servings

SQUASH CASSEROLE

2 pounds yellow squash,
 chopped

1 cup shredded Colby
 Jack cheese mixture

1 cup chopped green
 onions

2 tablespoons (heaping)
 chopped fresh
 dillweed

3 eggs, beaten

1 teaspoon salt

1/2 teaspoon pepper

1/2 cup butter

2 1/4 cups fresh Italian or
 French loaf bread
 crumbs

3/4 cup shredded Colby
 Jack cheese mixture

- Steam the squash in a steamer for
  10 minutes or until tender; drain.

- Process the squash in a food
  processor until coarsely chopped.

- Combine 1 cup cheese mixture,
  green onions, dillweed, eggs, salt
  and pepper in a bowl and mix
  well. Stir in the squash.

- Heat the butter in a skillet over
  medium heat until melted. Stir in
  the bread crumbs.

- Cook for 4 minutes or until crisp
  and brown, stirring frequently.
  Remove from heat. Fold 1/2 of
  the bread crumbs into the squash
  mixture. Spoon into a buttered
  9x13-inch baking dish.

- Mix 3/4 cup cheese mixture into
  the remaining bread crumbs in
  the skillet. Sprinkle over the top.

- Bake at 350 degrees for 35
  minutes or until golden brown.
  Let stand for 10 minutes
  before serving.

- May substitute 2 teaspoons dried
  dillweed for the fresh dillweed.

Six to Eight Servings

EASY SQUASH DRESSING

Terrific fall or winter dish with pork roast.

2 cups mashed cooked
 squash

2 cups crumbled corn
 bread

1 (14-ounce) can chicken
 broth

2 eggs, beaten

1/2 cup melted butter or
 margarine

1/4 to 1/2 cup chopped
 green onions or
 yellow onion

1 medium green bell
 pepper, chopped

Salt and pepper to taste

- Combine the squash, corn bread,
  broth, eggs, butter, green onions,
  green pepper, salt and pepper in
  a bowl and mix well.

- Spoon the squash mixture into a
  9x12-inch baking dish.

- Bake at 350 degrees for 30 to
  40 minutes or until brown
  and bubbly.

Eight Servings

BROILED TOMATO CUPS

5 or 6 tomatoes

$1/2$ cup sour cream

$1/2$ cup mayonnaise

$1/4$ cup grated Parmesan
   cheese

3 green onions, chopped

Juice of 1 lemon

1 teaspoon garlic salt

1 teaspoon chopped fresh
   parsley

- Cut the tomatoes horizontally
  into halves. Place cut side up on
  a baking sheet.

- Combine the sour cream,
  mayonnaise, cheese, green
  onions, lemon juice, garlic salt
  and parsley in a bowl and mix
  well. Top each tomato half with
  a small amount of the mixture.

- Broil until bubbly.

Ten to Twelve Servings

SCALLOPED TOMATOES

1 small onion, chopped

2 ribs celery, chopped

1 (16-ounce) can whole
   tomatoes, chopped

1 tablespoon sugar

1 teaspoon salt

$1/2$ teaspoon pepper

2 slices bread, torn into
   cubes

Butter or margarine

- Sauté the onion and celery in a
  nonstick skillet until tender. Stir
  in the undrained tomatoes, sugar,
  salt and pepper. Spoon into a
  baking dish.

- Top with the bread cubes; dot
  with butter.

- Bake at 350 degrees until brown
  and bubbly.

Two to Three Servings

GRILLED VEGETABLES

1 large yellow squash

1 large zucchini

1 large red bell pepper

1 large carrot, peeled

12 small asparagus
spears, trimmed

1/2 cup olive oil

1/2 cup balsamic vinegar

2 shallots, chopped

1 tablespoon Dijon
mustard

1 tablespoon lemon juice

1 tablespoon chopped
fresh thyme

1 teaspoon rosemary

Salt and pepper to taste

Chopped fresh herbs of
choice

- Slice the yellow squash and zucchini horizontally into quarters. Cut the bell pepper into 1-inch strips. Slice the carrot horizontally into halves. Cut each half into 2-inch pieces.

- Place the yellow squash, zucchini, red pepper, carrot and asparagus in a sealable plastic bag.

- Combine the olive oil, balsamic vinegar, shallots, Dijon mustard, lemon juice, thyme and rosemary in a bowl and mix well. Pour over the vegetables and seal the bag tightly.

- Marinate in the refrigerator for several hours, turning occasionally. Drain, reserving the marinade. Arrange the vegetables in a grilling basket.

- Grill over hot coals until slightly charred, turning and basting with the reserved marinade frequently.

- Transfer the vegetables to a serving platter. Sprinkle with salt, pepper and fresh herbs.

Four to Six Servings

VEGETABLE GRATIN

Florets of 1 pound
broccoli

Salt to taste

3 small yellow squash,
chopped

3 small zucchini,
chopped

1 large onion, coarsely
chopped

4 green onions (white
part only), chopped

1 tablespoon olive oil

1 tablespoon basil

3 cloves of garlic,
crushed

8 eggs

Pepper to taste

1/2 cup grated Parmesan
cheese

1/2 cup shredded Swiss
cheese

- Blanch the broccoli in boiling salted water in a saucepan for 2 to 3 minutes or until it turns bright green; drain.

- Blanch the yellow squash and zucchini in boiling salted water in a saucepan for 2 to 3 minutes or until tender-crisp; drain.

- Sauté the onion and green onions in the olive oil in a skillet over medium heat for 4 to 5 minutes or until tender.

- Combine the broccoli, yellow squash, zucchini, onions, basil and garlic in a bowl and mix well. Spoon into a 1 1/2-quart shallow baking dish.

- Beat the eggs in a mixer bowl. Beat in salt, pepper and Parmesan cheese. Pour over the vegetable mixture. Sprinkle with the Swiss cheese.

- Bake on the center oven rack at 350 degrees for 20 to 25 minutes or until set.

- Cool to room temperature before serving.

Six Servings

ZUCCHINI CASSEROLE

3 medium zucchini,
  sliced

1 pound Monterey Jack
  cheese, shredded

2 cups cooked rice

2 cups sour cream

1 (7-ounce) can green
  chiles, drained,
  chopped

2 large tomatoes, sliced

2 tablespoons finely
  chopped green bell
  pepper

2 tablespoons finely
  chopped onion

1 tablespoon finely
  chopped fresh parsley

1 teaspoon oregano

1 teaspoon salt

- Combine the zucchini with
  enough water to cover in a
  saucepan. Bring to a boil.

- Boil for 3 minutes; drain.

- Combine the zucchini, cheese,
  rice, sour cream, chiles,
  tomatoes, green pepper, onion,
  parsley, oregano and salt in a
  bowl and mix gently. Spoon into
  a greased baking dish.

- Bake at 350 degrees for 35 to
  40 minutes or until brown
  and bubbly.

Twelve Servings

ZUCCHINI STUFFED WITH CORN CONFETTI

For a tasty variation, sprinkle the tops of the stuffed zucchini with shredded cheese and heat in a 350-degree oven until bubbly.

4 medium zucchini

3 tablespoons melted
  butter

2 cups (about 4 ears)
  fresh corn kernels

1/2 medium red bell
  pepper, chopped

1 tablespoon minced
  fresh parsley

1/2 teaspoon pepper

1/4 teaspoon salt

- Bake the zucchini on a baking
  sheet in a moderate oven just
  until tender. Cut the zucchini
  horizontally into halves. Scoop
  out the pulp and seeds carefully
  from each half to form shallow
  boats. Brush the zucchini boats
  with 1 tablespoon of the butter.

- Combine the remaining 2 tablespoons butter, corn, red pepper,
  parsley, pepper and salt in a
  saucepan and mix well.

- Cook over medium-low heat
  for 3 minutes or until heated
  through, stirring frequently.
  Spoon the corn mixture into
  the zucchini boats.

- Arrange the zucchini boats on a
  serving platter. Serve immediately.

- May prepare in advance, store
  in the refrigerator and reheat in
  the oven or microwave just
  before serving.

Four Servings

CRANBERRY APPLE CASSEROLE

3 cups cranberries

3 cups chopped unpeeled
    apples

1 cup sugar

1 cup rolled oats

1/2 cup packed brown
    sugar

1/2 cup chopped pecans

1/4 cup melted margarine

- Combine the cranberries, apples and sugar in a bowl and mix well. Spoon into a greased 9x12-inch baking dish.
- Combine the oats, brown sugar, pecans and margarine in a bowl and mix well. Spread over the prepared layer.
- Bake at 325 degrees for 45 minutes.

Eight to Ten Servings

SAUTEED CORN CAKES

10 ounces frozen whole
    kernel corn, thawed

1 egg yolk, lightly beaten

1 cup chopped yellow
    bell pepper

3 1/2 tablespoons white
    cornmeal

3 tablespoons flour

2 tablespoons milk

1 tablespoon chopped
    chives

1 teaspoon fresh thyme
    leaves

1/8 to 1/2 teaspoon
    crushed red pepper, or
    to taste

Salt and black pepper
    to taste

3 egg whites, stiffly
    beaten

2 cups crème fraîche or
    sour cream

- Process 2/3 of the corn in a food processor or blender until puréed.
- Combine the puréed corn, remaining whole kernel corn, egg yolk, yellow pepper, cornmeal, flour, milk, chives, thyme, red pepper, salt and black pepper in a bowl and mix well. Stir in 1/3 of the egg whites. Fold in the remaining egg whites.
- Pour 1/8 to 1/4 cup of the batter onto a hot greased griddle. Pat lightly with a spatula.
- Bake until golden brown on both sides, turning once. Repeat the process with the remaining batter.
- Serve with crème fraîche or sour cream.

Twelve to Fifteen Servings

CREAMY YELLOW GRITS

3 cups chicken stock or
  bouillon

1/4 cup finely chopped
  onion

1 tablespoon nutmeg

1 teaspoon cayenne

Butter or vegetable oil

1 cup stone-ground
  yellow grits

1/2 cup whipping cream

Salt and white pepper
  to taste

- Bring the chicken stock to a boil
  in a saucepan.

- Sauté the onion, nutmeg and
  cayenne in butter in a saucepan
  until the onion is tender. Stir in
  the boiling stock. Bring to a boil.
  Whisk in the grits.

- Cook for 4 minutes or until
  thickened, whisking frequently.

- Remove from heat. Stir in the
  whipping cream. Season with salt
  and white pepper.

Eight Servings

SAUSAGE AND GRITS DRESSING

*This dressing is delicious served with turkey and giblet gravy
at Thanksgiving.*

1 cup grits

1 pound mild bulk
  sausage

1 cup chopped onion

1 cup chopped celery

1 cup chicken or turkey
  broth

1 slice white bread,
  crumbled

2 eggs, lightly beaten

1/2 teaspoon poultry
  seasoning

1/4 teaspoon sage

Salt and pepper to taste

- Cook the grits using package
  directions. Season to taste

- Brown the sausage in a skillet,
  stirring until crumbly. Transfer
  the sausage to a bowl with a
  slotted spoon, reserving the
  pan drippings.

- Sauté the onion and celery in
  the reserved pan drippings until
  tender; drain.

- Combine the grits, sausage,
  onion mixture, broth, bread,
  eggs, poultry seasoning and
  sage in a bowl and mix well.
  Season with salt and pepper.
  Spoon into a buttered 9x13-
  inch baking dish.

- Bake at 350 degrees for
  30 minutes.

- The dressing should have a
  moist consistency and will firm
  during baking.

Six to Eight Servings

SHRIMP AND YELLOW GRITS

2¹/2 cups chicken broth

1 tablespoon butter

³/4 cup yellow grits

3 tablespoons cream cheese

2 tablespoons half-and-half

¹/2 cup chopped scallions

1 pound deveined peeled shrimp

3 tablespoons butter

2 tablespoons lime juice

- Bring the broth and 1 tablespoon butter to a boil in a saucepan. Stir in the grits gradually. Bring to a boil; reduce heat.

- Simmer for 5 minutes. Stir in the cream cheese and half-and-half.

- Simmer, covered, for 7 minutes. Remove from heat. Stir in the scallions. Cover to keep warm.

- Sauté the shrimp in 3 tablespoons butter in a skillet until the shrimp turn pink. Stir in the lime juice.

- Spoon the shrimp over the grits on a serving platter.

Four Servings

BAKED RICE WITH PEPPERS

1 onion, chopped

3 tablespoons butter

1 cup long grain white rice

2 cups chicken stock

1 cup white wine

1 or 2 hot green chiles, seeded, chopped

1¹/2 cups sour cream

1 red bell pepper, chopped

1 green bell pepper, chopped

¹/2 cup chopped celery

¹/2 cup shredded Swiss cheese

¹/2 cup shredded Cheddar cheese

- Sauté the onion in the butter in a skillet until tender but not brown. Add the rice, stirring until coated. Stir in the stock, white wine and chiles. Bring to a boil, stirring frequently. Spoon into a baking dish.

- Bake, covered, at 350 degrees for 15 minutes or until the liquid is absorbed. Remove from oven. Increase the oven temperature to 400 degrees.

- Combine the rice mixture, sour cream, red pepper, green pepper, celery, Swiss cheese and Cheddar cheese in a bowl and mix well. Spoon into a lightly buttered baking dish.

- Bake for 20 minutes or until brown.

Six to Eight Servings

CHILE CHEESE RICE

3 cups sour cream

1/2 cup chopped sweet
   green chiles

1/2 cup chopped hot
   green chiles

Salt and pepper to taste

3 cups cooked rice

12 ounces Monterey Jack
   cheese, cut into strips

1/2 cup shredded Cheddar
   cheese

- Combine the sour cream, chiles, salt and pepper in a bowl and mix well. Stir in the rice.

- Layer the rice mixture and Monterey Jack cheese 1/2 at a time in a buttered 2-quart baking dish. Sprinkle with the Cheddar cheese.

- Bake at 350 degrees for 25 minutes or until the cheese melts.

- May increase or decrease the amount of chiles according to desired taste.

- May be prepared in advance and stored in the refrigerator or frozen for future use.

Six to Eight Servings

SAUSAGE AND RAISIN RICE

1 1/2 cups raisins

2 (6-ounce) packages
   long grain and wild
   rice

5 cups chicken broth

1/2 teaspoon curry
   powder

1 pound hot sausage

2 cups chopped celery

2 cups sliced mushrooms

1/2 cup chopped onion

1/2 cup chopped green
   bell pepper

1/2 cup sliced almonds

- Plump the raisins in boiling water in a bowl; drain.

- Cook the rice using package directions, substituting the chicken broth for the liquid and adding curry powder.

- Brown the sausage in a skillet, stirring until crumbly. Remove the sausage to a bowl with a slotted spoon, reserving the pan drippings.

- Sauté the celery, mushrooms, onion and green pepper in the reserved pan drippings until tender; drain.

- Combine the raisins, rice, sausage, celery mixture and almonds in a bowl and mix well. Spoon into a baking dish.

- Bake, covered, at 350 degrees for 30 minutes.

Twelve Servings

SOUTHWESTERN RISOTTO

1/2 cup chopped onion

2 cloves of garlic, minced

2 tablespoons butter

1 cup medium grain rice

1/2 cup dry white wine

6 cups broth

1/2 cup whipping cream

2 medium tomatoes, seeded, chopped

1/2 cup chopped green onions

1 jalapeño, seeded, chopped

2 to 3 tablespoons minced fresh cilantro

- Sauté the onion and garlic in the butter in a saucepan over medium heat. Stir in the rice.
- Cook for 2 to 3 minutes, stirring constantly. Add the white wine and mix well.
- Cook until the liquid is absorbed, stirring constantly. Add 1 cup of the broth, stirring constantly.
- Cook over medium-high heat until the liquid is absorbed, stirring constantly. Add the remaining broth 1 cup at a time, cooking after each addition until the broth is absorbed. The rice will be creamy in texture. Stir in the whipping cream, tomatoes, green onions, jalapeño and cilantro.
- Cook for 2 minutes. Spoon into a serving bowl. Sprinkle with additional minced fresh cilantro.

Six Servings

Cranberry Chutney makes a great accompaniment to any holiday meal. Bring 1 cup chopped Granny Smith apple, 1 cup raisins, 1 cup chopped onion, 1 cup sugar, 1 cup white wine vinegar, 3/4 cup chopped celery, 3/4 cup water, 12 ounces fresh cranberries, 2 teaspoons cinnamon, 1 1/2 teaspoons ginger and 1/4 teaspoon ground cloves to a boil in a saucepan; reduce heat. Simmer for 30 minutes, stirring occasionally. The flavor is enhanced if the chutney is prepared 1 to 2 days in advance.

VEGETABLE RISOTTO

6 cups chicken stock

8 ounces small zucchini, cut diagonally into $^1/_2$-inch slices

8 ounces carrots, cut diagonally into $^1/_2$-inch slices

8 ounces green beans, cut into 1-inch pieces

$^1/_2$ cup butter

8 ounces snow peas, cut into 1-inch pieces

6 medium mushrooms, sliced

4 ounces frozen green peas

3 cups arborio rice

$^1/_4$ cup butter

$^1/_2$ cup whipping cream

1 cup freshly grated Parmesan cheese

$^1/_4$ cup finely chopped fresh parsley

Freshly ground pepper to taste

1 tablespoon chopped fresh chives

- Bring the stock to a boil in a saucepan; reduce heat to simmer.
- Sauté the zucchini, carrots and green beans in $^1/_2$ cup butter in a saucepan for 3 to 4 minutes. Add the snow peas, mushrooms and green peas and mix well.
- Sauté for 1 minute. Stir in the rice.
- Cook for 2 minutes, stirring constantly. Add 1 cup of the hot stock and mix well.
- Cook for several minutes or until the liquid is absorbed, stirring constantly. Add the remaining stock 1 cup at a time. Cook until the liquid is absorbed after each addition, stirring constantly. Stir in $^1/_4$ cup butter and whipping cream. Remove from heat.
- Add $^2/_3$ of the cheese and $^2/_3$ of the parsley and mix well. Season generously with pepper. Spoon into a serving bowl. Sprinkle with the remaining cheese, the remaining parsley and the chives. Serve immediately.

Six Servings

WILD PECAN RICE

8 ounces bacon, chopped

1/2 cup chopped onion

1/2 cup minced celery

1 1/4 teaspoons salt

1/2 teaspoon cayenne

1 tablespoon butter

1/2 cup pecan pieces

1 unpeeled Granny Smith
apple, chopped

1 (7-ounce) package wild
pecan rice

2 cups water

1 cup chopped boiled ham

1/2 cup chopped green onions

2 tablespoons minced fresh
parsley

- Fry the bacon in a skillet until crisp; drain.
- Sauté the onion, celery, salt and cayenne in the butter in a saucepan over medium-high heat for 3 to 4 minutes or just until the vegetables are tender. Stir in the pecans.
- Cook for 4 minutes, stirring frequently. Add the apple and rice.
- Cook for 1 minute, stirring constantly. Stir in the water. Bring to a boil; reduce heat to medium.
- Cook, covered, for 20 minutes. Remove from heat. Add the bacon, ham, green onions and parsley and mix well.
- Let stand for 3 minutes before serving. Spoon into a serving bowl.

Six Servings

TANNY'S BRANDIED CRANBERRIES

Delicious served during the holidays with turkey or pork.

1 large package
   cranberries

2 cups sugar

3 tablespoons brandy

- Remove the stems from the cranberries. Rinse and drain. Spread the cranberries in an 8x8-inch baking pan. Sprinkle with the sugar.

- Bake, covered, at 325 degrees for 1 hour. Stir in the brandy.

- Spoon the cranberry mixture into hot sterilized 6-ounce jars, leaving a 1/4-inch headspace; seal with 2-piece lids.

- Let stand until the lids pop.

- To sterilize jars, wash in warm soapy water, rinse and dry. Place the jars in a 250-degree oven for 20 minutes.

Four (Six-Ounce) Jars

BREAD AND BUTTER PICKLES

7 pounds small
   cucumbers, sliced

3 pounds onions, sliced

1/2 cup salt

5 cups vinegar

4 1/2 cups sugar

2 tablespoons turmeric

2 teaspoons white
   mustard seeds

2 teaspoons celery seeds

1/2 teaspoon ground
   cloves

- Combine the cucumbers, onions and salt in a nonreactive container and mix well. Pack ice on top of the cucumber mixture.

- Let stand for 3 hours in ice. Drain the cucumber mixture and place in a stockpot.

- Combine the vinegar, sugar, turmeric, mustard seeds, celery seeds and cloves in a bowl and mix well. Pour over the cucumber mixture.

- Cook just until heated through, stirring occasionally; do not boil.

- Ladle into hot sterilized jars, leaving a 1/2-inch headspace; seal with 2-piece lids.

Twelve to Fifteen Pints

PEACH PRESERVES

1 quart chopped peeled
  peaches

2 cups sugar

Juice of 1/2 lemon

1 tablespoon butter

2 cups sugar

- Bring the peaches, 2 cups sugar, lemon juice and butter to a boil in a saucepan over medium heat.

- Boil for 10 minutes, stirring frequently. Stir in 2 cups sugar.

- Cook for 12 minutes longer, stirring constantly. Remove from heat.

- Let stand for 5 minutes. Ladle into hot sterilized jars, leaving 1/2-inch headspace; seal with 2-piece lids.

- Invert the jars on a wire rack for 5 minutes.

- May double the recipe.

Four (Six-Ounce) Jars

SPICED CRANBERRY APRICOT RELISH

Wonderful addition to your table during the Thanksgiving and Christmas holidays.

1 pound fresh or frozen
  cranberries

2 1/2 cups water

2 cups chopped dried
  apricots

1 cup chopped seedless
  golden raisins

1 tablespoon grated
  orange peel

1/4 teaspoon ginger

1 cup sugar

- Combine the cranberries, water, apricots, raisins, orange peel and ginger in a saucepan and mix well. Bring to a boil over high heat; reduce heat.

- Simmer for 10 minutes or until the cranberries pop and are tender, stirring occasionally. Remove from heat. Stir in the sugar.

Five Cups

DESSERTS

DESSERTS

DESSERT ON THE PATIO

In 1868, Governor James L. Orr called attention to the "commodious building" commanding a picturesque view of Columbia and the valleys of the Congaree, Broad, and Saluda rivers. Known today as the Governor's Mansion, silver glints and flowing waters grace its patio.

Opposite:

Toffee Pecan Brownies

Raspberry-Glazed Strawberries

Almond Meringue Torte with Lemon Curd and Hazelnuts

Company Carrot Cake

APPLE DUMPLINGS
WITH HONEY VANILLA SAUCE

To prepare Honey Vanilla Sauce, combine 1¹/₂ cups sugar, 1¹/₂ cups water, 1 vanilla bean (split and scraped), zest of 1 orange, zest of 2 lemons and 3 whole cloves in a saucepan. Cook over high heat until the sugar dissolves and the vanilla scrapings are dispersed, whisking constantly. Bring to a boil. Boil for 5 minutes; do not stir. Strain into a bowl. Let the sauce stand until cool. Stir in 1¹/₂ tablespoons honey.

This dessert takes a little extra time but the results are well worth the effort.

4 Granny Smith apples

¹/₂ cup butter, softened

¹/₄ cup packed light brown sugar

¹/₄ cup almond paste

1 tablespoon sugar

1 egg and 1 egg yolk

1 tablespoon finely grated orange zest

1 teaspoon almond extract

6 tablespoons cake flour

¹/₄ teaspoon baking powder

¹/₄ cup chopped almonds

¹/₂ apple, peeled, grated

¹/₂ cup coarsely chopped dried fruit of choice

1 pound phyllo pastry

1 cup clarified butter

Honey Vanilla Sauce (at left)

Confectioners' sugar

Toasted almonds

- Peel the 4 apples and cut into halves. Arrange the apples cut side down on a baking sheet.

- Heat ¹/₄ cup of the butter in a saucepan until melted. Brush the apples with the butter. Sprinkle with the brown sugar.

- Broil until light brown but firm. Let stand until cool.

- Beat the remaining ¹/₄ cup butter, almond paste and sugar in a mixer bowl until light and fluffy. Add the egg, egg yolk, orange zest and almond extract.

- Beat until blended. Stir in the cake flour and baking powder. Fold in the almonds, grated apple and dried fruit.

- Layer 4 sheets of the phyllo pastry on a work surface, brushing each sheet with some of the clarified butter. Cut the layers into halves.

- Place 1 apple half cut side up on each half. Spread each apple half with ¹/₈ of the almond mixture. Bring the edges of the pastry together in the middle. Clinch tightly just above the filling, leaving a flowery top. Place on a baking sheet. Repeat the procedure with the remaining phyllo pastry, clarified butter, apples and almond mixture.

- Bake at 400 degrees until light brown. Drizzle each dumpling with Honey Vanilla Sauce and sprinkle with confectioners' sugar and toasted almonds.

Eight Servings

ALI'S CHOCOLATE SILK DESSERT WITH RASPBERRY SAUCE

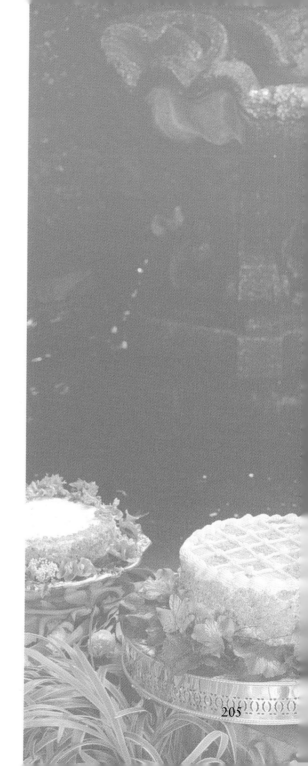

Raspberry Sauce

2 (10-ounce) packages frozen raspberries, thawed

2 tablespoons superfine sugar, or to taste

2 tablespoons framboise or kirsch (optional)

1 tablespoon lemon juice, or to taste

Chocolate Silk Dessert

16 ounces semisweet chocolate chips

3/4 cup butter, softened

4 eggs, lightly beaten

1 tablespoon sugar

1 tablespoon flour

Crème fraîche

Sprigs of mint

- For the sauce, process the raspberries in a food processor until puréed.

- Press the purée through a sieve into a bowl to remove the seeds. Stir in the sugar, framboise and lemon juice.

- Store, covered, in the refrigerator until serving time.

- For the dessert, grease a 9-inch round baking pan; line with foil.

- Heat the chocolate chips and butter in a double boiler until blended, stirring frequently.

- Combine the eggs and sugar in a double boiler. Heat just until warm, stirring frequently and being careful not to cook the eggs. Beat for 5 minutes or until tripled in volume. Stir in the flour. Add the chocolate mixture and mix well. Spoon into the prepared pan.

- Bake at 400 to 425 degrees for 15 minutes.

- Let stand until cool. Freeze, covered, for 8 to 10 hours.

- Let stand at room temperature for 20 minutes before serving. Serve with the sauce. Garnish with crème fraîche and sprigs of fresh mint.

Six to Eight Servings

GERMAN CHOCOLATE CHEESECAKE

Hampton Street Vineyard in Columbia is known for its German Chocolate Cheesecake.

Crust

Chocolate wafers, crushed

2 to 3 tablespoons (about) melted butter

Cheesecake Filling

24 ounces cream cheese, softened

1 cup sugar

4 eggs

3 egg yolks

Topping

3/4 cup evaporated milk

3/4 cup sugar

2 egg yolks

2 tablespoons butter

2 tablespoons semisweet chocolate

1 1/2 cups shredded coconut

1 cup chopped pecans

- For the crust, combine the chocolate wafer crumbs and butter in a bowl and mix well. Pat over the bottom and up the side of a 10-inch springform pan.

- For the filling, beat the cream cheese, sugar, eggs and egg yolks in a mixer bowl until light and fluffy. Spoon into the prepared pan.

- Bake at 350 degrees for 1 hour or until set. Turn off the oven.

- Let stand in the oven with the door slightly ajar until the cheesecake is room temperature. Chill in the refrigerator.

- For the topping, whisk the evaporated milk, sugar and egg yolks in a saucepan until blended. Add the butter and chocolate.

- Cook over medium heat for 5 minutes or until thickened, stirring constantly; do not boil. Stir in the coconut and pecans.

- Let stand until cool. Spread over the chilled cheesecake.

- Chill until serving time. Store in the refrigerator.

Sixteen Servings

HEATH BAR CHEESECAKE

Crust

2¹/2 cups vanilla wafers

¹/2 cup melted butter

¹/4 to ¹/2 cup pecans

Cheesecake Filling

24 ounces cream cheese, softened

1 (14-ounce) can sweetened condensed milk

3 eggs

2 teaspoons vanilla extract

4 Heath candy bars, coarsely crushed

- For the crust, process the vanilla wafers, melted butter and pecans in a food processor until finely ground.

- Press the crumb mixture over the bottom and up the side of a 10-inch springform pan.

- Chill in the refrigerator.

- For the filling, beat the cream cheese in a mixer bowl until light and fluffy. Add the condensed milk.

- Beat at medium speed until smooth, scraping the bowl occasionally. Add the eggs and vanilla.

- Beat until blended. Stir in the crushed Heath bars. Spoon into the chilled crust.

- Bake at 300 degrees for 1 hour or until set.

- Let stand until cool. Chill until serving time. Store in the refrigerator.

Sixteen Servings

DOT-DOT'S PEACH COBBLER

4 cups sliced peeled peaches

Lemon juice

1 cup sugar

1 cup self-rising flour

1 egg

¹/2 cup melted butter

- Toss the peaches with lemon juice in a bowl. Spoon into an 8x8-inch baking dish.

- Combine the sugar, flour and egg in a bowl and mix well. Spread over the peaches. Drizzle with the butter.

- Bake at 350 degrees for 30 minutes.

- Substitute apples, blueberries or blackberries for the peaches for variety.

Eight Servings

ORANGE ESPRESSO FLAN

1 cup sugar

1/4 cup water

1/2 teaspoon fresh lemon juice

4 eggs

2 egg yolks

3 1/2 teaspoons instant espresso powder

1 1/2 teaspoons vanilla extract

3 cups whole milk

1/3 cup sugar

1 cinnamon stick

1 tablespoon grated orange peel

- Arrange six 3/4-cup custard cups in a heavy baking pan.
- Combine 1 cup sugar, water and lemon juice in a saucepan and mix well. Cook over medium-low heat until the sugar dissolves, stirring constantly. Bring to a boil.
- Boil until the syrup turns a deep amber in color, brushing down the side of the pan with a pastry brush dipped in water and occasionally swirling the pan; do not stir. Spoon into the custard cups. Let stand until cool.
- Whisk the eggs, egg yolks, espresso powder and vanilla in a bowl until blended.
- Combine the whole milk, 1/3 cup sugar, cinnamon stick and orange peel in a saucepan. Bring to a boil, stirring occasionally. Remove from heat.
- Stir a small amount of the hot milk mixture into the egg mixture; stir the egg mixture into the hot milk mixture. Strain into a bowl. Ladle into the prepared custard cups.
- Add hot water to the baking pan to reach halfway up the sides of the custard cups.
- Bake at 350 degrees for 40 minutes or until set. Remove the custard cups from the water. Let stand until cool. Chill, covered with plastic wrap, for 8 to 10 hours.
- Loosen the custard by running a sharp knife around the sides of the custard cups. Dip the cups into a bowl of hot water for 15 seconds. Invert onto dessert plates, allowing the caramel to drizzle down the sides of the custards.

Six Servings

Blueberry Gingerbread
With Lemon Sauce

This unusual gingerbread is delicious with or without the Lemon Sauce.

3 cups flour

1 tablespoon cinnamon

2 teaspoons baking soda

1 teaspoon ground cloves

1 teaspoon ginger

3/4 teaspoon salt

1 1/2 cups sugar

1 cup vegetable oil

1 cup unsulfured light
    molasses

1/2 cup water

2 eggs

1 tablespoon minced peeled
    gingerroot

1/2 cup fresh or dried
    blueberries

1/4 cup chopped crystallized
    ginger

1/4 cup chopped golden
    raisins

Lemon Sauce (at right)

- Sift the flour, cinnamon, baking soda, cloves, ginger and salt into a bowl and mix well.

- Combine the sugar, oil, molasses, water, eggs and gingerroot in a bowl and mix well. Stir in the blueberries, crystallized ginger and raisins. Add the dry ingredients and mix well. Spoon into a buttered and floured 10-inch springform pan.

- Bake at 350 degrees for 1 hour or until a knife inserted in the center comes out clean.

- Cool in the pan on a wire rack for 1 hour. The gingerbread may fall in the center. Run a sharp knife around the side of the pan to loosen. Remove the side of the pan. Slice and serve warm or at room temperature with the hot Lemon Sauce.

- May be prepared 1 day in advance and stored, covered with foil, in the refrigerator. Bring to room temperature before serving.

Ten Servings

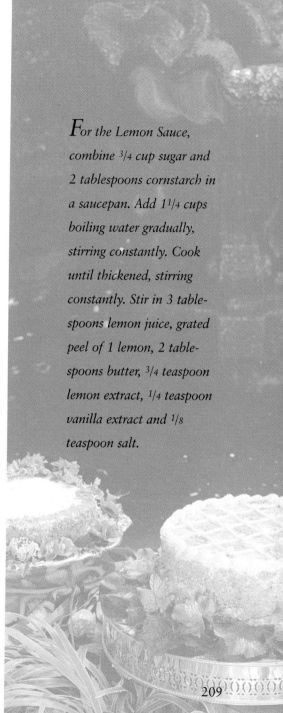

For the Lemon Sauce, combine 3/4 cup sugar and 2 tablespoons cornstarch in a saucepan. Add 1 1/4 cups boiling water gradually, stirring constantly. Cook until thickened, stirring constantly. Stir in 3 tablespoons lemon juice, grated peel of 1 lemon, 2 tablespoons butter, 3/4 teaspoon lemon extract, 1/4 teaspoon vanilla extract and 1/8 teaspoon salt.

CARAMEL ICE CREAM

1¹/4 *cups sugar*

4 *teaspoons flour*

¹/8 *teaspoon salt*

4 *cups milk*

2 *egg yolks, lightly
beaten*

2 *cups whipping cream*

1 *teaspoon vanilla
extract*

2 *cups sugar*

1 *cup hot water*

- Combine 1¹/4 cups sugar, flour and salt in a double boiler and mix well. Stir in ¹/2 cup of the milk. Add the egg yolks and remaining 3¹/2 cups milk and mix well.

- Cook over boiling water until thickened, stirring frequently. Remove from heat. Stir in the whipping cream and vanilla.

- Chill, covered, in the refrigerator.

- Heat 2 cups sugar in a cast-iron skillet over medium heat until melted, stirring constantly. Add the hot water, stirring constantly. Stir into the milk mixture. Pour into an ice cream freezer container.

- Freeze using manufacturer's directions.

Six Servings

PUDDING POPS FOR KIDS AND PARENTS

1¹/2 *cups cold milk*

1 *(4-ounce) package any
flavor instant pudding
mix*

1 *cup whipped topping*

¹/2 *cup mashed banana*

- Whisk the milk and pudding mix in a bowl until blended. Fold in the whipped topping. Stir in the banana gently.

- Spoon into six 5-ounce paper or plastic cups. Insert a wooden popsicle stick in the center of each cup.

- Freeze until firm.

- May substitute crumbled chocolate sandwich cookies, miniature marshmallows, miniature chocolate chips or chopped nuts for the banana.

Six Servings

AMARETTO BREAD PUDDING

Carmella Roche at Columbia's Villa Tronco was most generous to share this specialty recipe.

Bread Pudding

2 tablespoons butter

1 loaf French bread

4 cups half-and-half

1 1/2 cups sugar

3 eggs

2 tablespoons almond extract

3/4 cup golden raisins

3/4 cup sliced almonds

Amaretto Sauce

1/2 cup butter

1 cup confectioners' sugar

1 egg, beaten

6 tablespoons amaretto

• Grease a 3-quart baking dish with the butter.

• For the bread pudding, tear the bread into bite-size pieces. Place in a large bowl. Pour the half-and-half over the bread.

• Let stand for 1 hour.

• Beat the sugar, eggs and flavoring in a bowl until blended. Stir into the bread mixture. Fold in the raisins and almonds. Spoon into the prepared baking dish.

• Bake at 350 degrees for 50 minutes.

• Cool in the baking dish on a wire rack. Cut into squares.

• For the sauce, heat the butter in a saucepan until melted. Stir in the confectioners' sugar.

• Cook over low heat until the sugar dissolves, stirring constantly. Remove from heat.

• Stir a small amount of the hot mixture into the egg; stir the egg into the hot mixture. Add the amaretto and mix well.

• Drizzle the warm sauce over the bread pudding.

Fifteen Servings

Serve Grand Marnier Dip with assorted fresh fruit for a quick and easy dessert. Combine 3 egg yolks, 1/2 cup sugar and 1/4 teaspoon salt in a saucepan. Cook over medium heat for 2 to 3 minutes or until the sugar dissolves, stirring constantly. Remove from heat. Stir in 1/4 cup Grand Marnier. Cool. Beat 2 cups whipping cream until stiff peaks form. Fold into the Grand Marnier mixture. Chill, covered, for 1 to 2 hours before serving.

BREAD PUDDING WITH WHISKEY SAUCE

This dessert, originally devised as a way to use leftover stale bread, has become one of the most popular New Orleans classics.

Bread Pudding

1 cup sugar

1/2 cup butter, softened

2 cups whipping cream

5 eggs, beaten

1/4 cup raisins (optional)

1 tablespoon vanilla extract

1/8 teaspoon cinnamon

12 slices fresh or dry French bread, 1 inch thick

Whiskey Sauce

1 cup whipping cream

1/2 cup sugar

1/4 cup bourbon

- For the bread pudding, beat the sugar and butter in a mixer bowl until creamy. Stir in the whipping cream, eggs, raisins, vanilla and cinnamon. Pour into a 9x9-inch baking pan, 1 3/4 inches deep. Arrange the bread slices cut side down in the egg mixture.

- Let stand for 5 minutes to soak up some of the liquid. Turn the bread over.

- Let stand for 10 minutes longer. Press the bread lightly so that most of the bread is covered by the egg mixture, being careful not to break the bread apart.

- Place the baking pan in a larger baking pan. Add enough water to the larger baking pan to come within 1/2 inch of the top of the smaller pan. Cover with foil.

- Bake at 350 degrees for 45 to 50 minutes, removing the foil 10 minutes before the end of the cooking process. The pudding should be soft, not firm.

- For the sauce, beat the whipping cream in a mixer bowl until slightly thickened. Add the sugar.

- Beat until thickened. Whisk in the bourbon.

- Serve with the warm bread pudding.

Six Servings

TIPSY PUDDING

This old-fashioned English dessert has become a special Christmas dessert in the South.

4 egg yolks, lightly beaten

1/4 cup sugar

1/8 teaspoon salt

2 cups whole milk, scalded

1 teaspoon sherry

1 small pound cake

Slivered almonds or pecan
    pieces

1/4 cup (about) sherry

1 cup whipping cream

1 tablespoon (or more) sugar

1/2 teaspoon vanilla extract
    or sherry

Red maraschino cherries

- Combine the egg yolks, 1/4 cup sugar and salt in a double boiler and mix well. Add the scalded milk gradually, stirring constantly.

- Cook over hot water until the mixture begins to thicken, stirring frequently. Remove from heat. Add 1 teaspoon sherry and mix well.

- Tear the pound cake into bite-size pieces.

- Line a 1-quart glass or crystal bowl with the cake pieces. Fill the center with the remaining cake pieces. Sprinkle with almonds; drizzle with 1/4 cup sherry. Spoon the custard over the prepared layers.

- Chill for 6 hours or longer.

- Beat the whipping cream in a mixer bowl until soft peaks form. Add 1 tablespoon sugar and vanilla and mix well. Spread the chilled layers with the whipped cream 1 hour before serving. Garnish with drained maraschino cherries.

- May substitute 2 packages ladyfingers for the pound cake.

Eight Servings

To prepare the Blueberry Sauce, combine 1 pint fresh blueberries, 1/2 cup sugar and 2 lemon slices in a nonreactive saucepan. Cook over medium heat for 5 minutes or until the blueberries give off their juices but keep their shape. Discard the lemon slices.

FROZEN LEMON SOUFFLE WITH BLUEBERRY SAUCE

1 1/2 teaspoons unflavored gelatin

1/2 cup lemon juice

1/3 cup sugar

3 egg yolks, chilled

Grated zest of 1 lemon

3 egg whites, chilled

1/2 teaspoon lemon juice

1/3 cup sugar

1 cup whipping cream, whipped

Blueberry Sauce (at left)

- Soften the gelatin in 1/2 cup lemon juice. Pour into a double boiler. Cook over hot water until the mixture is warm and the gelatin dissolves, stirring constantly. Remove from heat.

- Beat 1/3 cup sugar and egg yolks in a mixer bowl until thick and pale yellow. Fold the lemon mixture into the egg yolk mixture. Return the mixture to the double boiler. Cook over medium heat for 8 minutes or until the mixture coats the back of a wooden spoon, whisking constantly. Fold in the lemon zest.

- Let stand, covered with plastic wrap, until cool.

- Beat the egg whites in a chilled mixer bowl until frothy. Add 1/2 teaspoon lemon juice and beat until blended.

- Add 1/3 cup sugar gradually, beating constantly until glossy stiff peaks form. Blend a large spoonful of the meringue into the cooled lemon mixture. Fold the remaining meringue into the lemon mixture. Fold in the whipped cream. Do not overblend; streaks of the meringue should be apparent. Spoon into a 1 1/2-quart soufflé dish or into parfait glasses.

- Freeze for 2 hours. Serve the soufflé with warm or room-temperature Blueberry Sauce. May allow the soufflé to stand at room temperature for 30 minutes before serving.

- Use chilled mixer bowls and beaters when preparing the meringue and whipped cream.

Four to Five Servings

MACADAMIA CREAM TARTS
WITH PAPAYA APRICOT GLAZE

Cookbook author Susan Fuller Slack contributed this delicious dessert recipe.

Tart Shells

1 recipe (2-crust) pie pastry
   or 2 all ready pie pastries

Macadamia Cream Filling

8 ounces cream cheese,
   softened

3/4 cup confectioners' sugar

1 to 2 tablespoons dark rum
   or 1 teaspoon vanilla
   extract

1 cup whipping cream

1/3 cup finely chopped
   macadamia nuts

Papaya Apricot Glaze

1 cup apricot preserves

1 tablespoon fresh lemon
   juice

1 red papaya or mango or
   2 peaches

- For the shells, roll the pie pastry on a lightly floured surface. Cut six 5 1/2-inch circles with a cutter. Press into six 4-inch French tart pans with removable bottoms. Prick the pastry with a fork. Chill in the refrigerator.

- Bake the pastry shells at 350 degrees for 20 minutes or until golden brown.

- Let stand until cool. Remove the tart shells.

- For the filling, beat the cream cheese, confectioners' sugar and rum in a mixer bowl until smooth.

- Beat the whipping cream in a mixer bowl until stiff peaks form. Fold into the cream cheese mixture. Fold in the macadamia nuts. Spoon into the cooled tart shells.

- Chill for 1 hour.

- For the glaze, heat the preserves in a saucepan until warm. Process in a blender until puréed.

- Combine the puréed preserves and lemon juice in a bowl and mix well. Spoon over the top of each tart.

- Peel the papaya and cut into halves. Remove the seeds, reserving several. Cut each papaya half diagonally into thin slices.

- Arrange 3 or 4 papaya slices in a fan design on top of each tart. Sprinkle with a few of the reserved seeds.

Six Servings

S'MORES ON THE GRILL

24 good-quality graham
crackers

1¹/₄ (3-ounce) bars good-
quality bittersweet
chocolate, broken into
36 pieces

12 marshmallows

- Place 12 graham crackers on twelve 8x8-inch sheets of foil. Arrange 3 pieces of chocolate in the shape of a triangle on each graham cracker.

- Toast the marshmallows over hot coals until golden brown. Place 1 marshmallow on top of each chocolate triangle. Top with the remaining graham crackers. Seal the foil to enclose.

- Place the foil packets on a grill rack 5 to 6 inches above the heat source.

- Heat for 1 minute on each side or until the chocolate melts.

Four Servings

RASPBERRY-GLAZED STRAWBERRIES

For an elegant dessert, serve a pyramid of ruby-glazed strawberries in a silver bowl sprinkled with pistachios. Serve with a dollop of whipped cream.

1 cup seedless raspberry
preserves

2 tablespoons Grand
Marnier

2 pints large ripe
strawberries

- Cook the preserves in a saucepan over low heat just until heated through, stirring frequently. Remove from heat. Stir in the liqueur. Cool slightly.

- Dip the strawberries lightly into the glaze. Tap the excess glaze into the saucepan.

- Arrange the strawberries in a crystal bowl.

- May arrange the strawberries in a bowl and drizzle with the glaze.

- For variety, substitute crème de fraise or framboise for the Grand Marnier.

Four to Five Servings

QUEEN OF TRIFLES

Time consuming, but worth every single minute.

24 macaroons

Bourbon

1/2 cup sliced almonds

Rose water

1 cup whipping cream

1 cup milk

1 cup sugar

3 eggs, lightly beaten

1 teaspoon vanilla
extract

2 cups whipping cream

1/2 teaspoon vanilla
extract

1 (3-ounce) package
ladyfingers

Maraschino cherries

- Soak the macaroons in enough bourbon to cover in a bowl for 8 to 10 hours. Soak the almonds in enough rose water to cover in a bowl for 8 to 10 hours; drain.

- Scald 1 cup whipping cream and milk in a double boiler. Remove from heat. Add the sugar and mix well. Stir a small amount of the hot mixture into the eggs; stir the eggs into the hot mixture.

- Cook the egg mixture until thickened, stirring constantly. Stir in 1 teaspoon vanilla. Fold in the macaroon mixture.

- Beat 2 cups whipping cream and 1/2 teaspoon vanilla in a mixer bowl until soft peaks form.

- Line a trifle bowl with the ladyfingers. Layer the macaroon mixture, almonds and whipped cream 1/2 at a time in the bowl. Top with cherries.

- Chill, covered, until serving time.

Ten to Twelve Servings

TIRAMISU

4 cups water

1/4 cup instant espresso
powder

Dark rum or brandy
to taste

24 ladyfingers

2 cups whipping cream

1 cup sugar

1 pound ricotta cheese or
mascarpone cheese

2 tablespoons baking
cocoa

- Bring the water to a boil in a saucepan. Remove from heat. Add the espresso, stirring until dissolved. Stir in rum or brandy.

- Pour over the ladyfingers in a bowl.

- Beat the whipping cream in a chilled mixer bowl until soft peaks form. Add 1/2 cup of the sugar and mix well. Add the cheese and remaining 1/2 cup sugar, beating until smooth.

- Layer the ladyfingers and ricotta cheese mixture alternately in a glass bowl until all of the ingredients are used.

- Chill, covered, for 8 hours or longer. Sprinkle with the baking cocoa just before serving.

- May substitute chocolate shavings or cinnamon for the baking cocoa.

Twelve to Fifteen Servings

ALMOND MERINGUE TORTE WITH LEMON CURD AND HAZELNUTS

In France, layer cakes are often made with ground nuts. Made with almonds, the layers are called fonds à succès. The layers can be made a week in advance and sealed in plastic wrap to preserve freshness. Buttercream is the traditional filling and frosting but for a quicker version try using sweetened, flavored whipped cream. Embellish each slice of this elegant dessert with one of the Raspberry-Glazed Strawberries, page 216.

Almond Meringues

1/3 cup sifted cornstarch

1/4 cup finely ground
   blanched almonds

3 egg whites, at room
   temperature

1 teaspoon vanilla extract

1/8 teaspoon cream of tartar

1/8 teaspoon salt

3/4 cup sugar

Torte

3/4 cup lemon curd

French Buttercream (at left)

1 1/2 cups finely chopped
   hazelnuts or almonds,
   toasted

- For the meringues, line 2 baking sheets with nonstick parchment paper. Draw a 9-inch circle on each sheet.

- Mix the cornstarch and almonds in a bowl.

- Beat the egg whites, vanilla, cream of tartar and salt in a mixer bowl until soft peaks form. Add the sugar gradually, beating constantly until stiff peaks form. Fold in the almond mixture.

- Spread 1/2 of the meringue inside each circle and smooth, or pipe the meringue mixture from a pastry tube fitted with a 3/8-inch tip.

- Bake 1 meringue at a time at 325 degrees for 25 minutes or until dry and slightly crisp. Transfer the meringues with a spatula to a flat surface to cool.

- For the torte, arrange 1 meringue on a serving platter. Spread with the lemon curd. Top with the remaining meringue. Spread French Buttercream over the side.

- Hold the torte from the bottom over a large pan and gently pat the hazelnuts over the side. Return the torte to the serving platter. Spread the top with the remaining French Buttercream. Chill for several hours before serving. May store in the refrigerator for several days.

Ten to Twelve Servings

Prepare French Buttercream by bringing 10 tablespoons sugar and 2 1/2 tablespoons water to a boil in a saucepan over medium-high heat. Boil until the sugar dissolves, stirring once or twice. Beat 4 egg yolks in a mixer bowl until blended. Add the hot sugar syrup in a fine stream, beating constantly until blended. Beat for 5 minutes or until thick and pale yellow. Let cool. Add 1 cup softened unsalted butter gradually, beating until blended. Beat in 2 tablespoons vanilla extract or fruit brandy. May be stored, covered, in the refrigerator for several days.

MERINGUES WITH LEMON SAUCE

Lemon Sauce

Grated peel of 2 lemons

1 1/2 cups sugar

6 tablespoons flour

2 cups hot water

3 egg yolks, beaten

Juice of 2 lemons

1 teaspoon butter

1/8 teaspoon salt

Meringues

3 egg whites, at room
    temperature

1 teaspoon vanilla extract

1/4 teaspoon cream of tartar

1/8 teaspoon salt

1 cup sugar

Ice cream

Whipped cream

Sprigs of fresh mint

- For the sauce, combine the lemon peel, sugar and flour in a double boiler and mix well. Add just enough of the hot water to moisten and mix well. Stir in the remaining hot water, egg yolks, lemon juice, butter and salt.

- Cook until thickened, stirring constantly.

- Let stand until cool. Store, covered, in the refrigerator.

- Serve chilled or at room temperature.

- For the meringues, line 2 baking sheets with parchment paper. Draw eight 3-inch circles on the parchment paper.

- Beat the egg whites, vanilla, cream of tartar and salt in a mixer bowl until soft peaks form. Add the sugar gradually, beating constantly until stiff peaks form. Spread over the circles using the back of a spoon to shape into shells and make depressions in the center.

- Bake at 250 degrees for 1 hour.

- Let stand until cool. Peel off the parchment paper.

- Fill each meringue with ice cream and drizzle with the sauce. Top with whipped cream and sprigs of mint.

Eight Servings

When you need sugar to dissolve quickly, such as in cold, unsweetened iced tea or when preparing caramel, use superfine sugar, a finely granulated form of refined sugar. It can also help prevent that unpleasant grainy texture in foods in which you must incorporate large amounts of sugar, such as meringues. Superfine sugar may be purchased at your local supermarket or prepared at home from regular granulated sugar. Just process the sugar in a food processor or blender, or in a mini-chopper for smaller quantities.

TWO-CHOCOLATE NUT TORTE

Store chocolate in a cool, dry environment such as a cupboard or pantry. Do not store in the refrigerator, as the chocolate will turn white.

Raspberry Sauce

2 tablespoons sugar

1 tablespoon water

1 (14-ounce) jar raspberry jam

1/2 cup sweet red wine

Torte

1 1/3 cups sugar

1/2 cup water

2 cups semisweet chocolate chips, chopped

1 cup unsalted butter

5 eggs, at room temperature, beaten

1/2 cup chopped pistachios

6 ounces white chocolate

4 to 6 tablespoons cream

- For the sauce, bring the sugar and water to a boil in a saucepan; reduce heat.

- Simmer until of a syrupy consistency, stirring frequently. Stir in the jam and red wine. Bring to a simmer, stirring frequently. Strain into a bowl. Chill, covered, until serving time.

- For the torte, butter a 9-inch round baking pan. Line the bottom with parchment paper.

- Bring the sugar and water to a boil in a saucepan; reduce heat. Simmer, stirring frequently. Add the chocolate chips and mix well.

- Simmer until smooth, stirring constantly. Add the butter gradually and mix well. Simmer until the butter melts, stirring constantly. Stir a small amount of the hot mixture into the eggs; stir the eggs gradually into the hot mixture. Spoon into the prepared pan. Sprinkle with the pistachios. Place the baking pan in a larger pan with water to reach halfway up the side of the baking pan.

- Bake at 350 degrees for 25 to 30 minutes. Let stand until cool.

- Heat the white chocolate and cream in a double boiler over simmering water until blended, stirring frequently. Drizzle over the baked layer.

- Chill for 6 hours or until firm. Loosen the torte by running a knife dipped in hot water around the edge.

- Spoon the sauce onto a serving platter; top with the torte.

Twelve Servings

Banana Cake With Cream Cheese Frosting

Cake

1 1/2 cups butter, softened

1 1/2 cups sugar

3 eggs

1 1/2 cups mashed ripe
    bananas

2 1/2 cups plus 2 tablespoons
    unbleached flour

1 tablespoon baking soda

3/4 teaspoon salt

1/2 cup buttermilk

1 1/2 teaspoons vanilla extract

Cream Cheese Frosting

16 ounces cream cheese,
    softened

6 tablespoons unsalted
    butter, softened

3 cups confectioners' sugar,
    sifted

1 teaspoon vanilla extract

Juice of 1/2 lemon (optional)

- For the cake, beat the butter and sugar in a mixer bowl until light and fluffy, scraping the bowl occasionally. Add the eggs 1 at a time, beating well after each addition. Stir in the bananas.

- Sift the flour, baking soda and salt together. Add to the creamed mixture, stirring until blended. Add the buttermilk and vanilla and mix for 1 minute. Spoon the batter into two 9-inch greased and floured cake pans.

- Bake on the middle oven rack at 350 degrees for 25 to 30 minutes or until the layers test done.

- Cool in the pans on a wire rack for 10 minutes. Invert onto the wire rack.

- Let stand for 2 hours.

- For the frosting, beat the cream cheese and butter in a mixer bowl until creamy, scraping the bowl occasionally.

- Add the confectioners' sugar gradually, beating constantly until of spreading consistency. Stir in the vanilla and lemon juice.

- Spread the frosting between the layers and over the top and side of the cake.

Twelve Servings

COMPANY CARROT CAKE

3 cups flour

2¹/₂ cups sugar

¹/₂ cup packed light brown sugar

1 tablespoon baking soda

2 teaspoons cinnamon

1 teaspoon nutmeg

1 teaspoon salt

¹/₄ teaspoon allspice

1¹/₂ cups corn oil

4 eggs

1 tablespoon vanilla extract

2 cups grated carrots

1 cup drained crushed pineapple

1 tablespoon grated orange peel

Cream Cheese Frosting (at left)

2 cups finely chopped pecans, toasted

¹/₄ cup pineapple preserves

¹/₄ cup orange marmalade

- Grease and flour two 9-inch round cake pans 2 inches in depth or two 10-inch round cake pans.

- Sift the flour, sugar, brown sugar, baking soda, cinnamon, nutmeg, salt and allspice into a bowl and mix well.

- Whisk the corn oil, eggs and vanilla in a bowl until blended. Add the carrots, pineapple and orange peel and mix well. Stir into the flour mixture. Spoon the batter into the prepared pans.

- Bake at 350 degrees for 35 to 40 minutes or until the layers test done.

- Cool in the pans on a wire rack for 30 minutes. Invert onto the wire rack to cool completely.

- Reserve 2 cups of the Cream Cheese Frosting. Place 1 cake layer on a serving platter. Spread with 1 cup of the remaining frosting. Top with the remaining cake layer. Spread the side and top of the cake with the remaining frosting. Pat 1¹/₂ cups of the pecans around the side of the cake.

- Spoon the reserved frosting into a pastry bag fitted with a star tip. Pipe horizontal lines 1³/₄ inches apart over the top of the cake. Pipe similar lines running vertically. Pipe a decorative edge with the remaining frosting.

- Combine the pineapple preserves and orange marmalade in a bowl and mix well. Spoon the preserves mixture and remaining pecans into alternating sections of the lattice design.

Twelve Servings

CHOCOLATE CAKE

This is the best low-fat cholesterol-free cake. Guests do not believe it is actually healthy!

1 cup flour

2/3 cup sugar

1/4 cup baking cocoa

3/4 teaspoon baking soda

1/2 cup skim milk

1/2 cup orange juice

1/3 cup canola oil

1 teaspoon grated orange peel (optional)

2 tablespoons confectioners' sugar

- Combine the flour, sugar, baking cocoa and baking soda in a bowl and mix well.

- Combine the skim milk, orange juice, canola oil and orange peel in a bowl and mix well. Stir into the flour mixture. Spoon the batter into an 8- or 9-inch cake pan sprayed with nonstick cooking spray.

- Bake at 350 degrees for 30 to 35 minutes or until a wooden pick inserted in the center comes out clean.

- Cool in the pan on a wire rack. Sprinkle with the confectioners' sugar just before serving.

- May sift confectioners' sugar over a fancy doily for a design.

Six Servings

BLUEBERRY POUND CAKE

2 cups fresh blueberries

1/4 cup flour

2 tablespoons butter

1/4 cup sugar

1 cup butter

2 cups sugar

4 eggs

1 teaspoon vanilla extract

2 3/4 cups flour

1 teaspoon baking powder

1/2 teaspoon salt

- Combine the blueberries and 1/4 cup flour in a bowl and mix gently.

- Spread 2 tablespoons butter over the bottom and up the side of a 10-inch springform pan. Sprinkle with 1/4 cup sugar.

- Beat 1 cup butter in a mixer bowl until creamy. Add 2 cups sugar gradually, beating until light and fluffy. Add the eggs 1 at a time, beating well after each addition. Beat in the vanilla.

- Combine 2 3/4 cups flour, baking powder and salt in a bowl and mix well. Add to the creamed mixture gradually, beating until blended. Fold in the blueberries. Spoon into the prepared pan.

- Bake at 325 degrees for 70 minutes or until the cake tests done.

- Cool in the pan on a wire rack for 10 minutes. Remove to a wire rack to cool completely.

Sixteen Servings

Brown Sugar Pound Cake

Cake

3 cups flour

1 teaspoon baking powder

1 cup butter, softened

1/2 cup vegetable shortening

1 cup sugar

1 (1-pound) package light
    brown sugar

5 eggs

1 cup milk

1 cup chopped pecans

1 teaspoon vanilla extract

Praline Sauce

2 cups dark corn syrup

1/3 cup sugar

1/3 cup boiling water

1 cup chopped pecans or
    small pecan halves

- Spray a large tube pan with nonstick cooking spray and sprinkle lightly with flour.

- For the cake, mix 3 cups flour and baking powder in a bowl.

- Beat the butter and shortening in a mixer bowl until creamy, scraping the bowl occasionally. Add the sugar and brown sugar gradually, beating until light and fluffy. Add the eggs 1 at a time, beating well after each addition.

- Add 1 cup of the flour mixture and mix well. Add the milk and remaining flour mixture 1/2 at a time, ending with the flour mixture and beating well after each addition. Spoon into the prepared pan.

- Bake at 300 degrees for 1 3/4 hours or until a long wooden skewer inserted in the center comes out clean.

- Cool in the pan for 10 minutes. Invert onto a serving platter.

- For the sauce, combine the corn syrup, sugar, boiling water and pecans in a saucepan. Bring to a boil over medium heat, stirring frequently. Remove from heat.

- Serve hot or cold with the pound cake.

- Store leftovers, covered, in the refrigerator. Great accompaniment with ice cream.

Sixteen Servings

CHOCOLATE SOUR CREAM POUND CAKE

Delicious and so easy to prepare. Children love to make this cake.

1 (2-layer) package yellow cake mix

1 (4-ounce) package chocolate instant pudding mix

1 cup sour cream

2/3 cup vegetable oil

1/3 cup water

3 eggs, lightly beaten

1 cup miniature chocolate chips

1/2 cup sugar

1/4 cup water

2 tablespoons butter or margarine

1/2 cup ground pecans or shredded coconut

- Combine the cake mix, pudding mix, sour cream, oil, 1/3 cup water and eggs in a bowl, stirring just until moistened. Fold in the chocolate chips. Spoon into a bundt pan or an angel food cake pan sprayed with nonstick cooking spray.

- Bake at 350 degrees for 50 minutes or until the cake tests done.

- Cool in the pan for 10 minutes. Invert onto a serving platter.

- Bring the sugar, 1/4 cup water and butter to a boil in a saucepan, stirring frequently.

- Boil gently for 3 minutes, stirring occasionally.

- Cool for 2 minutes. Drizzle over the hot cake. Sprinkle with the pecans or coconut; press gently into the glaze.

- May allow the cake to cool before drizzling with the glaze.

Sixteen Servings

POPPY SEED CAKES

Cakes

3 cups flour

2¹/4 cups sugar

1¹/2 cups milk

1 cup plus 2 tablespoons
   vegetable oil

3 eggs

1¹/2 tablespoons poppy seeds

1¹/2 teaspoons salt

1¹/2 teaspoons baking powder

1¹/2 teaspoons butter
   flavoring

1¹/2 teaspoons almond
   extract

1¹/2 teaspoons vanilla extract

Orange Glaze

³/4 cup sugar

¹/4 cup orange juice

¹/2 teaspoon butter flavoring

¹/2 teaspoon almond extract

¹/2 teaspoon vanilla extract

- For the cakes, combine the flour, sugar, milk, oil, eggs, poppy seeds, salt, baking powder and flavorings in a mixer bowl.

- Beat for 1 to 2 minutes or until mixed, scraping the bowl occasionally. Spoon into 2 lightly greased loaf pans, a tube pan or several miniature loaf pans.

- Bake at 350 degrees for 1 hour or until a wooden pick inserted in the center comes out clean.

- Cool in the pans for 5 minutes. Remove to a serving platter.

- For the glaze, combine the sugar, orange juice and flavorings in a saucepan.

- Cook until blended, stirring frequently. Drizzle the hot glaze over the warm loaves.

Sixteen Servings

CARAMEL HEAVENLIES

A good recipe for kids to prepare, but adults usually prefer it to eat.

12 double graham
  crackers

2 cups miniature
  marshmallows

3/4 cup butter

3/4 cup packed brown
  sugar

1 teaspoon cinnamon

1 teaspoon vanilla
  extract

1 cup sliced almonds

1 cup flaked coconut

- Arrange the graham crackers in a single layer in a 10x15-inch baking pan. Sprinkle with the marshmallows.

- Combine the butter, brown sugar and cinnamon in a saucepan.

- Cook over medium heat until the brown sugar dissolves, stirring constantly. Remove from heat. Stir in the vanilla. Drizzle over the marshmallows; sprinkle with the almonds and coconut.

- Bake at 350 degrees for 12 to 14 minutes or until light brown.

- Cool in the pan on a wire rack. Cut into 3-inch squares; cut each square into halves to form triangles.

- Store in an airtight container in the refrigerator for up to 2 weeks or freeze for up to 3 months.

Thirty Servings

PECAN PRALINES

3 cups sugar

1 cup buttermilk

1/2 cup light corn syrup

1 teaspoon baking soda

3 cups pecans

3 tablespoons margarine

1/2 teaspoon vanilla
  extract

- Combine the sugar, buttermilk, corn syrup and baking soda in a saucepan.

- Cook to 234 to 240 degrees on a candy thermometer, soft-ball stage, stirring frequently. Stir in the pecans just before removing from heat. Remove from heat.

- Add the margarine and vanilla and mix well. Stir until the mixture begins to thicken and cool slightly.

- Drop by spoonfuls onto greased waxed paper. Let stand until firm.

- Store in an airtight container.

Fifty Pralines

ALMOND MACAROONS

2 (7-ounce) cans almond
    paste

1 cup sugar

2 cups sifted confectioners'
    sugar

1/2 cup egg whites

2 teaspoons rose water,
    vanilla extract or liqueur

1/8 teaspoon salt

1 cup almond slivers, toasted,
    chopped

- Line 2 or 3 cookie sheets with parchment paper.

- Separate the almond paste into 1/4 cup portions. Place in a mixer bowl. Add the sugar.

- Turn the mixer on and off several times to draw the sugar into the mixture so it does not fly out of the bowl.

- Beat at low speed until the mixture forms coarse even crumbs. Add the confectioners' sugar. Beat at low speed for 1 minute. Beat at medium speed for 1 to 2 minutes or until smooth and the mixture begins to adhere to the side of the bowl, scraping the bowl occasionally. Add the egg whites, rose water and salt.

- Beat at medium speed until blended, scraping the bowl occasionally.

- Beat at medium-high speed for 2 minutes or until the mixture is light in texture and almost white in color. Add 1/2 of the almonds. Beat at low speed until combined.

- Use 2 tablespoons to shape the dough into small mounds on the prepared cookie sheets, leaving 2 inches between each mound. Sprinkle with the remaining almonds; press lightly.

- Bake at 325 degrees for 25 to 28 minutes or until puffed and light. The macaroons will feel soft but not wet.

- Cool on the cookie sheets on wire racks. Remove the cookies carefully from the parchment paper.

- Store in an airtight container at room temperature.

Two to Three Dozen Cookies

TOFFEE PECAN BROWNIES

Brownies

4 ounces unsweetened
  chocolate, chopped

1/2 cup unsalted butter

1 1/4 cups packed light brown
  sugar

1 tablespoon cinnamon

1/4 teaspoon salt

3 eggs

1 teaspoon vanilla extract

3/4 cup flour

1 cup chopped Heath candy
  bars

Brown Sugar Topping

1 cup packed light brown
  sugar

1/4 cup whipping cream

1 tablespoon unsalted butter

3/4 teaspoon vanilla extract

1/2 cup chopped pecans

- For the brownies, line an 8x8-inch baking pan with foil, extending foil over the sides.

- Combine the chocolate and butter in a saucepan.

- Cook over low heat until blended, stirring constantly.

- Cool for 5 minutes. Whisk in the brown sugar, cinnamon and salt. Add the eggs 1 at a time, whisking well after each addition. Stir in the vanilla. Whisk for 2 minutes or until smooth. Add the flour, whisking just until blended. Stir in the chopped candy bars. Spoon into the prepared pan, smoothing the surface.

- Bake at 325 degrees for 35 minutes or until a wooden pick inserted in the center comes out with a few moist crumbs attached.

- Cool in the pan on a wire rack.

- For the topping, combine the brown sugar, whipping cream and butter in a saucepan.

- Bring to a boil, whisking constantly until smooth. Remove from heat. Stir in the vanilla.

- Let stand for 10 minutes. Whisk until of spreading consistency. Stir in the pecans. Spread over the brownies.

- Let stand for 1 hour or until set. Serve cold or at room temperature.

- Store, covered, in the refrigerator.

- May be prepared 1 day in advance.

Sixteen Brownies

Having a chocolate emergency? Substitute a mixture of three tablespoons unsweetened baking cocoa and one tablespoon butter for one ounce of unsweetened chocolate.

Most home cooks are accustomed to using regular baking cocoa for baking and hot chocolate. Now, more and more grocery stores are carrying European-style or Dutch process cocoa, resulting in confusion over the difference between the two and which will render superior results. Untreated chocolate, like the cocoa most Americans are accustomed to, is slightly acidic. Dutch cocoa has been treated with an alkaline solution to raise its PH, thereby neutralizing the acidity of the cocoa.

(continued at right)

BEST-EVER BROWNIES

1 cup vegetable oil

5 tablespoons baking cocoa

4 eggs, lightly beaten

2 cups sugar

1¹/₂ cups sifted self-rising flour

2 teaspoons vanilla extract

2 cups chopped pecans

- Combine the oil and baking cocoa in a bowl and mix well. Stir in the eggs. Do not use an electric mixer. Add the sugar, self-rising flour and vanilla and mix well. Fold in the pecans.

- Spoon the batter into a greased 9x13-inch baking pan.

- Bake at 350 degrees for 30 to 35 minutes or until the brownies test done.

Three Dozen Brownies

BUTTERSCOTCH CREAM CHEESE BARS

These bars are worth every calorie and fat gram!

2 cups butterscotch chips

¹/₃ cup butter

2 cups graham cracker
   crumbs

1 cup chopped pecans

8 ounces cream cheese,
   softened

1 (14-ounce) can sweetened
   condensed milk

1 egg

1 teaspoon vanilla extract

- Combine the butterscotch chips and butter in
  a saucepan.
- Cook over low heat until smooth, stirring constantly.
  Remove from heat. Stir in the graham cracker crumbs
  and pecans.
- Press ¹/₂ of the crumb mixture over the bottom of a
  greased 9x13-inch baking pan.
- Beat the cream cheese in a mixer bowl until fluffy. Add
  the condensed milk, egg and vanilla.
- Beat until blended. Spread over the prepared layer. Top
  with the remaining crumb mixture.
- Bake at 350 degrees for 25 to 30 minutes or until a
  wooden pick inserted in the center comes out clean.
- Cool to room temperature on a wire rack. Chill,
  covered, in the refrigerator, before cutting into bars.

Two Dozen Bars

This results in a more mellow flavor and a darker color. Which to use? Dutch process cocoa produces better results in hot chocolate but generally does not make a better brownie or devils food cake. The harshness of natural cocoas is overcome by the higher sugar and fat content of brownies and cakes and delivers more flavor than the milder Dutch process cocoa. Keep using regular baking cocoa for baking, but give the European-style cocoa a try the next time you crave a cup of hot chocolate.

WHITE CHOCOLATE LACE OATMEAL COOKIES

1 3/4 cups cake flour

1 teaspoon baking soda

1 teaspoon cinnamon

1 teaspoon allspice

1 teaspoon salt

1 cup butter or margarine, softened

1 cup packed light brown sugar

1 cup sugar

2 eggs

1 teaspoon vanilla extract

3 cups old-fashioned rolled oats

1 cup broken pecans

6 ounces white chocolate

- Sift the cake flour, baking soda, cinnamon, allspice and salt into a bowl and mix well.

- Beat the butter, brown sugar and sugar in a mixer bowl until creamy, scraping the bowl occasionally. Add the eggs 1 at a time, beating well after each addition. Add the vanilla and mix well.

- Stir the flour mixture into the butter mixture. Fold in the oats and pecans.

- Drop by rounded tablespoonfuls onto a greased and floured cookie sheet.

- Bake at 350 degrees for 9 to 10 minutes or until light brown.

- Cool on the cookie sheet for 3 minutes. Remove to a wire rack.

- Heat the white chocolate in a double boiler over hot water until melted, stirring frequently. Drizzle over the top of each cookie in a lacy design.

Three Dozen Cookies

Oatmeal Cookies

1 cup vegetable
  shortening

1 cup packed brown
  sugar

1 cup sugar

2 eggs, beaten

1 teaspoon vanilla
  extract

1^1/$_2$ cups flour

1 teaspoon baking soda

1 teaspoon nutmeg

1 teaspoon cinnamon

1 teaspoon salt

3 cups rolled oats

1 cup chopped pecans

- Beat the shortening, brown sugar and sugar in a mixer bowl until creamy, scraping the bowl occasionally. Add the eggs and vanilla and beat well.

- Combine the flour, baking soda, nutmeg, cinnamon and salt in a bowl and mix well. Add to the creamed mixture gradually, mixing well after each addition. Fold in the oats and pecans.

- Drop by tablespoonfuls onto a nonstick cookie sheet; flatten slightly.

- Bake at 350 degrees for 8 to 10 minutes or until light brown.

- Cool on the cookie sheet for 2 minutes. Remove to a wire rack to cool completely.

Three Dozen Cookies

Luella's Cookies

1/2 cup butter

1 cup sugar

2 egg yolks

1^1/$_2$ cups flour

1 teaspoon baking
  powder

1/2 teaspoon salt

1 teaspoon vanilla
  extract

1 cup packed brown
  sugar

2 egg whites, beaten

1 cup chopped nuts

- Beat the butter and sugar in a mixer bowl until creamy, scraping the bowl occasionally. Add the egg yolks and beat well.

- Sift the flour, baking powder and salt together. Add to the creamed mixture and mix well. Stir in the vanilla. Spoon into an 8x10-inch baking pan.

- Bake at 325 degrees for 20 minutes or until the mixture rises.

- Spread the baked layer with a mixture of the brown sugar, egg whites and nuts.

- Bake until golden brown. Cool in the pan on a wire rack.

- Cut into bars with a sharp knife.

Three Dozen Bars

POUND CAKE COOKIES

This is a South Carolina State Fair winner.

1 cup sugar

1 cup butter

2 cups cake flour, sifted

1 egg yolk

1 teaspoon rum

1/2 teaspoon salt

1/2 teaspoon vanilla
extract

Pecan halves

- Beat the sugar and butter in a mixer bowl until creamy. Add the cake flour and egg yolk and beat well. Stir in the rum, salt and vanilla.

- Chill, covered, until firm. Shape into 1/2-inch balls. Place on a nonstick cookie sheet. Press 1 pecan half into each cookie.

- Bake at 350 degrees for 10 minutes.

- Cool on the cookie sheet for 2 minutes. Remove to a wire rack to cool completely.

Two to Three Dozen Cookies

TOFFEE BARS

Graham crackers

1 cup butter

1 cup packed light brown
sugar

2 cups milk chocolate
chips

Bits o' Brickle or
chopped nuts
(optional)

- Line a 10x15-inch baking pan with foil.

- Arrange graham crackers in a single layer in the prepared pan.

- Combine the butter and brown sugar in a saucepan. Bring to a boil.

- Boil for exactly 3 minutes, stirring occasionally. Drizzle over the graham crackers.

- Bake at 400 degrees for exactly 5 minutes. Remove from the oven. Sprinkle with the chocolate chips and spread with a buttered spatula. Sprinkle with the brickle.

- Cool to room temperature. Chill until set. Cut into bars.

- Store the bars, covered, in the refrigerator.

Thirty Bars

Tortilla Flats

Reprinted from Mexican Medley *with permission from author Susan Fuller Slack and The American Cooking Guild. These crunchy spice cookies contain oats, pine nuts and a surprise ingredient—tortilla chips. Use unsalted, unseasoned tortilla chips. For your next fiesta, drizzle the cookies with melted semisweet chocolate.*

2 cups packed light brown sugar

^{1}/$_2$ cup unsalted butter

^{1}/$_2$ cup vegetable shortening

1 egg

2 teaspoons cinnamon

1 teaspoon Mexican vanilla extract or any vanilla extract

^{1}/$_2$ teaspoon baking soda

^{1}/$_4$ teaspoon salt

1^1/$_2$ cups rolled oats, lightly toasted

1^1/$_2$ cups coarsely ground tortilla chips

1^1/$_4$ cups flour

^{1}/$_2$ cup pine nuts or chopped pecans, toasted

- Beat the brown sugar, butter and shortening in a mixer bowl until creamy. Add the egg, cinnamon, vanilla, baking soda and salt, beating until blended. Add the oats and mix well. Stir in the tortilla chips, flour and pine nuts.

- Drop by heaping tablespoonfuls 2 inches apart onto a greased and floured cookie sheet. Flatten the cookies into 2-inch rounds with a glass dipped in sugar.

- Bake at 350 degrees for 8 to 9 minutes.

- Cool on the cookie sheet for 2 to 3 minutes. Remove to a wire rack to cool completely.

- Store in an airtight container.

Fifty-Four Cookies

Watermelon Cookies

1 recipe sugar cookie dough

Red food coloring

Miniature chocolate chips

Confectioners' sugar

Water

Green food coloring

- Tint the cookie dough with red food coloring.

- Roll the dough on a lightly floured surface. Cut with a round cookie cutter. Cut the circles into halves. Place on a nonstick cookie sheet. Sprinkle chocolate chips in the center of each cookie dough half to represent seeds; press lightly.

- Bake at 375 degrees for 10 to 12 minutes or until light brown. Cool on the cookie sheet for 2 minutes. Remove to a wire rack to cool competely.

- Combine the confectioners' sugar and water in a bowl, stirring until of a spreading consistency. Tint with green food coloring.

- Dip the outside round edge of each cookie in the icing.

- May tint ready-made icing green and substitute for the confectioners' sugar icing.

Variable Servings

World's Best Cookies

The name says it all!

3¹/2 cups flour

1 teaspoon baking soda

1 teaspoon salt

1 cup butter, softened

1 cup sugar

1 cup packed brown sugar

1 egg

1 cup vegetable oil

1 cup rolled oats

1 cup crushed cornflakes

¹/2 cup shredded coconut

¹/2 cup chopped pecans

1 teaspoon vanilla extract

- Sift the flour, baking soda and salt together.

- Beat the butter in a mixer bowl until creamy. Add the sugar and brown sugar gradually.

- Beat until light and fluffy, scraping the bowl occasionally. Stir in the egg, oil, oats and cornflakes. Add the dry ingredients and mix well. Fold in the coconut, pecans and vanilla. Drop by teaspoonfuls onto an ungreased cookie sheet.

- Bake at 350 degrees for 15 minutes. Cool on the cookie sheet for 2 minutes. Remove to a wire rack to cool completely.

Ten Dozen Cookies

BUTTERMILK PECAN AND RAISIN PIE

6 tablespoons unsalted
    butter, cubed

1¹/3 cups sugar

¹/2 teaspoon salt

3 eggs

²/3 cup buttermilk

¹/2 cup chopped pecans,
    toasted

¹/2 cup finely chopped raisins

1 (baked) 9-inch pie shell

• Heat the butter in a double boiler over simmering water until melted. Remove the top boiler pan from heat. Add the sugar and salt, stirring with a wooden spoon until blended. Beat in the eggs. Add the buttermilk, beating until smooth. Return top boiler pan to the double boiler.

• Cook until the mixture registers 130 degrees on a candy thermometer or is shiny and warm, stirring frequently. Remove from heat. Stir in the pecans and raisins.

• Place the baked pie shell if not still warm in a 275-degree oven. Heat for 3 to 5 minutes or until warm. Spoon the raisin mixture into the warm shell.

• Bake on the center oven rack at 275 degrees for 50 to 60 minutes or until the center is set but is still soft and gelatinous.

• Cool on a wire rack for 4 hours or until cooled completely. Serve at room temperature or reheat in moderate oven.

Six Servings

KEY LIME PIES

Chef Waverly Dickerson of South Carolina shares one of his favorite recipes.

3¹/₂ cups graham cracker crumbs

¹/₄ cup melted butter

15 egg yolks

1 (5-pound) can sweetened condensed milk

1 cup Key lime juice

- Combine the graham cracker crumbs and butter in a bowl and mix well. Pat over the bottoms and up the sides of three 9-inch pie plates.

- Bake at 325 degrees for 5 minutes or until brown. Cool for 2 minutes.

- Whisk the egg yolks, condensed milk and Key lime juice in a bowl until blended. Spoon into the baked shells.

- Bake at 325 degrees for 10 minutes.

Eighteen Servings

JUMPIES PEAR PIE

4 large pears, peeled, chopped

1 (unbaked) 9-inch pie shell

1 cup sugar

¹/₄ cup flour

¹/₄ cup melted butter

2 eggs, lightly beaten

1 teaspoon vanilla extract

¹/₄ teaspoon nutmeg

¹/₂ teaspoon cinnamon

- Arrange the pears over the bottom of the pie shell.

- Combine the sugar, flour, butter, eggs, vanilla, nutmeg and cinnamon in a bowl, stirring until blended. Pour over the pears.

- Bake at 325 degrees for 55 to 60 minutes or until golden brown. The filling will be of a custard consistency.

Six Servings

SUMMERTIME PIE

A cool, sweet ending for a summer supper.

3/4 cup sugar

3 tablespoons cornstarch

1 1/2 cups water

1 (3-ounce) package any
   flavor red gelatin

1 cup blueberries

1 cup raspberries

1 cup sliced strawberries

1 (9-inch) graham
   cracker pie shell

2 cups whipped topping

- Combine the sugar and
  cornstarch in a saucepan and mix
  well. Add the water gradually,
  stirring until blended.

- Cook over medium heat until the
  mixture comes to a boil, stirring
  constantly.

- Boil for 1 minute. Remove from
  heat. Add the gelatin, stirring
  until dissolved.

- Cool to room temperature. Stir
  in the blueberries, raspberries
  and strawberries gently. Spoon
  into the pie shell.

- Chill for 3 hours or until set.
  Spread with the whipped topping
  just before serving.

- Store leftovers in the refrigerator.

- May choose to use only 2 of the
  above berries but make sure the
  total fruit measures 3 cups.

Six to Eight Servings

ABRAMS' SWEET POTATO PIE

*You'll find this pie is delicious even when served cold right out of
the refrigerator.*

3 sweet potatoes

1/4 cup butter or
   margarine, softened

1/2 cup sugar

1 egg, beaten

1/4 cup milk

1 teaspoon vanilla
   extract

1 (unbaked) 9-inch pie
   shell

- Bake the sweet potatoes on a
  baking sheet at 350 degrees for
  1 hour or until tender. Scoop
  the pulp into a mixer bowl. Add
  the butter.

- Beat at low speed until blended.
  Add the sugar and egg.

- Beat until smooth, scraping the
  bowl occasionally. Mix in the
  milk and vanilla. Spoon into the
  pie shell.

- Bake at 350 degrees for 30 to
  40 minutes or until the pie tests
  done. Serve plain or with honey.

Six to Eight Servings

OTHER GOOD STUFF

When I was asked to write for the Junior League of Columbia's new cookbook, I felt it was a privilege but I had a few preconceived ideas about the task at hand. I thought it would be challenging because the book was being compiled in Columbia and would, consequently, have a definite Southern accent.

Surprise! Surprise! When I read an advance copy of the new book, I discovered a global cookbook, a true potpourri of different cultures, the image of the melting pot that America is.

So, let's talk food and wine. First, wine is not only a beverage but a condiment. This being said, not every wine goes with every food. I would like to destroy a myth immediately—white wine with white meat is a fallacy—so is the rest of that commonplace sentence. Remember, drinking wine is a pleasure and should stay that way. Consequently, you should always drink what you like with what you want. No exceptions!

Your taste buds are as good as those of anyone else, so trust yourself and have confidence. If not, you should find a wine merchant who inspires your confidence, choosing in the same way you select a decorator or doctor.

When planning a meal look at the origin of the recipe. If it is Italian, look into Italian wines. If Northern Italian, check into wines from Piedmont or the Friuli. If from Firenze, search for white or red wines from Tuscany. If Lebanese, ask your wine merchant for one of the great wines of the Mediterranean that comes from Lebanon.

Greek food calls for spicy full-bodied wines like those from the Rhone Valley in France or one from the Rhone Rangers, as we call those from California. And yes, Greece, the cradle of our civilization, produces some very good if not outstanding wines.

With recipes coming from the West Coast, particularly California, we find the ultimate multi-cultural cuisine or "Pacific Rim Culture," where Asia meets Central and South America. The wines of California are the best accompaniment without any doubt, and there are plenty from which to choose.

Again, make your life simple and keep in mind some rules: French recipes, French wine; Spanish recipes, Spanish wine, etc. What about recipes coming from countries that do not produce wine? For example, Northern Germany: in many cases a good beer, a pilsner, will be the appropriate accompaniment. Beers, ales, and stouts are beverages that can be very complex, with great bouquets and incredible taste.

And since Asian cuisine can be very challenging, here is some advice: sometimes beer is your only answer. But with sweet-and-sour tastes, as well as with hot peppers, riesling, chenin blanc, or gewürztraminer-based wines are your answers.

What about light fare—a luncheon or a brunch where you often want to serve a salad or something cold that is seasoned with a dressing made with vinegar or lemon? According to the French "adage," you cannot serve wine!

It is true of French wine but not true of California chardonay or sauvignon blanc, which I would highly recommend in such context. Very often, as a matter of fact, the accompanying dressing gives a lift to these wines, which often are low in acidity.

Of course, if all the preceding is too confusing and you are ready to give up—please hold it right here! Close your eyes and think Champagne. Yes, Champagne or very good sparkling wine from the West Coast.

What about "bubbly" you are asking yourself? The wine for special occasions, birthdays, anniversaries, graduations, etc. Yes and no, because Champagne is not only that; Champagne is your best friend as a host. "C'est le vin passe partout." This is the wine for everything, a wine for everyday, a wine that makes every day a special day.

Champagne is a great aperitif. Champagne is a great hors d'oeuvre wine. Champagne goes well with seafood and fish. Heavier-bodied Champagne will marry well with white or red meat. And at last, Champagne goes well with dessert, but here do yourself and your guest a favor.

Forget about "Brut" or dry Champagne with dessert. Serve a demi sec (half dry) or semisweet Champagne. They are made to be served in the context of sweets. And these kinds of Champagnes are a glorious end to a great dinner.

Remember, Champagne is our salvation in case of dilemma and will always make an ordinary day a special day. You and your guests deserve that special "Je ne sais quoi" that you only find in Champagnes.

—Jean Pierre Chambas

MENUS

NEW YEAR'S EVE DESSERT BUFFET

Fresh Fruit with Grand Marnier Dip
Tipsy Pudding
Pound Cake Cookies
Toffee Pecan Brownies
Company Carrot Cake
Heath Bar Cheesecake

WINE

Sparkling Blanc de Noirs
Late Harvest Riesling
Sauterne

DINNER FOR TWO

Spinach Salad with Goat Cheese
Chicken with Champagne Sauce
Green Beans with Garlic and Basil
Broiled Tomato Cups
Orange Espresso Flan

WINE

Pinot Noir

FOURTH OF JULY PICNIC

Slaw for Barbecue
Mrs. Chandler's Potato Salad
Congaree Ribs
Corn on the Cob
Marbleized Deviled Eggs
Dot-Dot's Peach Cobbler

WINE

Red Zinfandel
Hand-Crafted American Ale

CHRISTENING LUNCHEON

Mixed Greens with Goat Cheese
   and Pine Nuts
Shrimp and Artichoke Casserole
Steamed Asparagus with Butter Pecan Sauce
New Potatoes with Spring Onion Vinaigrette
Queen of Trifles

WINE

Pinot Blanc

SUPER BOWL PARTY

White Chili
Red Pepper and Onion Corn Bread Muffins
Butterscotch Cream Cheese Bars

WINE

Hand-Crafted American Ale
Lager Cabernet Sauvignon

THANKSGIVING DINNER

Royal Anne Cherry Salad
Carolina Deep-Fried Turkey
Spiced Cranberry Apricot Relish
Carolina Oyster Casserole
Sausage and Grits Dressing
Squash Casserole
Sweet Potato Soufflé
Nell's Green Beans
Grandmother's Rolls
Tipsy Pudding

WINE

Gewürztraminer
Red Zinfandel

VIP Dinner

Stilton Salad with Walnuts
Beef Tenderloin Stuffed with Lobster
Broccoli Timbales
Wild Pecan Rice
Tiramisù

Wine

Chardonnay

Cocktail Buffet

Tomato Galette with Fresh Rosemary
Cocktail Sauce for Shrimp or Crudités
Smoked Salmon Gâteau
Greek Spinach Squares
Mushroom Pâté
Apricot Brie Spread
Cucumber Rounds
Shrimp and Feta Cups
Fillet-Topped Baguettes with
    Walnut Parsley Pesto

Wine

Chardonnay
Pinot Noir

Supper Club Social

Crunchy Romaine Salad
Grilled London Broil
Vegetable Gratin
Southwestern Risotto
Almond Meringue Torte with
    Lemon Curd and Hazelnuts

Wine

Merlot

Hot Summer Night Celebration

Pont Neuf Salad
Barbecue Shrimp
Steamed Rice
French Bread
Caramel Ice Cream

Wine

Sauvignon Blanc

Ladies Luncheon

Roslyn Drive Mint Tea
Caprese
Pickled Shrimp
Steamed Asparagus
Sour Cream Biscuits
Brown Sugar Pound Cake with Praline Sauce

Wine

Sauvignon Blanc

Tailgate Get-Together

Marinated Chicken Wings
Aunt Sallee's Vegetable Pizza
Buttered Pecans
Muffuletta
Pasta Greco
Oatmeal Cookies
Toffee Bars

Wine

Chardonnay

*Check index for recipes included in the menus.

CONTRIBUTORS

Clarissa T. Adams

Jo Simmons Aiken

Mary Alexander

Susan Ellenbast Anderson

Diana B. Ayers

Laura Baker

Terri Barnett

Lynn Barron

Cindy C. Barwick

Beth Baxley

Harvin Belser

Leslie Woods Bennett

Rebecca C. Best

Krista Buyck Birchmore

Kathy Hill Blackmon

Louise Rooker Bohannon

Marty Rankin Bonds

Caroline Marchant Borucki

Bramley Bowers

Amelia S. Bowie

Bitsey Bruce Box

Cary B. Boyd

Ashley Brantley

Katherine H. Brazell

Alice L. Brooker

Blanche J. Bryan

Kim D. Buchanan

Stephanie Bulter

Lelia Freeman Byars

Karen F. Bybee

Kathy B. Cantey

Margaret Kelley Carter

Melissa McCullough Carter

Trina Carter

Susan Watts Case

Libby Lee Castles

Elizabeth Clare

Andrea Clarke

Sarah Bull Clarkson

Vicki E. Collins

Katherine G. Crosthwaite

Rita B. Cullum

Verd Craig Cunningham

Betsy Daniel

Teri J. Daniels

Grace McCutchen
      Daughtridge

Brandon Davidson

Char Davis

Kelly J. Davis

Theresa Counts Davis

Allison DeLoache

Betsy DesChamps

Mary DesChamps

Lynn M. Dority

Ellen Seastrunk Dozier

Suzanne Eaddy

Angie Easterlin

Lanie Epting

Harriet G. Fairey

James W. Fant

Diane Farr

Deans Richardson Fawcett

Terry Floyd

Emily S. Folline

Elizabeth Chachere Freeman

Walter Hal Freeman

Melissa Fritz

Katherine G. Fritze

Laurie Fuller

Liz Fuller

Retta Gantt

Elizabeth M. Gilbert

Jane Gillespie

Ann B. Gilpin

Susan Graham

Sherri Greenberg

Carolina M. Gribble

Leila Grimbal

Maria Heath Hackney

Anna A. Haltiwanger

Ellen Hamilton

Tonya Hammond

Mrs. George C. Hart

Susan R. Harvin

Anne Sullivan Haynie

Lee Rooker Heath

Mary Ann S. Heath

Melanie Heath

Tammy Heath

Betsy Hemlepp

Sarah Waites Hennig

Mrs. Albert R. Heyward III

Sharmin Hill

Catherine Horne

Robyn A. Hornsby

Polly T. Howser

Denise Hubbard

Karen M. Hudgens

Martha Hudgens

Susan Hutcherson

Libby Anne Kepley Inabinet

Gloria Cassels Jackson

Gail Rawls Jeter

Lisa Jones

Kathy Paget Joye

Polly Judd

Mary Haynes Kaminsky

Fain Ravenel Kapeluck

Susan D. Kay

Marty Keels

Traci H. Kennedy

Amy Kinard

Mary Karl Kinard

Memi Kinard

Stephanie S. Kirkland

Julia Foster Krebs

Becky Laffitte

Helen Harvey Laffitte

Nell Laffitte

Jennie P. Lambe

Caroline LaMotte

Lillian Bollin Lawrence

Mrs. John T. Lay

Kathy Linnette

Betty Lovelace

Debbie Lowe

Catherine A. Luce

Teresa E. MacGillivray

Lois Marsha

Carolyn G. Mason

Leck Paschal Mason

Mary Louise Mason

Barbara McArthur

Patricia B. McCallum

Tara D. McClary

Frazer J. McCrorey

Celmira T. McDaniel

Betsy McDonald

Blair McDow

Katie McElveen

Mrs. Wilson A. McElveen III

Clare Nissen McGill

Sarah Ellis McKay

Jodie Watt McLean

Mary Carlisle McLeod

Galen S. McWilliams

Lita Middleton

Kay F. Miefert

Ann Miller

Bet Miller

Larry Miller

Susan N. Minter

Jan Guerry Moore

Mary Dallas Moore

Meribeth Walton-Moore

Totsie Moore

Nancy B. Moorer

Kirsten J. Moorman

Page Morris

Meg Morrison
Shirley Munn
Betty Murdaugh
Sandra Myrick
Julie O'Neal
Robin O'Neil
Alice Hopkins Otis
Susan C. Owen
Nelle S. Palms
Debra T. Paysinger
Jim Pesci
Elizabeth A. Phillips
Louise S. Pinckney
Frances A. Plyer
Alice Powell
Betsy Powell

Peggy Powers
Lindsay Pressley
Gwen Holliday Pruett
Carol Ragsdale
Carolyn Ragsdale
Marie-Louise Ramsdale
Kimberly Reaser
Tracey Reddic
Carol Renshaw
Caroline R. Reutter
Valerie H. Reynolds
Virginia McGee Reynolds
Harriet M. Rice
Francis LaMotte Robinson
Robin Abrams Rutledge
Lyn Schultz

Debra W. Scott
Jean Selman
Elaine Shedd
Margie Shelburg
Ann Cheves Sherard
Susan Poston Shirley
Nancy Shultz
Murray Simmons
Dorothy Smart
Dorothy Brown Smith
Martha B. Smith
Gwenn Smyth
Mary Rhett Sparkman
Lauri B. Stevenson
Lannie Stinnette
Margaret B. Stover

Frances Stuckey
Helen C. Summer
Margaret Anne Tarbox
Jane B. Taylor
Nancy D. Theus
Elizabeth Clare Thomas
Melanie T. Thompson
Emily P. Tompkins
Linda A. Truluck
Elizabeth Lane Trzcinski
Melissa J. Tuten
Laura Twitty
Jane F. Watson
Mary Moore M. C. Watson
Starlene Watson
Kitty Weiland

Mindy Weiss
Catherine M. Wendt
Deana West
Betsy Dye Westfall
Mary Jane White
Jane B. Whiteside
Debbie Whitlark
Ingrid W. Williams
Mason K. Williams
Mrs. R. C. Wimberly
Anne Guerry Woods
Pamela M. Woods
Margaret G. Yeakel
Mary Jane Zimmerman

PROFESSIONAL CREDITS

Cellars Restaurant, David Williamson
Waverly Dickerson, Professional Chef
Fleur de Lys, Francois Fisero
Frank's Restaurant & Bar, Chef Pierce Culliton
Bill Goulding, Restaurant Owner
Hampton Street Vineyard
Mr. Friendly's New Southern Cafe, Kristian Niemi

Restaurant at Cinnamon Hill, Andy Marchant
Richard's, Executive Chef Tim Freeman
Saluda's, Rob Patterson
Susan Fuller Slack, CCP, Food Styling and Prop Coordination
Stellinis
Villa Tronco, Carmella Roche

COOKBOOK COMMITTEE

Maria Heath-Hackney . . . . Chairman, Creative Director
Gwen Holliday Pruett . . . . Marketing
Catherine McGregor Wendt . . . . Non-recipe Copy
Vicki Eberhart Collins . . . . Recipe Collection
Harriet McElveen Rice . . . . Recipe Testing
Melissa Phillips Fritz . . . . Treasurer
Betsy Thompson Bakhaus . . . . Photography

RECIPE TESTING COMMITTEE

Mary Echols Barwick	Susan DesChamps Kay	Katherine Lydon Moore
Lelia Crouch Byars	Gina Wurthmann Lesslie	Meg Kramer Morrison
Sarah Theresa Daniels	Betsy Felder McDonald	Joie Potter Ray
Tonya Hammond	Margaret Ann Wade McMullen	Fran Davis Sadler
Susan F. Hutcherson	Susan Nelson Minter	

1. Famous Piggy Park mustard-based barbecue sauce (regular, spicy hot or hickory), hams, smoked turkey and pork barbecue.
   Maurice Bessinger's Piggy Park
   P.O. Box 6847
   West Columbia, South Carolina 29171
   1-800-Maurice (628-7423)

2. American Classic Tea
   Only tea native to America, grown on Wadmalaw Island, South Carolina.
   Charleston Tea Plantation
   P.O. Box 12810
   Charleston, South Carolina 29412
   1-803-559-0383

3. Blenheim Ginger Ale
   Extra spicy Jamaican ginger ale. "Mild" Extra Pale or "Hot" Old Number Three.
   Blenheim Bottling Company
   Box 62, Mineral Spring Road
   Blenheim, South Carolina 29516

4. Fine quail raised and processed for over twenty-five years. Call to locate a grocer or mail-order source in your area.
   Manchester Farms
   P.O. Box 97
   Dalzell, South Carolina 29040
   1-800-845-0421

5. Crawfish meat and boiled crawfish. Fifty-dollar minimum, shipped overnight.
   P & J Oyster Company
   1039 Toulouse
   P.O. Box 20104
   New Orleans, Louisiana 70112
   1-800-La Bayou (522-2968)

6. Vidalia Onions
   Famous sweet onions.
   Bland Farms
   P.O. Box 606
   Glennville, Georgia 30427
   1-800-Vidalia (843-2542)

7. Country ham, stone-ground grits, muscadine products.
   Callaway Gardens Resort, Inc.
   P.O. Box 2000
   Pine Mountain, Georgia 31822-2000
   1-800-280-7524

8. Andouille (Cajun-smoked pure pork sausage), tasso, boudin, chaurice (winter only). Ten-pound minimum.
   Poche's Meat Market
   3015-A Main Highway
   Breaux Bridge, Louisiana 70517
   1-800-Poches (376-2437)

9. Adluh short-patent, soft wheat flour (self-rising and plain), white and yellow cornmeal, seafood and chicken breader, hush puppy mix, biscuit mix, Miller's bran, whole wheat flour.
   Allen Brothers Milling Co.
   P.O. Box 1437
   Columbia, South Carolina 29202
   1-800-692-3584

10. Fruit Chutneys
    Raggy-O Traditions
    P.O. Box 1626
    Smithfield, North Carolina 27577
    1-888-4-Chutney
    (1-888-424-8863)

INDEX

DOWN BY THE WATER

A Collection Of Recipes From The Junior League Of Columbia, Inc.

Please send me _____ copies of *Down By The Water* @ $22.95 each $ _____

Shipping @ $4.00 each $ _____

TOTAL $ _____

Name _____

Address _____

City _____ State _____ Zip Code _____

Daytime Phone   (   ) _____

Method of Payment

☐ VISA   ☐ MasterCard   ☐ Check or Money Order

Account Number _____ Expiration Date _____

Signature _____

How did you hear about *Down By The Water*?

☐ Friend   ☐ Media   ☐ Gift   ☐ Other _____

If you know of a business interested in carrying our cookbook, please send the appropriate information with your order.

Photocopies Accepted

MAIL ORDERS
TO

The Junior League
of Columbia
2926 Devine Street
Columbia, South Carolina 29205

(803) 252-4552
(803) 254-0805

*Proceeds from the sale
of this cookbook are
returned to the community through
The Junior League
of Columbia projects.*

255